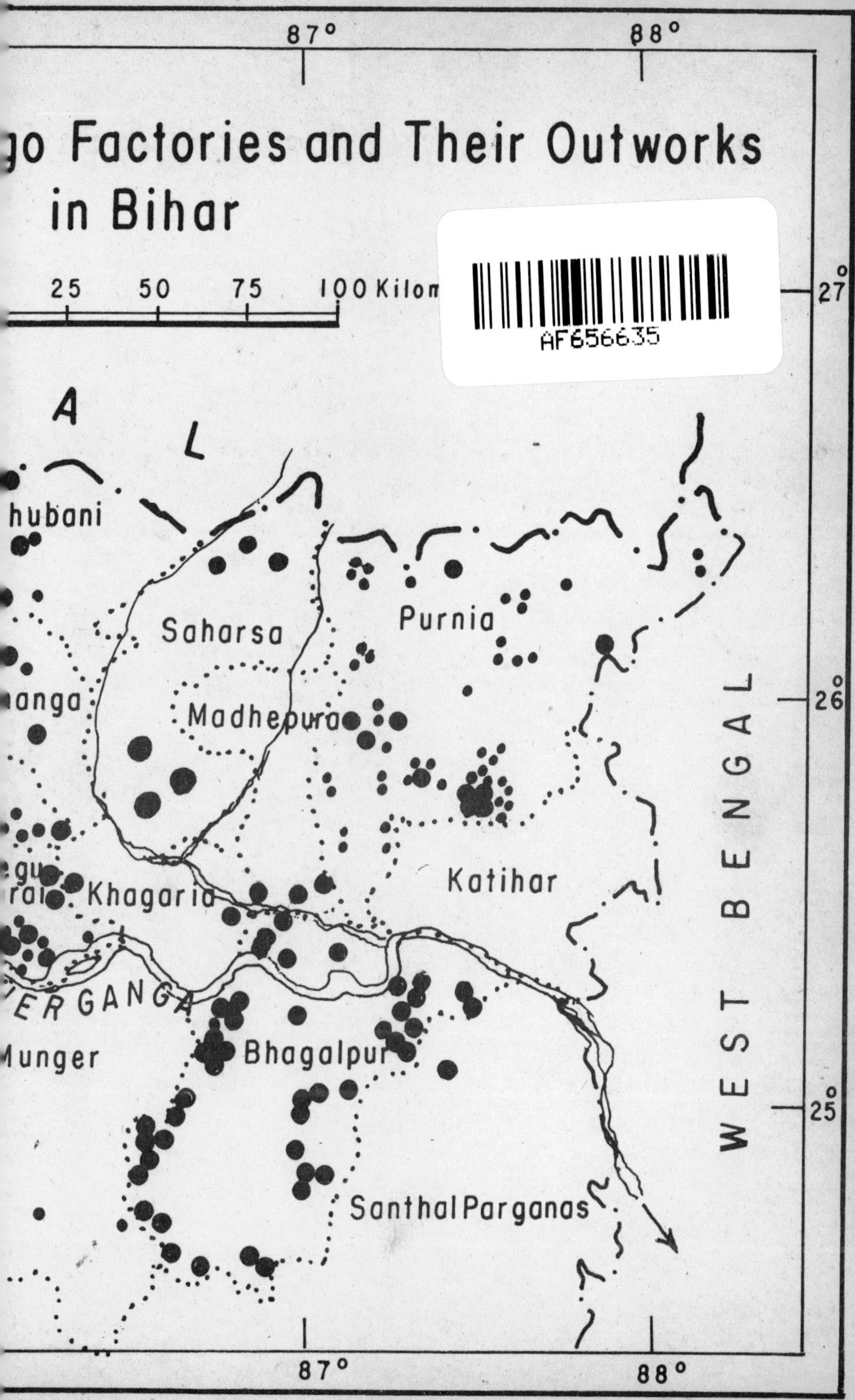
go Factories and Their Outworks
in Bihar
87°
88°
25
50
75
100 Kilom
27°
26°
25°
A
L
hubani
anga
Saharsa
Madhepura
Purnia
Katihar
gu
rai
Khagaria
ER GANGA
Munger
Bhagalpur
Santhal Parganas
WEST BENGAL
87°
88°

INDIGO AND THE RAJ

Peasant Protests in Bihar 1780-1917

To the memory of my father

JANAK SUKUL

Preface

Indigo has a long and chequered history. In medieval times its cultivation was voluntarily pursued by the tenants in Karnataka, Madras, Surat, Ahmedabad, Sindh and Agra. In the *Ain-i-Akbari*, the Persian account of Akbar's administration (1590), the indigo produced in Agra is spoken of as being of superior quality. Tirhut and Bengal are also described but no mention is made of the indigo grown in the lower provinces of Bengal.

Indigo became indispensable once again in the eighteenth century when British cloth merchants were in dire need of the dye. As such the colonists -- the French, the Spanish and the Portuguese -- took to indigo cultivation in the late eighteenth century. They began to utilise their skill and enterprise to lay a firm foundation for indigo cultivation in India.

Due to the American War of Independence in 1776, the relations between America and Great Britain became strained. As a result America stopped supplying the dye to Great Britain. The slave revolt in the West Indies also gave a big jolt to the supply of indigo to Great Britain. In such a situation the British manufacturers became dependent on foreign countries for the dye. All such developments took place at a time when British mercantilism was established in India.

Indigo plantation was a purely private and capitalist enterprise. None the less it gradually received official patronage, protection and pecuniary support from the Directors of the East India Company from 1780 onwards. Some districts of lower Bengal were chosen for indigo cultivation. Keeping in view the fertility of the soil in the Gangetic plain, Purnia, Bhagalpur and Muzaffarpur districts of Bihar were selected first for its cultivation. The officers of the Company were permitted to take up the indigo business besides performing their official duties. The planters were also given permission to go to the interior dehat for establishing indigo factories. In this process the colonisation of thousands of villages had started.

According to the Report of the Proceedings of the East India Company (Calcutta, 1836, p.IV) in regard to the culture and manufacture of indigo, the dependence of British manufacturers at the mercy of foreign countries for this dye was not liked by the Directors of the Court. They made "extraordinary efforts to increase its production and improve its quality". As the industry established itself very soon, no further material support from the Company was required. It was therefore left to the planters themselves to pursue indigo cultivation on their own. The huge capital generated in this business enabled the officers of the East India Company to transmit their "fortunes" to Great Britain. This remittance was considered by the Court of Directors as "legal, advantageous and adequate". In course of time the quality of indigo produced in Bengal and Bihar surpassed all countries and it became the "chief source of supply to the rest of the world". Its importance was so great for the "mother country" that in 1789 Britain imported indigo from India to the tune of 371,461 lbs.

The approach to the understanding of the process of colonisation and the working of British imperialism in India had undergone a fundamental change in recent years. Many new aspects including the literary works of the colonial era have been critically studied by historians. One of the aspects has been the agrarian problems of colonial India. Of late the studies on peasant movements in India have also received the attention of historians. The subject has been taken up in a wider context, and historians are no longer ready to treat the peasant movements of colonial India as merely a "law and order problem". Instead, they now look at these movements as expressions of popular rejection of colonial control over the lowest level of Indian society. This, indeed, is a welcome trend.

Yet, much more remains to be done in regard to the study of agrarian problems. First, studies done so far have been able to cover only a fraction of the problem and it demands an in-depth study at the village level. Second, the existing approach to the subject still needs to be freed from a few prejudices. For example, the elements of "protests" and "tensions" in agrarian life have been seen by the historians mostly in a political context and, in the process, other aspects of agrarian life have been overlooked. Studies of these aspects, especially of the socio-economic life of the raiyats in relation particularly to the Government and non-official white-born indigo planters are equally important. This may throw light on the whole process of colonisation at the lowest level. The usefulness of the study of peasant movements in the indigo growing areas of Bihar is more apparent when one understands how the peasantry gave a jolt to the colonial system, which ultimately collapsed. These are some of the assumptions which have been examined in the present study.

Indigo plantation in Champaran has often been referred to in connection with the launching of Gandhiji's political agitation but no in-depth study of indigo plantation itself has been done so far. The implications of indigo plantation for British rule is without doubt far greater than has generally been presumed until now. This is because indigo was cultivated not only in Champaran but in most parts of Bihar. This area constitutes a major part of the fertile Gangetic plain in eastern India. Moreover, this study has revealed the existence of a close proximity between the European planters and the local society leading to social interaction. This had significant consequences with considerable political and economic ramifications. In course of time, the *Gora Saheb* or the planters, emerged as an important factor in the local society thanks to the patronage they received from the British authorities and the rapport they enjoyed with the local population. Because of this rapport and their influential position, they quietly carried on the process of colonisation to the grass root levels and thus contributed towards providing a foothold to the Empire in the region which was most hostile to the British rule. It may be noted here that the 1857 Revolt was more manifest in Bihar than anywhere else.

It is no surprise that the reluctant Gandhiji chose to launch his first political agitation here at Champaran in north Bihar. Once the imperial stronghold was endangered here, it became difficult for the rulers to maintain their hold elsewhere, and ultimately the mightiest power collapsed thirty years later. This broad understanding forms the basis of the discussion of the present study.

Chapter One aims at examining the British policy towards indigo cultivation from its beginnings to 1917. It discusses how colonisation of the villages was started through the planters. Intrusion of Europeans into the countryside for indigo cultivation and their penetration among the natives served and sustained the interest of the *Raj* from below. In this connection it would be our endeavour to examine the nature and scope of the relations between the planters and Government, and to find out how this relationship helped the planters penetrate into the remote villages and provide a base for the Empire at village level.

The second chapter brings out the districtwise distribution of the indigo *kothis* and discusses the various systems of plantation. It also examines the economic consequences of indigo plantation. The third chapter discusses the agrarian relations affected by the collusion between the zamindars, the planters and the Government. It attempts to study how the feudal forces in the countryside were further strengthened. Chapter Four examines the overall impact of indigo plantation on the tenantry and the labour. Chapter Five is devoted to the study of the peasant protests against the planters and the Government. It discusses how the anti-planter movement was not "instigated" by the affluent raiyats alone; the formidable combination of the raiyats cut across the barriers of caste, community and class to challenge the authority of the Government in the second half of the nineteenth century and the first half of the twentieth century.

A map indicating the number of indigo *kothis* in Bihar, a bibliography, a glossary, an index and four appendices have also been provided in the study.

In the preparation of the book I have received constant encouragement and guidance from my supervisor Professor Sita Ram Singh to whom I record my deep sense of gratitude. The scholar to whom I am most indebted and beholden is Dr V. Jha whose brotherly affection, constant encouragement and mature guidance at every stage of writing the book have enabled me to publish it on time. I am thankful to my revered teachers Professors R.S. Sharma, Q. Ahmad and D.N. Jha for their encouragement in the pursuit of the work. My elder brother, Professor R.L. Shukla, has been a constant source of inspiration to me.

I am indebted to Professor Irfan Habib, Chairman, ICHR, who had granted me study leave to prepare the book and also offered me silent encouragement.

I acknowledge with thanks the expertise of Professor Bharat Prasad Mishra, Department of Geography, University of Bihar, Muzaffarpur, for preparing a map of the indigo growing places in the districts of Bihar.

I would like to record my thanks to the National Archives of India, New Delhi; West Bengal Record Office, Calcutta; Bihar State Archives, Patna; Record Room of Muzaffarpur Collectorate; Nehru Memorial Museum and Library, New Delhi; L.S. College

Library, Muzaffarpur; and the Library-cum-Documentation Centres of the ICHR and the ICSSR for extending all possible help and cooperation.

I am thankful to Dr Suhash Chakravarty, Department of History, Delhi University and Professor H.C. Satyarthi, University of Bihar, Muzaffarpur, who have helped me to select the subject. Professor Raghunath Jha, Department of History, University of Bihar, Muzaffarpur, took keen interest in the subject. He took me to Kanti in 1986 and showed me the relics of the Kanti concern which was one of the oldest and largest indigo factories in Bihar. I must express my thanks to him. I am equally thankful to my other friends and colleagues. These include Dr T.R. Sareen, Shri P.N. Sahay, Shri S.A. Hasham, Dr B.K. Pandeya, Ms Indira Gupta, Ms Savitri Das Sinha, Shri Shabi Ahmad, Shri S.M. Mishra, Shri Tasneem Ahmad, Dr B. Ram, Professors R.B. Chaudhary, N.K.P. Sinha, and O.P. Jaiswal, Shri J.N. Sinha, Shri V.R. Mani, Dr T.K.V. Subrahmaniam, Dr K.K. Sharma, Shri G.P. Sharma, Dr S.B. Roy, Dr V.N. Dixit, Dr Abhaya Kumar Singh, Shri S.P. Das and Shri Tara Sharan Sinha. I am equally thankful to my brother-in-law, Dr. Nalin Bilochan for his assistance in this work.

My friends Dr Deepak Kumar, NISTAD, New Delhi, and Shri Ishrat Alam, C.A.S. in History, AMU, Aligarh, offered comments and suggestions for which I am obliged.

I am obliged to Shrimati Shanti Jha, wife of Dr V.Jha, for her keenness about the early publication of the book. I cannot adequately express my gratitude to my wife, Shabnam, who helped me not only in the collection of material from the INSA library but also anxiously watched its progress. My son, Kinshuk, too, has through his playful pranks and sweet smile made my work a pleasure.

I have great pleasure in acknowledging the unstinting support and sincere encouragement provided by my colleague Ms Kalyani Subramanyan in bringing out this book. I am also grateful to Shri Buddhadev Bhattacharya for his valuable advice from time to time.

Deputy Director (Research) PRABHAT KUMAR SHUKLA
ICHR, New Delhi
27 November 1992

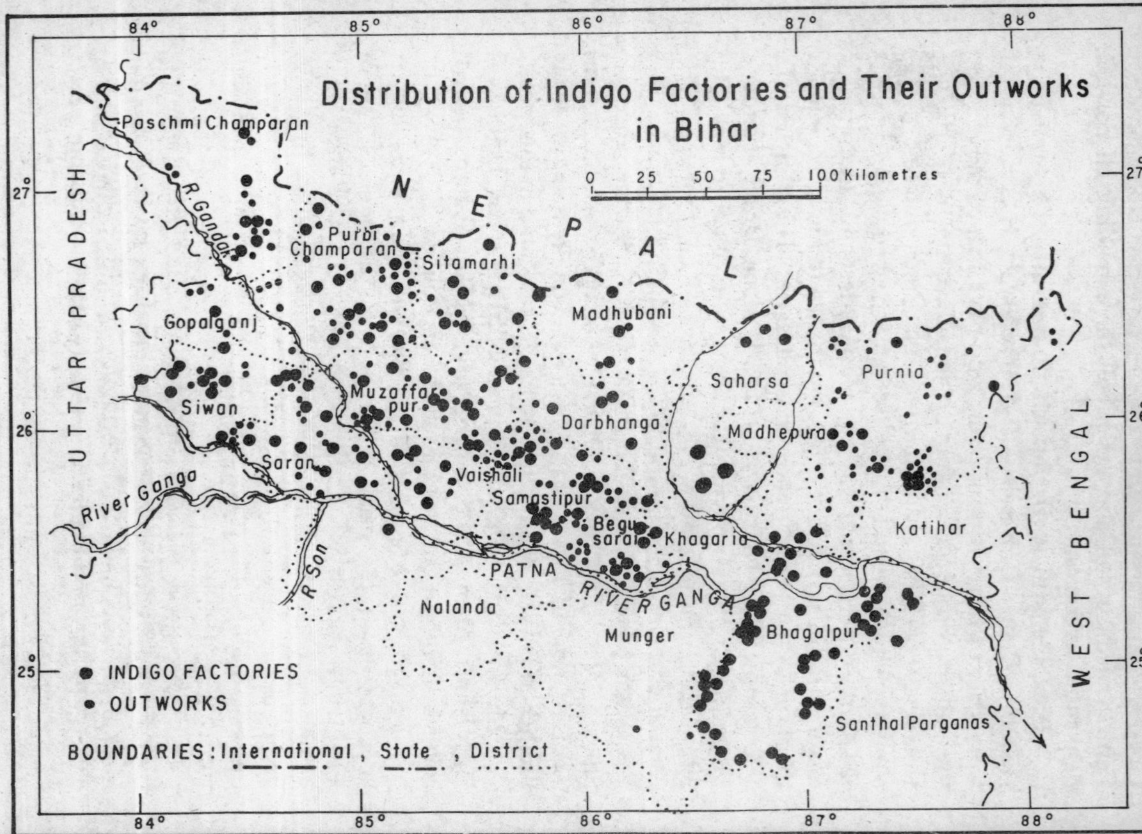
Distribution of Indigo Factories and Their Outworks in Bihar
0 25 50 75 100 Kilometres
NEPAL
UTTAR PRADESH
WEST BENGAL
Paschmi Champaran
Purbi Champaran
Sitamarhi
Madhubani
Saharsa
Purnia
Gopalganj
Siwan
Saran
Muzaffarpur
Vaishali
Darbhanga
Madhepura
Samastipur
Begusarai
Khagaria
Katihar
PATNA
Nalanda
Munger
Bhagalpur
Santhal Parganas
R. Gandak
River Ganga
RIVER GANGA
R Son
INDIGO FACTORIES
OUTWORKS
BOUNDARIES : International , State , District
84°
85°
86°
87°
88°
25°
26°
27°

CHAPTER I

British Policy Towards Indigo Cultivation in Bihar: A Survey

An attempt is being made in this chapter to discuss the policy of the British government towards indigo cultivation in Bihar. In its insatiable greed for profit the East India Company not only encouraged the indigo planters in various ways but it also gave them administrative and legal protection against the raiyats. Although a private enterprise, the cultivation of indigo was determined by the needs of the European cloth markets as well as those of the remittance trade. While commenting on the report of the Indigo Commission, even J.P.Grant, Lieutenant Governor of Bengal and a member of the Indigo Commission, who was very critical of the whole system of indigo planting, underlined the importance of indigo trade, and of the great political advantage of having a large body of European gentlemen widely dispersed over the country. To him its importance lay in its trade to the tune of two million pounds sterling a year.[1]

Bihar alone produced 32,699 maunds of indigo (i.e. nearly 31 per cent of the total yield) out of the total of 106,887 maunds of indigo then produced.[2] But there was no demand in Bihar for a special law in favour of any party as in Bengal. This does not mean that Bihar was not affected by the various legislative and administrative measures adopted by British government. The rapid increase in the demand for indigo in the foreign market led to the establishment of a number of indigo factories.[3] By the end of the eighteenth century the war against France occasioned an increased consumption of indigo by the great military establishments maintained by the belligerent powers whose troops were clothed in blue. In Tirhut, for instance, twenty-five factories were established with the help of the Government by the year 1803. According to a report (1810) of the Collector of Tirhut, the district sent 10,000 maunds of indigo to Calcutta every year. In Purnia, at the time of Buchanan's survey more than seventy-five factories came into existence under European management and started manufacturing indigo. There were seven other factories which belonged to two Hindu zamindars of

Purnia and a native Portuguese. In Patna and Gaya districts the cultivation and manufacture of this plant was relatively unimportant, but in the district of Shahabad it was in a better state. Indigo factories were also established in the district of Bhagalpur before the close of the eighteenth century. In all such establishments, the Government of India extended patronage to the planters besides issuing licence for the cultivation of indigo plant. Thus for about twenty-two years (1780-1802) the East India Company directly supported the indigo factories and placed India in the foremost of indigo producing countries of the world.[4] When pecuniary help was no longer necessary, the Company withdrew from the direct ownership of the factories.

The Board of Directors of the Company were of the view that merchants should have their own resources from the substantial profit accruing to them and these should be utilized to further promote their indigo transactions. But the Company continued to make large purchases and to trade in indigo. It also set up a mart in Calcutta in 1806 for cash purchase to help develop the trade further. As a sort of incentive it also advanced cash to the manufacturers from whom the Company proposed to purchase the dye, though direct supervision was discontinued.[5] In a Statement of Advances on the Remittance Plan the Company was shown as having advanced from 1786 to 1804 a million pounds towards their purchase. When loss was incurred by the Company on account of the indigo investment in 1788, the Court of Directors desisted from actively involving itself in the indigo business and left the trade altogether in the hands of private individuals. But the Governor-General in Council modified the Court's instruction and decided to advance funds to the individuals on their undertaking to deliver indigo in the Company s warehouses. The sum so advanced by the Company in India was to be repaid to it in London. Thus the inflow of colonial wealth and commodities into Britain in the latter half of the eighteenth century had a crucial relationship with accumulation of capital in England. Such accumulation certainly determined to a very large degree the pace and intensity of colonial expansion and exploitation.[6] If gave impetus to the process of Industrial Revolution in England. England like the other countries of Europe desired that the colonies of its own race should be opened up chiefly for the command of its markets.

The other colonies were looked down upon as "plantations" where raw produce was grown to be sent to the mother country.[7]

The Company brought experienced planters from the West Indies. Its offices were encouraged to engage in the trade and the other persons were issued licences to go to the interior and set up plantations. Although trade was a monopoly, in order to encourage it the Company permitted anyone to deal in it for three years and offered low rates on shipments to England.[8]

Planters seldom came from Europe with capital. They depended entirely on the capital supplied by the Agency Houses in Calcutta. Even the advances on account of indigo from the Company were received by them through these Agency Houses. In fact, the Agency Houses acted as a watchdog to safeguard the interests of the planters,[9] although the interest rates were very high (often 10 to 12 per cent besides a 2½ per cent commission).[10] In the case of indigo the British Agency Houses were involved in each stage of production from the growing of the plant to its manufacture as saleable indigo and finally to its export to Europe and other parts of the world. Although production of many primary commodities including silk suffered from the shortage of credit due to the collapse of Agency Houses, indigo and opium were spared. The Union Bank partly supplied the needs of the European merchants.[11] Increased credit was also provided by the company to private merchants on hypothecation of goods meant for exports. Besides local banks and the Company, East India Houses in London also extended credit to many private merchants in Bengal. Thus the control of the Europeans over new enterprise such as indigo was assured by directness of their contacts and their control over overseas markets.[12]

Quite a few of the high-ups in the Company's government were opposed to the settlement of private British subjects among the peasantry apprehending that it would undermine the supremacy of the Company and cause dissatisfaction with British rule; even so, the Company had to encourage indigo cultivation because it "badly needed Indian products for remittance purposes".[13] Before 1813 the administrators of the Company were apprehensive that private British subjects might emulate the American precedent and try to establish a settler-dominated government in Bengal.[14] But the urge for enormous profit from the colony was so strong that the Company was ready to take the risk.

In 1823 Lord Amherst (1823-28), the Governor-General, empowered the indigo planters to recover advances from the raiyats through summary suits. The planters were also given lien on any crop produced on land for which they had given advances. He also extended support to the planters and shielded them against the interference of the zamindars. It was he who first opened the door to the leasing of land to Europeans in 1824.[15]

When a sound economic base for the prosperity of indigo trade was established by 1823, it became a principle with the Government of India to consider the indigo trade in all its branches as one that was left to regulate itself. The spirit of free competition was the main reason of its prosperity. The Government of India was of the view that the prosperity of the planters lay in their own initiative and exertion as well as competition among themselves, and if necessary they could take recourse to regular courts of law to settle their disputes and differences. It therefore saw no reason to legislatively interfere in the matter.[16]

As regards the planters' complaints that the raiyats took advances even from another person while being committed to one earlier, the Governor-General in Council expressed the view that this phenomenon was not confined to indigo trade only and was experienced in a greater or lesser degree in every transaction which involved the outlay of capital in the form of advances to the agricultural classes.[17] Lord William Bentinck (1828-35), took a less lenient view of the situation and Regulation V of 1830 authorized the summary criminal trial and imprisonment of those raiyats who violated duly entered indigo contracts. Bentinck favoured the presence of Europeans in the *mufassil* as it would help "civilize" the Indians by disseminating European arts and science among them.[18] By the Charter Act of 1833 the British subjects were permitted to settle in any territory which had been under the rule of the Company in 1800. Further, the Act IV of 1837 gave British subjects unrestricted right of entry.

Since the Government of India did not want the "American precedent" to be repeated in India, it imposed certain restrictions on the Europeans holding land and becoming landed proprietors.[19] To this J. P. Pattle, a member of the Board of Revenue, took strong objection and said that the Resolution of the Government of India was a great hindrance to the British subjects taking land. He was of the opinion that the existence of such restrictions would retard the government of the country. He therefore felt that the restrictions were unnecessary and hence these be abolished so as to encourage British subjects to occupy lands and become landed proprietors. He considered this a pre-requisite for the advancement of the revenue of the state, which would enable the government to maintain a large establishment of public officers. His argument was based on political consideration also. He asserted: "Our permanency in this country must always be uncertain until attachment to the government is unquestionably the common interest of a principal and influential portion of the population. Such a state of things, I imagine, can only be induced by facilitating and encouraging the settlement of British subjects in India and by abolishing every hindrance by which their settling is obstructed and no means can be devised so certain of advocating the welfare, happiness and prosperity of the whole population and therefore necessarily the 'permanency of our possession'".[20]

As Pattle was fully conscious of the need of the colonial empire, he observed that "it was only capitalists and their principal agents that will colonize" India.[21] According to him "their number should be at first small, gradually increasing as experience of success might afford encouragement, but not for half a century to come, amounting to any considerable number". He was equally conscious of the 'natural resources' of the country which were vast and "imperfectly developed". In view of all this Pattle was convinced that the unrestricted introduction of "European capital, enterprise, skill and science" was the only means by which these resources could be adequately developed and their value realised.[22]

Such a colonial view like the one expressed openly by Pattle was quite meaningful. In England there were two wings of thought. The evangelical humanitarian wing wanted to diffuse British civilization and Christianity in India. One important medium of this diffusion was that the British settlers should live among the people in India while the other wing, known as the Lancashire group, was interested in the growing of cotton within the empire under the supervision of British settlers.[23] The debate with regard to the methods by which India was to be colonised reached its climax in 1858. The movement favouring European colonization in India was discussed in British Parliament. In Parliament it was led by humanitarian elder statesman William Ewart supported by other humanitarians. Its opponents were the Indian authorities' shareholders of the East India Company. Ultimately the Parliament appointed a "Select Committee" on European colonization and settlement in India which collected evidence for two years.[24] Though critical of the indigo planters, the Committee called on the Government of India to encourage settlement by reforming the administration of the judiciary and the police, and improving roads and communication. It dispelled all doubts about the right of Europeans to settle in India.

The Board of Revenue also obtained the local officers' opinion. It felt that the Resolution of the Government of India of 1824 had been "almost entirely inoperative". But at the same time it argued in favour of unrestricted European landholding. It held the opinion that these matters should safely be left to be regulated by self-interest or to be adjudicated by the Courts of Justice should disputes occur.[25]

The restrictions imposed by the Resolution of 1824 were ultimately removed after the passing of the Act of 1833 which conferred upon the natural born British subjects the right to proceed to, and reside in, major parts of the Company's territories on giving simple information to the customs officer at the port of their landing. The other restrictions became unnecessary after the passing of the Act of 1836, and Act VI of 1843, which rendered amenable all persons without reference to birth or descent, to the civil courts of the country. Being essentially a British trading monopoly corporation, the administration of the Company put some check on the flow of population from the United Kingdom, although the flow of capital in India went on increasing. Since the policy of free trade for the exploitation of raw material suited the early colonisers, Adam Smith and Ricardo advocated its application as against the mercantilist policy of protection. The application of free trade to countries lacking an independent capitalist class "doomed India to the position of supplier of raw material and grain".[26] Moreover, "one way free trade" led to the underdevelopment of the capitalist classes as the Indian home market was not allowed to develop.[27]

The Charter Act of 1833 had opened the interior of India to British capital and led to some diversification of the industry. Indigo remained the most important private export of Bengal. In the peak years of 1842 indigo accounted for 46 per cent of the value of goods exported from Calcutta.[28]

The abolition of the monopoly of the East India Company in 1833 gave new impetus to the indigo entrepreneurs in India for free exploitation of the raw material. The planters wanted to act as free exploiters in a colonial country. It is proved by their reaction to the *Parwana* of the Magistrate of Tirhut on the indigo system in the districts of Bihar. The *Parwana* (28 May 1839) underscored the point that indigo contracts would be invalid without the consent of the zamindar. In a petition[29] submitted to the Government of Bengal the planters of Tirhut, Saran and Munger prayed that they should be allowed to have a lien on the land on which they gave advances and that the raiyats be enabled by regulation to compel fulfillment of engagements on the part of the planters. Since the interests of the colonial government and the planters were identical, the latter argued that they were the producers of a staple commodity, the supply of which was of vast importance to the commercial prosperity of the mother country.[30] According to the estimate of the planters the annual amount raised in the districts of Tirhut, Saran and Munger was valued at forty to sixty lakhs of rupees. The capital invested in block was estimated to be half a million sterling. But the Government of Bengal was not convinced by the arguments of the planters and wanted to ascertain the situation from different districts of Bihar. Although there was no clash of interest between the planters and the government, the *Parwana* issued by the Magistrate of Tirhut was found "entirely unobjectionable" as any open support to the planters would have antagonised the zamindars whose support for the exploitation of the agricultural population was essential.

Sir Frederick Halliday, the Lieutenant Governor of Bengal, was also partial to the planters. He believed that the economic future of Bengal depended upon the enterprise of Europeans in the *mufassil*. He felt that if the planters were given responsibility for their own good behaviour and shown respect by the government, they would themselves curb their excesses and reform the system.[31] Ignoring the petition presented to him by the indigo growing natives Halliday devoted a good deal of his attention to the complaints of the planters who wanted a law to enforce indigo contracts in the criminal courts. He was, in fact, in favour of a pro-planter legislation to prevent the disputes, but his intention to enact such legislation did not materialise due to the Revolt of 1857. Pointing out the abuses connected with the cultivation of indigo in Nadia, A. Scene, the Judge of Nadia, recommended to the Lieutenant Governor that the commissioners should be appointed to inquire into the relation of the planters and the raiyats. Scene's recommendation was necessitated by the fact that "all the servants and labourers of the planters, boatmen, hack drivers were forced to work for inadequate wages". According to him the raiyats had nothing except labour and land but they were treated as mere "working cattle".[32] To the suggestions of the Judge of Nadia Sir Halliday observed that the "laws were inefficient and the tribunal would be of no avail". While rejecting the proposal for an inquiry he said that this interpretation was based partly on the character of the people, which should be improved through the slow advance of knowledge and civilization, and partly to the errors of law and system.[33]

The indigo disputes started occurring between the raiyats and the planters and therefore it was thought essential to keep constant watch on the whole system of indigo planting in Bengal and Bihar. The Government of Bengal sent a circular letter to all the commissioners asking for reports from the indigo growing districts about the disputes.[34] The Commissioner of Bhagalpur reported to the government that there were only two cases filed by the raiyats against the planters. Several cases relating to injury by cattle trespass were brought forward by the planters. Complaints of forcible sowing with indigo were found in Munger.[35] In the district of Purnia there were only two cases of complaints while in Tirhut there were thirty-eight complaints. But since these complaints did not create law and order problem, the government did not interfere with the disputes between the planters and the *maliks*.

The revolt of 1857 was more serious in Bihar than anywhere else in India. The indigo planters in North Bihar proved to be strong props of Company's rule. They fought against the mutineers, guarded Muzzaffarpur and helped the Company restore its rule. As a result of this, the attitude of the government became much more favourable to them.[36] It was widely rumoured in Tirhut that "all natives were to be made Christians".[37] The report of bullock's and pig's fat being used in the cartridges was denied by the Commander-in-Chief, but the people were not convinced. All the Europeans, particularly the planters, were scattered in the interior of the *dehat* and therefore the Magistrate of Muzzaffarpur thought it proper to protect them from the attack of the mutineers. He summoned all the planters for a meeting in Muzzaffarpur. Trouble was expected from the *Mujeebs* -- a provincial battalion who supplied men as guards for the treasury. The government asked the planters to be ready for mutual help in case of need. The Magistrate asked the Europeans to keep guard as *santaris*, but the planters expressed their desire to disarm suspects and take the treasure to Patna, if necessary, in their factory cars under their escorts. The planters from far off districts began to arrive and soon there were over 300 men, women and children at Muzzaffarpur.[38]

Since the mutiny of the Native Infantry created panic among the Europeans, they formed two camps and messes for protection from the mutineers. All the ladies and children occupied the houses at one place, while the gentlemen slept in the tents. Each of the camps supplied two *santaris* and the planters had to do two hours watch and ward every night.

A native *daroga* (head inspector of police) named Warris Ali was suspected of inciting the people. The government planned to arrest him. Three Europeans and a magistrate were asked to accomplish the task. One of the planters informed the magistrate of the *daroga* approaching with his friends to annihilate the Europeans. When the *daroga* was surrounded, he was writing letters to the "rebels" of 1857. Ultimately he was arrested with the help of the indigo planters and was kept in charge of three "gentlemen of the Blue at Muzzaffarpur". Later he was taken to Patna where he was hanged. Before he was hanged, he was reported to have said that the King of Delhi should be informed that he was true to the King of Delhi to the last.[39]

Baddeley, a planter of the Daulatpur factory had to leave it and hide at Muzzaffarpur. In his absence a small zamindar declared himself the king of those parts. He was trying to take possession of the Daulatpur factory as he thought the British *raj* had passed away. He was also supported by the people of the area. But he was arrested, tried and imprisoned for ten years.[40] De Begg was the planters' doctor and ran an agency of the indigo seed. During the revolt of 1857 all members of his family were killed by the mutineers. Gerstin was managing Attur factory. He volunteered his services to the government during the mutiny. He went to Arrah to help the government but he was wounded by the rebels. The owner of Shahpur Oundie (now Shahpur Patori) Justin Finch supplied his six-foot gun to the government at Muzzaffarpur.[41] George Toomey was a nephew of James Cox, a planter of Dholi. George came out just before the revolt of 1857. He was one of those who, with others, started to retake Muzzaffarpur after the civilians and the rest of the residents had been ordered away by W. Taylor, Commissioner of Patna. In this way the indigo planters help the government to restore its rule.

It was hoped that an alliance between the planters, zamindars and the British government would form a strong bulwark to buttress the British rule. The appointment of European planters and zamindars as honorary magistrates by the government of Bengal at the instance of the Government of India and the Secretary of State for India in 1860-61 illustrates the pursuance of this policy.[42] As in Awadh and Punjab the landholders of Bengal were vested with the judicial powers of the Magistrate and made honorary Magistrates. It was desired by Her Majesty's Government that the "influence", services and means of information of the landholders and the European residents in the *mufassil* should be more largely utilised than previously for the proper administration of the country. J.P. Grant translated such a policy by appointing 45 honorary magistrates to the *mufassil* and 45 in Calcutta.[43] The experience of the Indian Mutiny and the abolition of Company's rule in 1858, however, brought home to the British government the expediency of an alliance with the Indian zamindars.[44]

Since J.P. Grant was critical of the whole system of indigo plantation, widespread rumour prevailed in the rural areas that the government was in favour of putting an end to the indigo cultivation. J. Forlong, a planter, wrote to the government of Bengal apprising them about the widespread rumour. He convinced the government that the raiyats were better in the indigo growing districts, for elsewhere they were little better than slaves to their *mahajans*. The opposition by the raiyats to the planters was attributed to the machinations of the middlemen and *mahajans* who were in the habit of supplying food to the raiyats at exorbitant rates.[45] To dispel the rumour the Government of Bengal requested the Government of India to direct the commissioners and the district officers to "spare no pains in impressing upon the villagers the duty of honestly fulfilling their agreements...".[46] The villagers were warned by the government of the ruinous consequences, if they failed to fulfil the agreement to cultivate indigo. As regard the proposed bill for the registration of the contracts for the delivery of the agricultural produces, the Lieutenant Governor concluded that the registration of indigo contracts would be largely ineffective. Thus the government took the side of the planters and refused to provide legal protection to the raiyats.

Contrary to the expectation of the raiyats who sought some relief, the majority members of the Commission were of the opinion that "no change of law and no changes in the system of administration were requisite or desirable".[47] The only remedy they recommended and which was within the power of the government was to apply effectively the execution of the existing law. It meant multiplication of sub-divisions with provision for better police and civil courts. The Lieutenant Governor, J.P. Grant, desired that the Governor-General in Council should issue a proclamation so as "to calm the minds of the ryots and to secure tranquillity of the country".[48] He believed that law could be made the sole instrument of change. According to him prosperity of agriculture and commerce depended more on the judges than on any other single office. [49] He was opposed to the indigo planters not on any doctrinaire principle. He believed that if their system were more sound, they could, like the planters of Banaras, become a blessing to the surrounding country. His major complaint was that they restricted the freedom of enterprise of the raiyats. [50]

It was a characteristic feature of the colonial administration and policy that they did not allow the freedom of enterprise to the raiyats. The need of the empire was more important than the interest of the cultivating classes. In order to safeguard the interest of the planters the Government of Bengal recommended to the Government of India the fulfillment of the valid contracts.[51] It was also suggested that a general notification should be issued to dispel the doubts in the minds of the raiyats that the government was opposed to indigo cultivation. His Excellency the Governor-General in Council approved of the proposal of the Government of Bengal and a notification was issued stating that the Government of India was not opposed to the cultivation of indigo.[52] As regards the relation between the indigo planter and the raiyats the Governor-General in Council felt that the matter should be settled by mutual adjustment without the intervention of the government.[53]

Reacting to the observation of the Lieutenant Governor on the report of the Indigo Commission, the Governor-General in Council observed that he estimated the local value of the indigo trade to be higher than that of the Governor-General of Bengal, as it brought profit and also gave employment to the agricultural classes. Besides, because of its trade "merchant's profit was derived from Russia, France, England and from all civilized countries in the world".[54] Thus the Government of India did not want to wish the break-down of the indigo trade of Bengal as the English capital was invested in the trade.[55] As regards investing the planters with the powers of the magistrate the Government of India strongly desired to seek the cooperation of the non-official gentlemen in indigo districts. The Governor-General in Council observed that such cooperation would be an aid to the government.

Keeping in view the importance of forging an alliance between the Indian zamindars and the planters, the Secretary of State for India proposed in 1862 the gradual extension of the Permanent Settlement to other parts and also advised the distribution of the wasteland to the planters at a nominal rates.[56] The Government of India expressed their views on this subject by a resolution on 17 October 1861. The main point in the resolution was the sale of wasteland to the European settlers. Charles Wood, the Secretary of State for India considered the question in detail and communicated his views to the Government of India in his Despatch No. 14 of July 1862. In para forty-seven of the same despatch he remarked:

"His Majesty's Government entertain no doubt of the political advantages which would attend a permanent settlement. The security, and, it may almost be said, the absolute creation of property in the soil which will flow from limitation in perpetuity of the demands of the state on owners of the land, cannot fail to stimulate or confirm their sentiments of attachment and loyalty to the government by whom so great a boon has been conceded, and whose existence its permanency will depend".[57] Thus from the time of Lord Minto (1810) to that of Lord Canning in 1859 the Government of India issued no strong statements condemning the behaviour of the indigo planters.

Condition in indigo plantation in Bihar were probably worse than in Bengal. Lawrence reported that the raiyat in Bihar was no better than a serf and the cultivation was being carried on under systematic pressure and terror. He believed that no final settlement of the indigo problem in Bihar was possible until there had been an outbreak such as had occurred in Bengal in 1860.[58]

The indigo question, which had subsided in the Nadia and Jessore districts of Bengal, assumed importance in Bihar. Disputes arose during the year 1866-67 with regard to indigo cultivation in the Pandaul concern where the raiyats asserted that the land seized by the manager of the factory was not the *zeerat* land. The planter on the other hand claimed that the raiyats were merely labourers cultivating the *zeerat* land of the factory.[59] In this dispute the local government sided with the planter. D.M. Barbour, Assistant Magistrate of Madhubani, was advised by the Officiating Magistrate of Tirhut to take action against the raiyats if they were repudiating the indigo contracts.[60] The raiyats filed two cases against the planter but the judgement was delivered in favour of the latter,[61] although the Assistant Magistrate admitted certain anomalies in the arrangements under which the factory possessed land for indigo. Since the dispute in Pandaul was considered to be of a serious nature, the Government of Bengal was duly informed by the Commissioner of Patna. The latter held the decision in one case and observed that the raiyats had been cowed down. The local government's policy evidently was oppressive to the raiyats in the Pandaul disputes. When the Manager of Darbhanga estate was approached to intervene in the matter, he adopted a posture of strict neutrality. [62] The Government of India, however, directed the officers not to interfere executively in the matter and asked them to maintain peace. The planters were asked to show the wisdom of viewing the subject in a broad and conciliatory spirit. The policy of Sir C. Beadon through out these disputes was to encourage an amicable settlement of disputes in every way.[63] But in most of the cases which came up for adjudication, the decisions of the court was in favour of the factory and thus the raiyats were convicted of criminal trespass under the Penal Code.

In similar raiyat-planter disputes in Motihari that followed the government adopted a much tougher stand towards the raiyats. In 1867-68 there was a strong demonstration by the raiyats against indigo cultivation in the district of Champaran. The main grievances of the raiyats related to the hard labour, inadequate wages, constant harassment by the factory servants and extortion of *dastoori* from them. Since the price of food grain had gone up, the raiyats wanted the rates of indigo plant to be increased. A number of petitions were sent to the government requesting them to redress their grievances. In a petition the raiyats of Tuppeh Madhole and Manore Seronah protested to the government against the cruelties meted out to them by the indigo planters.[64] They bought to the notice of the government how their standing food crops were damaged by the planters. They alleged that each factory had about 200 *lathials* ready to destroy and plunder the food crops. [65] The planters usually paid an advance of Rs 2 or 3 per *bigha* to the raiyats and promised to pay the rest of the amount after the indigo plants were ready. They however did not keep their promise. This breach of promise infuriated the raiyats who sometimes filed petitions recording their complaints and seeking redressal of grievances. But as the case of Dauli Sahu showed, the government paid no heed to such complaints.[66] When the raiyats protested against the forcible conversion of their land into *zeerat* land by the factories, they had to pay a fine varying from Rs 40, Rs 50 to Rs 100. The oppressive and coercive methods of the planters sometimes forced the raiyats to leave their hearths and homes and take refuge in the Nepal *terai*.[67] As a result their indignation manifested itself in the form of an assembly of twenty thousand people at Motihari. They made joint and vociferous complaints to the divisional commissioner on their arrival at Mothari for amelioration of their plight.[68] But the commissioner's callous indifference underlined their utter helplessness and disappointment. Another petition to the Lieutenant-Governor requesting for an increase in their wages and hiring rates for bullock carts fared no better as the Lieutenant-Governor pleaded his lack of jurisdiction in the matter.[69]

The local government in connivance with a planter named Balpin released some of the intelligent men among the raiyats while the majority of the innocent raiyats were detained in the *hajat*. The influential raiyats were released because the planters thought that they would take advantage of their presence in the countryside by forcing the poor raiyats to grow indigo, although the charges against all the raiyats were the same. In this way discriminatory attitude was adopted by the government to divide the raiyats.

Since there was no appeal under the contract law to the High Court, the raiyats were compelled to bring their hard cases before the Lieutenant-Governor of Bengal. In a petition the indigo raiyats of Bajaria within the zamindari of the Maharaja of Bettia complained to the Lieutenant-Governor about the obligatory cultivation of indigo.[70] They alleged that their rice land was being converted into indigo land. Their complaints to the zamindars and the police did not bear fruit because of the influence of the powerful planters. Refuting the allegation against himself Baldwin, an indigo planter, attributed this to the instigation of Mahashaya Singh and Daulat Singh of Bhawanipur village. In this case the Government of Bengal directed Metcalfe to exercise his influence to induce the raiyats to act upon their engagements. He was also directed to neutralise the "pernicious influence" of the influential persons who were instigating the trouble. [71] The Governor-General in Council, however, made a query from the Government of Bengal regarding the complaints of the raiyats. The Government of Bengal in reply stated that "nothing indeed would be more likely to lead to serious mischief than direct interference on the part of the Government".[72]

The Lieutenant-Governor anticipated that the immediate consequence of direct interference would create widespread rumour among the people that the government was opposed to indigo cultivation followed by immediate losses to the planters who had invested their capital. According to him the planters in Tirhut were very reasonable and modest and therefore they did not deserve loss owing to the interference of the government.[73] Even the Governor-General in Council was satisfied with the system and disfavoured any "pressure" against it.[74] As a result of the query made by the Governor-General in Council, the indigo planters enhanced the rate from Rs 8 or Rs 9 per *bigha* to Rs 12 per *bigha* and guaranteed the full payment to the raiyats. The Governor-General, however, maintained that indigo planting must remain an issue between the planters and the raiyats. According to him the leasing of estates by the landlords to the planters should be entirely left to the parties concerned.[75] Anticipating the possibility of agrarian disturbance, he warned the planters and asked them to take pre-emptive steps to protect English capital and energy. He advised them to be moderate and conciliatory and not to force any confrontation with the raiyats. He wanted to make indigo cultivation a "source of wealth" and contentment rather than a source of oppression and discontent to the people. Since so much of English capital was invested, the government was prepared to do everything that was in its power to assist the planters provided the latter established satisfactory relations between the cultivators and themselves.

Notwithstanding the desire for a harmonious planter-raiyat relationship Lawrence was realist enough to foresee that friction between the two might develop and the government may be left with no alternative but to interfere to adjust matters.[76] In fact Lawrence felt that it was in the interest of the planters to conciliate the raiyats. H.S. Maine, another member of the Board of Revenue, however, held different opinion on this issue. According to him the active interference would be a delicate undertaking. He wanted the planters to concede "such prices for the indigo plant as will produce contentment among the cultivating population".[78] He endorsed the view of the Lieutenant-Governor of Bengal that "if the indigo interests were destroyed by a combination among the ryots, native *thikadars* would be substituted by the zamindars for present European leaseholders, and that, under their exactions the condition of the peasantry would be much and permanently worse than at present".[79]

As regards the policy of A. Eden, Lieutenant-Governor of Bengal, towards indigo cultivation in Bihar it may be said that he was awaiting the result of the measures of reforms which the planters themselves had promised to initiate.[80] He was ready to consider any suggestions which the planters might make so that the relations between the zamindars, planters and the raiyats, could be placed on an equitable basis. He was fully convinced that the downfall of the indigo industry in Bihar would be a public calamity.[81] To safeguard the immensely lucrative nature of the industry in Bihar he wished the adoption of cordial and conciliatory attitude by the planters. Unlike Richard Temple, Lieutenant-Governor of Bengal, Ashley Eden supported the cause of the planters against the raiyats. Richard Temple had been a liberal and firm supporter of the rights of the raiyats. He had also initiated an enquiry into the conduct of those magistrates who had sided with the planters.[82]

The attention of the government was drawn during the years 1877-78 to the abuses which were allowed to continue in connection with indigo cultivation. After a detailed study a report was submitted by the Commissioner of Patna to the Government of Bengal. The report concluded that the system as it existed involved an amount of lawlessness and oppression, principally in the shape of extorted agreements to cultivate indigo. Seizure of ploughs and cattle was also brought to the notice of the government. But the recommendation of the Commissioner was not acceptable to the Lieutenant-Governor, Sir Richard Temple. He observed that "the appointment of commission would be a serious matter; by itself it would create a considerable disturbance, it would excite feelings which would not subside; it would shatter vested interests, place capital in jeopardy and proprietary status and occupancy rights into uncertainty for a time".[83]

Instead of appointing a commission of inquiry the Government of Bengal extended its patronage to the formation of Planters Association at Muzaffarpur in 1877 with its headquarters in London. Ashley Eden was made its patron. Some of the leading planters and officials of the government were consulted through the Commissioner of Patna. The main object of the Association was to do nothing which would unduly excite the minds of the raiyats. Although most of the planters who had disputes with the raiyats had not enrolled themselves as members of the Association, it formulated some rules for a regulation of what was known as *tinkathia* system. According to it a raiyat in a *tinkathia* village was to cultivate not more than three *kathas* of indigo per *bigha*. The raiyats who agreed to do so were not to have their rent enhanced. But the rules formulated by the Association were found satisfactory to the government.[84]

Reacting to the formation of the Planters Association in Bihar the *Samachar Chandrika* of 27 August 1877 remarked: *badmashas*, united a body, do more mischief than any one of them individually. The Association of the Bihar Planters will probably prove a combination to ruin the tenantry. They should never be permitted to combine; even as dacoits are not allowed to form themselves into gangs...".[85] The paper requested A. Eden to prevent the formation of an association by the planters, which was more likely to produce evil than good. The *Hindu Hitoishini* of 17 March 1877 contended that the indigo-planters of Bihar had become very bold during the tenure of Richard Temple. The civilians became friends of the planters and spent much of their time in their houses, where they also held courts. The intimacy between them strongly affected the tenantry. In view of the collusion between the government machinery and the planters, the raiyats had no courage to speak the truth.[86]

One of the weak points in Bihar and specially in Tirhut was the absence of tenants' right to the land. This gave an opportunity to the indigo planters to convert raiyats' land into *zeerat* land. While admitting the failure on the part of the government to bestow on tenants right to land, Temple wrote to Salisbury:

"I would not like to say in public nor in such a way as might annoy the large interests concerned.... Indigo system inevitably has the effect of depressing the status of the peasantry. The planters become landlord proprietors with a view to influencing the ryots to cultivate indigo. And a powerful interest thus arises which has strong motive for keeping the peasantry in that condition which will make them obedient to their masters".[87]

Salisbury, the Secretary of State for India, was more concerned about formidable indigo troubles in Bihar than about "vagaries of Cabul" and intrigues of Salarjung. The discontent of millions of raiyats appeared to him to be "a series of symptoms" to the government.[88]

Although the Bengal Tenancy Act of 1885 conferred upon the occupancy raiyats the right to lands, the landlords and the planters frequently infringed upon their rights because of some loopholes left in the Act. The tenants were assured against any enhancement of rents except in certain special circumstances including possible increase in the food prices. Due to the pressure of the landlords and the planters one clause was inserted in the Act, and according to which a raiyat, if he had held land at a specially low rate of rent in consideration of a particular crop for the convenience of the landlords, nothing was to prevent the raiyat from agreeing to pay such rent as he might deem fair and equitable.[89] When the Bill relating to Bengal Tenancy Act of 1885 was placed before the Select Committee, Section 29(iii) did not exist. It dealt with the enhancement of rent. Griffith Evans, a barrister, objected in the Council to the limit for enhancement of rent in view of the fact that the planters had let their land at a very low rate in consideration of raiyats growing indigo. To put a limit would have caused hardship to the planters. Ultimately Sir Stuart Bayley, who piloted the Bill, agreed to the amendments of Griffith as they protected the planters against the raiyats.[90]

Discovery of the synthetic dye in Germany and the consequent decline in the indigo trade in Bihar brought about some change in the attitude of the government. Lord Curzon established in Pusa a research station and college in 1905. Bernard Coventry, Manager of the Dalsingsarai factory, was appointed Director of the College. An experimental indigo farm was also started at Dalsingsarai through the efforts of the indigo planters and the government.[91] The main object of the College and the research station was to find out how the cultivation of indigo could be made cheaper and more remunerative, especially in view of the discovery of the synthetic German dye.

In spite of the so-called conciliatory spirit shown by the planters to the raiyats through the Planters Association, the protests of the raiyats did not stop. The raiyats become more vociferous in their attacks on the planters than earlier in view of the fact that they had to pay a number of *abwabs* to the planters in lieu of the loss the planters incurred in the indigo trade in the international markets. It was at this time that nascent nationalism was taking shape in Bihar. Fresh indigo troubles started in 1907 within the limits of Tilhara factory which resulted in the murder of its manager, Bloomfield. This was occasioned by the refusal of the manager to recognise the transfer of his sale to certain holdings. The next manifestation of the trouble came from the Sathi area where the raiyats refused to supply labour to the factory. It lead to violence from both sides. The other issues involved in the trouble pertained to the payments of indigo compensation and *abwabs*, service conditions and the rates of the carts. But the planters were so powerful and close to the government that they managed to secure the conviction of a large number of tenants.

The raiyats had become very conscious by the beginning of the twentieth century. They were ready for collective action. They organised themselves into groups, collected common funds to fight the planters in the civil courts, and also made several representations to the Government of Bengal. Their chief representative Sital Rai was arrested and some four thousand men followed him to Bettia where he was kept in the lock-up. The indigo planters, on the other hand, held a special meeting in Motihari and called up the government to take strong punitive measures to curb the disturbances. In such a situation marked by violent clashes between the planters and the raiyats, the Government of Bengal promised a full confidential inquiry into the agrarian conditions in Champaran.[92] Although the local administration and the Inspector-General of Police were opposed to any inquiry, the Commissioner of Patna recommended it. W.R. Gaurlay, the Director of Agriculture, was appointed by the Bengal Government to conduct a confidential inquiry. Gaurlay made a detailed study of the troubles and submitted his report to the government in April 1909. When he returned to Patna after making a inquiry he carried a few packing boxes. When the boxes were opened it was found that they contained both *rabbi* (wheat) and indigo plants. The inquiry clearly revealed that the raiyats were forced to cultivate indigo.[93] Gaurlay observed: "Any immediate change of a drastic nature in the terms of the contract between the factory and the producers will ruin many of the concerns...".[94] The issue that seriously concerned the government now was whether it would be desirable from a general point of view to destroy the indigo industry of Champaran and possibly in other parts of Bihar. While appreciating Gaurlay's findings, the Lieutenant-Governor admitted that the raiyats were not wholly free agents in the cultivation of indigo. He felt that the raiyats might refuse to cultivate it, if they were not obliged to do so. He wanted that indigo industry should stand on a commercial footing and should not depend on compulsion and pressure.[95]

Since the trouble in Champaran caused anxiety to the Government of Bengal as it involved a law and order problem, it announced some concessions to the raiyats. These included an increase in the rates of the price per acre paid for indigo cultivation to the raiyats from Rs 12 to Rs 13, i.e. 12½ per cent over those conceded in 1878; payment of full rates to the raiyats irrespective of the land sown with indigo; the reduction of the area under cultivation from three *kathas* to two *kathas* in a *bigha* and the reduction in the period of contract up to a limit of nine years. Although these recommendations of the government were discussed by the representatives of the planters and the local government officers, the planters did not fully implement them. But the government did not take any action. The Lieutenant-Governor on the other hand addressed the conference of the Planters Association held at Darjeeling in 1910 and expressed full confidence in them.[96] It gave an encouragement to the planters to oppress the raiyats.

In order to oppress the tenants punitive force was posted in Bettia. When a telegram was sent by the raiyats to the Lieutenant-Governor for redressal of grievances, they got no response.[97] Instead Baldeo Tiwari, a high caste Brahmin, was asked to supply *rasad* to the punitive force stationed there.[98] The raiyats were not allowed to assemble at one place and hold meetings. Two hundred warrants of arrest were issued to the tenants. Without verifying the facts the Lieutenant-Governor justified the posting of the punitive force surrounding the villages of Guraulia, Batua, Mathan and Bajahi within *thana* Bettia and Mathia, Darma, Lakhanpur, Kalan Barua, Gubauli and Chand Barua within the Shikarpur *thana*. The inhabitants of these villages were found responsible for the trouble.[99] The unhelpful attitude of the government was highlighted by the Calcutta journals, the chief of them were the *Bengali, Amrit Bazar Patrika*, the *Bharat Mitra*, the *Hindi Bangavasi*, the *Hitavadi* and the *Basumati*.

During the years from 1910 to 1914 the raiyats continued their struggles against the planters. They assembled at Narkatiaganj railway station on 11 December 1911 and registered their grievances to George V, the King Emperor of India, when he was on his way back from Nepal. A series of articles appeared in the *Beharee* newspaper in which the system of indigo cultivation was attacked. But the indigo planters continue to realise *tawan* from the raiyats without any check by the local government. Towards the end of 1914 a number of petitions were sent to the Lieutenant-Governor by the tenants of Champaran complaining of *abwabs* illegally collected by the planters. But the government did not pay any attention to the plight of the raiyats till the indigo question became a national issue. It was initially started by Raj Kumar Sukul of village Satwaria of Lawria Police Station. He attended the Provincial Congress session held at Chapra in 1915 and then the Indian National Congress session held in Lucknow in 1916. It was he who tried to convince Gandhiji at Lucknow about the condition of the raiyats in Champaran.

To conclude, from the inception of indigo cultivation till 1917 the attitude of the government remained the same, that is, it allowed uninterrupted this practice in Bihar. Despite immense harassment and continuous oppression leading even to the flight of the raiyats to Nepal *terai*, the government remained committed to the planters. The change of rule from the Company to the Crown did not change the system of cultivation as such; rather it added a number of administrative units which caused intense exploitation of the tenantry in Bihar. Since indigo cultivation was geared to the needs of the empire, the petitions filed by the tenants were unattended or were ignored under the facade of the non-interference policy. The system of cultivation and indigo manufacture was so carefully evolved by means of advance from the merchant capitalists to the raiyats that a handful of Europeans acquired not only a claim to the product but also exercised control over millions of producers. The planters had the advantage of imperial backing and political superiority and therefore they reaped enormous profit.

It may not be out of place to mention that like the Dutch the British also organised plantations for producing indigo, sugar, coffee, tea and rubber in India in order to obtain the lion's share of the surplus of the dominated economies.[100] The policy of free trade pursued in India after 1813 helped open India fully to the influence of the world capitalist market and provided new levers for extracting the surplus from India. The surplus realised through trade in indigo and other goods such as opium and cotton. etc. was utilised to extend the British domination over the rest of India and to balance the trade accounts with China. 7 or 8% of the national income invested by Britain during the period from 1757 to 1813 of her Industrial Revolution inflicted heavy damage to the Indian economy.[101] The internal transit and town duties abolished in 1856 in most parts of India ushered in the era of formal free trade as it did not involve any reciprocal concessions either by Britain or by other countries trading in indigo. As a result of the pursuance of free trade India, particularly the indigo growing areas of Bihar, was reduced to a position of a supplier of agricultural goods and raw material to the industrialising countries of the West, particularly Britain. Thus in a colonial country like India the *raj* enjoyed the executive power under the policy of "constructive imperialism". Chamberlain argued that the empire was like a vast landed estate and that the British, like any other landlord, had a duty to develop their estates. In the doctrine of *laissez-faire* the role of the State in the colonial development was seen mainly in terms of "opening up" colonies to trade, investment or settlement.[102]

REFERENCES

1 *Minute* by Lieutenant-Governor of Bengal on the *Report of the Indigo Commission* (1860), p. 19. After the indigo disturbances in Lower Bengal the Government passed an Act XI of 1860 to enforce the fulfillment of indigo contracts and to provide for the appointment of a Commission of Inquiry. The Commission consisted of Seton Karr, the Secretary to the Government of Bengal as its president, Richard Temple, W.F. Fergussion, a nominee of the Indigo Planters Association, Rev. John Sale, a Christian missionary and Babu Chander Mohan Chatterjee, a nominee of the British Indian Association.

2 Ibid., p.20. The old districts producing indigo in Bihar included Patna, Shahabad, Munger, Bhagalpur, Saran and Tirhut (Tirhut comprised both Muzaffarpur and Darbhanga).

3 H.R.Ghosal, *Economic Transition in Bengal Presidency (1793-1833)* (Calcutta, 1966), p. 76.
4 George Watt, *A Dictionary of Economic Products of India*, Vol. IV (Reprint, 1972), para 158, p. 395.
5 Ibid.
6 Sayera Irfan Habib, *Colonial Exploitation and Capital Formation in England in the Early Stages of the Industrial Revolution*, Proceedings of the Indian History Congress, 36th Session, Aligarh, 1975, p. XXVI.
7 *Nineteenth Century studies*, No. 8, October 1974 (Trade and Commerce), Calcutta, p.487.
8 D.H.Buchanan, *The Development of Capitalist Enterprise in India* (New York, 1934), pp. 36-37.
9 S.B.Singh, *European Agency Houses in Bengal, 1783-1833* (Calcutta, 1966), p. 213.
10 H.R.Ghosal, op.cit., p. 37.
11 Amiya Kumar Bagchi, *The Evolution of the State Bank of India*, The Roots, 1806-1876, Part I, The Early Years, 1806-1860, (Oxford University Press, Delhi, 1987), p.165.
12 Ibid., p.165.
13 Blair B. Kling, *The Blue Mutiny, the Indigo Disturbances in Bengal, 1859-1862* (Philadelphia, 1966), p. 38.
14 *Pearl Papers* 1831-32, VIII, quoted in Blair B. Kling, op.cit., p.38.
15 Ibid., p. 41.
16 The *Resolution of the Government of India*, 7 July 1823, W.B. Baylay, Chief Secretary to the Government of India to S.P. Lower Provinces.
17 Ibid.
18 Blair B. Kling, op.cit., p. 42. Also see Amiya Kumar Bagchi, *The Evolution of the State Bank of India*, The Roots, 1806-1876, Part I, The Early Years, op.cit., p.141.
19 *Board of Revenue* No. 57, J.P.Pattle's minute, 20 November 1833. The Government of India adopted a resolution on 7 May 1824 according to which some restrictions were imposed on the planters becoming landed proprietors.
20 Ibid.
21 Ibid.
22 Ibid.

23 Blair B. Kling, op.cit., p. 47. The evangelical humanitarian wing wanted to diffuse British civilization and Christianity in India while the Lancashire group was interested in the growing of the cotton within the empire.
24 Ibid. See also Hansard's *Parliamentary Debates*, Vol. CXLIX, 16 March 1858, pp.269-93.
25 *Board of Revenue* No. 59, from R.D. Mangles, Acting Secretary to the Board of Revenue to the Government of Bengal, 29 November 1833.
26 Amiya Kumar Bagchi, The *Political Economy of Underdevelopment*, (Cambridge University Press, Cambridge, 1982), p.17.
27 Amiya Kumar Bagchi, "Reflection on the Nature of the Indian Bourgeoisie", *Social Scientist*, Nos 214-15, New Delhi, 1991, pp.12-13.
28 Blair B. Kling, op.cit., p. 21.
29 *Judicial Criminal Proceedings* No. 26, from Messrs Taler Mackinnan H. Hill (representing the indigo planters of Tirhut, Saran and Munger) to F.J.Halliday, Secretary to the Government of Bengal, Fort William, 27 December 1839.
30 Ibid.
31 Blair B. Kling, op.cit., p. 65.
32 *Judicial Proceedings*, Minute of Halliday, the Lieutenant-Governor of Bengal, Minute No.122A, 5 June 1854.
33 Ibid.
34 *Judicial Proceedings* No. 27, 12 June 1856. The letter was issued by C.T.Buckland, Joint Secretary to the Government of Bengal, 7 June 1856, Fort William.
35 *Judicial Proceedings* No. 77 from the Commissioner of Bhagalpur to the Secretary to the Government of Bengal, 30 August 1856, Fort William.
36 Girish Mishra, "Indigo Plantation and the Agrarian Relations in Champaran during the Nineteenth Century", *Indian Economic and Social History Review*, Vol.3, No. 4, 1966.
37 Minden Wilson, *History of Bihar Indigo Factories* (Calcutta, 1908), pp. 196-97.
38 Ibid., p. 199.
39 Ibid., p. 201. The Europeans suspected that all the Muslims would revolt against them. Warris Ali was having close contacts with the royal family of Delhi. Some of the papers

seized from him proved that he was in league with Ali Karim of Patna.

40 Ibid., p. 203.

41 Ibid., p. 235.

42 C.E.Buckland, *Bengal Under Lieutenant Governors,* Vol.I (Reprint 1976), pp. 227-28.

43 Quoted in B.B.Misra, *Select Documents on Mahatma Gandhi's Movement in Champaran (1917-18),* (Government of Bihar, Patna, 1963), p. 2. People sharply reacted to the hanging of Warris Ali. All soldiers from Tirhut revolted. The government wanted to arrest all of them. Both the banks of rivers Gandak and Ganges were guarded. Zamindars were asked to give information about the soldiers who were rebellious. The planters were asked to help the zamindars to find out the whereabouts of the rebellious soldiers of Tirhut.

44 C.E. Buckland, op.cit., pp.227-28.

45 From J. Forlong, an indigo planter, to E.H. Lushington, Official Secretary to the Government of Bengal, 24 November 1859.

46 Ibid.

47 *Judicial Progress,* September 1860, No.238. Lieutenant-Governor's *Minute* on the Report of the Indigo Commission. The Legislative Council as an occasional and temporary measure passed the Indigo Enforcement Act No.XI of 1860 which promised an inquiry into the system of indigo planting.

48 Ibid.

49 Blair B. Kling, op.cit., p. 75.

50 Ibid., p. 76.

51 *Home Department* No.4849, 17 September 1860, from W.S. Seton Karr, Officiating Secretary to the Government of Bengal to the Secretary, Government of India.

52 Ibid., No.1814, 22 September 1860, from W. Grey, Secretary to the Government of India to the Officiating Secretary to the Government of Bengal.

53 Ibid.

54 *Home Department* No. 393, from W. Grey, Secretary to the Government of India to W.S.Seton Karr, Secretary to the Government of Bengal, 27 February 1861.

55 Ibid.

56 *Bengal Land Revenue Proceedings* Nos 5-9, 18 August 1859, Despatch No.2, 31 December 1858. The policy of granting wastelands to the European settlers was communicated to the Government of India under Lord Stanley, Secretary of State for India.

57 B.B.Misra, op.cit., p.3.

58 S.Gopal, *British Policy in India, 1858-1905* (Cambridge University Press, Great Britain, 1965), p. 34.

59 *Judicial Proceedings* No.129, February 1867 from J.W.Dalrymple, Commissioner of Patna Division to the Secretary to the Government of Bengal, No.50, 7 February 1867. In a petition to the Commissioner of Patna the raiyats alleged harassment by the planters and expressed anger about the maltreatment meted out to them. Not only their ploughs and cattle were taken, they were confined in the *moorgi khana*. They demanded an inquiry against the planter with a view to taking *mokchas* from the indigo planters.

60 *Judicial Proceedings* No. 40, from A.T. Maclean, Officiating Magistrate of Tirhut to the Assistant Magistrate of Madhubani, No. 11, 19 January 1867.

61 Ibid. One case was filed by Lakshman Paswan and Magho Raut against H.L. Gale, Manager of Pandaul factory, while the other case was filed by Tribhuban Tante and Bachoo Tante. Both Lakshman Paswan and Magho Raut had been found committing criminal tresspass and they were imprisoned for one month and one day. Tribhuban Tante and Bachoo Tante were ordered to be jailed for four weeks.

62 Ibid.

63 C.E.Buckland, op.cit., p. 328. It is a narrative of the principal events and public measures during their period of office (1854-98).

64 *Judicial Proceedings* No. 85, May 1868 (undated).

65 Ibid.

66 Ibid.

67 Ibid.

68 Ibid.

69 *Judicial Proceedings* No. 79, Resolution by His Honour the Lieutenant-Governor of Bengal, 30 March 1866, Fort William.

70 *Judicial Proceedings* No. 34, July 1868 (undated). The petitioners were Mahashaya Singh, Daulat Singh, Gopal Roy, Chhattar Mahto, Ganesh Mehta, Bhigali Mehra, Chattar Roy, Joothi Goala, Began Ojha and Randhir Roy.

71 From Officiating Secretary to the Government of Bengal to the Commissioner of Patna, No. 6787, 31 December 1867.

72 *Home Department* No. 5581, from H.L.Dampier, Officiating Secretary to the Government of Benagal to the Secretary to the Government of India, 17 October 1868, Fort William.

73 Ibid., para 20.

74 Ibid., para 6.

75 Ibid., para 15.

76 *Home Public Proceedings* No.110, 9 January 1869, *Minute* by Lawrence, 23 December 1868.

78 *Home Public Department Proceedings* No. 114, 9 January 1869, *Minute* by H.S.Maine, 8 January 1869.

79 Ibid.

80 C.E. *Buckland, Bengal under the Lieutenant Governors, 1854-1898*, Vol. II (Reprint 1976), p. 703.

81 Ibid.

82 B.B. Misra, *Select Documents on Mahatma Gandhi's Movement in Champaran*, op.cit., p.11.

83 *General Miscellaneous, Department Proceedings* Nos 1-4, July 1876. It contains Richard Temple's *Minute*, 15 July 1876

84 Ibid., p. 704.

85 *Report on the Native Newspapers of Bengal*, 1877, *Samachar Patrika*, 27 August 1877.

86 *Report on the Native Newspapers of Bengal* op.cit.

87 *Salisbury Papers*, Reel 818 (NAI)(Temple to Salisbury, 26 March 1876.

88 Ibid., Reel 811 (NAI), Microfilm, *Private Papers, Salisbury to Richard Temple*, 1 September 1875.

89 *Bihar and Orissa Land Revenue Department Confidential File, Agriculture & Commerce*, A&B. Proceedings, 1911-18.

90 B.B.Misra, op.cit., p. 13.

91 *Report on the Native Newspapers of Bengal*, 1904, *Sanjivani*, 10 March 1904.

92 Ibid., p. 15.

93 *Bihar District Gazetteer*, Champaran (Patna, 1960).

94 *Bengal Revenue Department Confidential File* No. 19, 1909. It contains Gaurlay's note to the Chief Secretary dated 11 December 1908.

95 Ibid.

96 *Bihar District Gazetteer*, Champaran, op.cit., p.274.

97 *Report on the Native Newspapers of Bengal*, November 1908, *Khulna*, 7 November 1908.

98 Ibid. The *Prabhat* of 11 November 1908 reported this episode in detail.

99 Ibid., p.375. The *Hitavadi*, 12 November 1908.

100 A.K. Bagchi, *The Political Economy of Underdevelopment* (Cambridge University Press, Cambridge, 1982), pp.78, 80.

101 Ibid., p. 82. Also see Sayera Irfan Habib, op.cit., p.XXIV According to her the colonial wealth furnished 4.8% of the British National Income (GNP) at the beginning of the nineteenth century.

102 Deepak Kumar, ed, *Science and Empire, Essays in Indian Context (1700-1947)* (New Delhi, 1991), p.15.

CHAPTER II

Indigo *Kothis* and Systems of Cultivation

Although indigo was a product of North Bihar long before the advent of the British, its cultivation in accordance with European methods[1] was started by M.F. Grand, the Collector of Tirhut, in 1782. It was from this time indigo cultivation began to develop into an industry.[2] In a report of 11 February 1788 the Collector prepared a list of eleven Europeans who lived within the collectorship of Tirhut.[3] By 1793 the number of indigo factories increased to nine in Tirhut. The places where these factories were established along with the names of the proprietors are as follows:

TABLE 1

Serial No.	*Name of the factory*	*Outworks*	*Names of proprietors*
1	Daudpur[4]	1 Arringpur 2 Musahari 3 Chhajan	William Orby Hunter
2	Saraiya[5]		William Orby Hunter
3	Dholi		"
4	Athar		James Gentil
5	Shahpur		Richardson Panzes
6	Kanti		Alexander Namell
7	Motihari		"
8	Deoria		Finch
9	Babera		Lewis Kick & Co (GMLS Shuman)

The Revenue Surveyor recorded that there were 86 factories in Tirhut district in 1850.[6] A number of factories which had previously been manufacturing sugar were subsequently converted into indigo factories. Aurai, previously a sugar factory, and Deoria, partly an indigo factory and partly a sugar factory, started the manufacture of indigo exclusively. It was a time when sugar was finally superseded by indigo under the management of Europeans. According to the *Report of the Survey and Settlement Operation* the following indigo factories belonging to Bihar Indigo Plantation Association existed in the district of Muzaffarpur.[7]

TABLE 2

Serial No.	*Name of the factory*	*Outworks*	*Thana*	*Remarks*
1	2	3	4	5
1	Agrail [8]	1 Bela		It belonged to Darbhanga Maharaj.
		2 Dubha	Mahua	Hajipur district
2	Belsand [9]	1 Bhagwanpur	Belsand	Sitamarhi
		2 Bellahi	Sitamarhi	district
3	Bataulia [10] (now Bhatauli)	1 Sakri	Mahua	All these places
		2 Mian Chapra	"	are now in
		3 Ramdaspur	"	Hajipur district.
		4 Rudstongunj (Rustamganj)	"	
4	Bhikhanpur[11]	1 Bochacha	Muzaffarpur	
		2 Sohagpur	"	
		3 Mirhab	"	
		4 Jhapaha	"	
		5 Sinirdha	"	
5	Chitwara[12] (now Chhatwara)			
6	Kanti[13]	1 Nariar	Muzaffarpur	
		2 Raghai	"	
		3 Lautan	"	
7	Dholi[14]		Muzaffarpur	
		1 Birauli	Darbhanga	
		2 Sarbnaha		
		3 Sakri		
8	Deoria[15]		Muzaffarpur	
		1 Karamwari	Paru	
		2 Sherpur	"	
		3 Majhaulia	"	

1	2	3	4	5
9	Daudpur[16]		Muzaffarpur	
		1 Arajpur	"	
		2 Mehsi	"	
		3 Chhajan	"	
10	Kutubpur		Hajipur	Now in Vaishali district.
11	Karhari		Mahua	Now in Vaishali district.
12	Karnauli[17]	1 Gaura	Paru	
		2 Monine	"	
		3 Tajpur	"	
13	Motipur[18]	1 Chaklauran	Paru	
		2 Jagannathpur	"	
		3 Mararpur	"	
		4 Bariarpur	"	
14	Athar		Muzaffarpur	
		1 Gosrama	"	
		2 Mohamadpur	"	
		3 Misraulia	"	
15	Pirikhpur		"	
16	Rajkhand[19]		Katra	
		1 Katra	"	
17	Runisaidpur[20]		Belsand	
		1 Pitaujhia	"	
18	Singhia[21]		Lalganj	Now in Vaishali district.
		1 Chakdaulat	"	"
		2 Nawada	"	"
		3 Paura	"	"
19	Saraiya		Paru	Now in Muzaffarpur district.
		1 Azijpur	Muzaffarpur	
		2 Mohamadpur	Paru	
		3 Kolpura	"	
		4 Kurnaji	Lalganj	In Vaishali district.
20	Tewarra		Katra	In Sitamarhi district.

1	2	3	4	5
21	Tharma		Darbhanga	
22	Shahpur Mircha[22]		Muzaffarpur	
		1 Susta	Katra	
23	Chaksikandar		Mahua	In Vaishali district.

Thus taken together there were twenty-three indigo factories with their forty-eight outworks in Muzaffarpur district. Besides, there were nine other indigo factories in Muzaffarpur, although these did not belong to Bihar Indigo Planters Association.[23] The most important of these was Jaitpur indigo factory.[24] There was an indigo factory at Dumra which was established in 1811. It had two outworks namely Panchor and Bathnaha.[25] An indigo factory existed in Poopri also with outworks. It was managed by M.J. Wilson in 1853-54. [26]Thus the total indigo concerns in the old district of Muzaffarpur come to about eighty.

As superior landlords, the planters held 17.59 per cent of the district area, but their landed interests were permanent and secure in over 2 per cent only.[27]

DARBHANGA

Indigo cultivation in Darbhanga by the Europeans goes back to the time of Permanent Settlement. Factories in Dalsingsarai, Jitwarpur, Tiwara and Kamtaul were established at the end of the seventeenth century. Between 1800 and 1900 indigo cultivation began in almost all parts of Darbhanga, although it was more prevalent in the south of Darbhanga than in the north. By 1874 Darbhanga had the largest indigo concern in India and probably in the world.[28] The factories cultivated directly in no less than 30,760 acres or 94 per cent of the total area under indigo,[29] although the actual areas under indigo cultivation is exactly not known because the records of rights were not available until the *Survey and Settlement Operation* (1890-1910) of this district. [30]

The following is the list of factories which were in existence in the *Survey and Settlement Report* covering the period 1896-1903. [31]

TABLE 3

Factories and Outworks in Darbhanga

Serial No.	*Name of the factory*	*Outworks*	*Thana*	*Remarks*
1	2	3	4	5
1	Jainagar[32]		Khajauli	
		1 Nardha	"	
2	Kewan[33]		Madhubani	
		1 Bakwa	Khajauli	
3	Pandaul[34]		Madhubani	
		1 Lohal	"	
		2 Lehra	Bahera	
4	Raiyam[35]		Benipatti	
5	Benipur[36]		Bahera	
		1 Harsingpur[37]		
6	Hati[38]		Bahera	
7	Mankauli		Darbhanga	
		1 Singhwara	"	
8	Jharma		"	Factory in Muzaffarpur
9	Anar[39]		"	
10	Hathauri[40]		Rosera	
		1 Rasalpur	Darbhanga	
		2 Baghauni	Rosera	
11	Daulatpur		Rosera	
		1 Meghaul[41]	"	
		2 Ramnagar	"	
12	Mangalgarh		"	
		1 Karsaul	"	
		2 Motipur	"	
13	Buchaulia		"	
14	Girpura		"	
15	Muktapur		Warisnagar	
		1 Kalayanpur	"	
		2 Chak Mehsi[42]	"	
16	Jitwara[43]		"	
		1 Hasauli	Samastipur	
		2 Daudpur		

1	2	3	4	5
17	Banhar		Warisnagar	
18	Agrail		Samastipur	The factory was located in Muzaffarpur district.
19	Harsingpur[44]		Samastipur	
		1 Balrampur	"	
		2 Bahimabad	"	
		3 Tajpur	"	
		4 Bhawara	"	
		5 Mehsi	"	
20	Ilmasnagar		Warisnagar	
		1 Masina	"	
21	Rewari		Samastipur	
22	Gangauli[45]		Warisnagar	
		1 Alampur	"	
23	Koeta		"	
		1 Kumhah	"	
		2 Chatra	"	
		3 Tupha	"	
		4 Govindpur	"	
		5 Shahpur	"	
		6 Pembarhauda	"	
24	Maniarpur[46]		Dalsingsarai	
		1 Kalayanpur	"	
		2 Budayah	"	
25	Shahpur Undi[47]		"	
26	Nandni		"	
27	Mau		"	
		1 Dharnapatti	"	
		2 Maniar	"	
		3 Birauli[48]	"	
		4 Sakri	"	
		5 Subnaha[49]	"	It was an outwork of Dholi in Muzaffarpur district.
28	Manji		Rosera	

Thus there were about twenty-eight indigo factories with thirty-six outworks in Darbhanga district.

CHAMPARAN

The cultivation of indigo in the district of Champaran was started by Colonel Hicky in 1813 after the Nepal War. Factories at Rajpur and Tarkaulia were established by Messrs Moran and Hill respectively. The sugar industry flourished in Champaran till 1850 when it was superseded by indigo. During the last decade of the nineteenth century when the indigo industry was at its peak in the district, there were twenty-one indigo factories with forty-six outworks.[50]

The following are the factories with outworks belonging to the Bihar Indigo Planters Association in Champaran district.[51]

TABLE 4

Serial No.	*Name of the factory*	*Outworks*	*Thana*	*Remarks*
1	2	3	4	5
1	Bara[52]		Kesaria	
		1 Manipur	Madhuwan	
		2 Jagaulia[53]	"	
		3 Mahuawa	Kesaria	
		4 Gondaha	"	
		5 Rasulpur	"	
2	Bairia[54]		Bettia	
		1 Nautan	"	
3	Lalsaraya[55]		"	
		1 Madhopur	"	
		2 Faraua	"	
		3 Rajghat	"	
4	Loharia[56]		"	
		1 Lugina		
5	Dhokraha[57]		"	
		1 Bhamachak	"	
6	Mallaya[58]		"	
		1 Sirsia	"	

1	2	3	4	5
7	Motihari[59]		Motihari	
		1 Sugaon	"	
		2 Mirpur	Dhaka	
		3 Puranhia	"	
		4 Bhelwa	"	
		5 Haraj	Motihari	
		6 Chailaha	"	
		7 Bishambharpur	Dhaka	
8	Murla[60]		Motihari and Adapur	
		1 Lakshmipur	Adapur	
		2 Pokhari	"	
9	Pipra[61]		Motihari	
		1 Madhuban	Pipra	
		2 Dakaha	Motihari	
		3 Jagirha	Kesaria	
		4 Dinamath	"	
		5 Dhabaulia	Pipra	
10	Rajpur[62]		Kesaria	
		1 Hussaini	"	
		2 Pakri	"	
		3 Jamunapur	"	
11	Parsa[63]		Shikarpur	
		1 Harpur	Bagaha	
		2 Sargina	"	
12	Sathi[64]		Shikarpur	
		1 Malaria	"	
13	Siraha[65]		Dhaka	
		1 Parewa		
		2 Pudamkair		
		3 Puttaihi		
		4 Nawadah		
		5 Murpah		
		6 Tilara		
14	Titaria[66]		Madhuban	
		1 Bala	"	
		2 Chauhani	"	

1	2	3	4	5
15	Tarkaulia[67]		Motihari	
		1 Chilaram (Chilram)	"	
		2 Olaha	Govindganj	
		3 Barharwa	"	
		4 Jalaha	"	
		5 Makhua	"	
		6 Dudahi	"	
		7 Gahiri	Bettia	
		8 Khairwa	Govindganj	
		9 Sakhwa (Sirni)	"	
		10 Tejpurwa	"	
16	Nawadah[68] (Nawada)			
		1 Rajpur	Dhaka	
		2 Parsauni	Sheohar	In Muzaffarpur district.
17	Kuria[69]		Bettia	
		1 Lalghar	"	
18	Marpa		Madhuban	In Sheohar (Muzaffarpur district).
19	Padamkia (Padamkar)		Dhaka	
20	Hardia[70]		Adapur	
21	Tilhara[71] (Telhara)		Dhaka	

From the above table it is obvious that indigo factories were more common in the Motihari subdivision. Out of 21 factories with 53 outworks, 12 were located there. Except Lalsaraya all the major factories such as Rajpur, Bara, Motihari and Tarkaulia were located in Motihari subdivision. In Champaran district the planters had the right as superior landlords in 46.03 per cent of the total area.[72] As superior landlords they had secure interest in the land in 17.67 per cent as against 2 per cent in Muzaffarpur district.[73] The planters held 58.55 per cent of the total area of Motihari subdivision under them as proprietors, intermediary tenureholders and under tenureholders while in the Bettia subdivision they had 34.9 per cent of the total land area under them.[74] Since transport facility in Bettia was not sufficiently available, the planters invested their capital more and more in Motihari subdivision.

SARAN

Indigo cultivation was introduced in Saran district in 1793-94, when Messrs Ivory and Blako obtained permission from the government to build a factory at Akbarpur (now Sitalpur) in Sonpur *Thana*.[75] Shore obtained permission to start a factory in 1794 at Darauli. A licence was granted to him to hold fifty *bighas* of land. Thus during the early part of the nineteenth century factories were established in all parts of the district. By 1850 indigo cultivation by Europeans coincided with the growth and manufacture of sugar industry. But between 1850 and 1898 sugar was practically replaced by indigo.[76]

The following is the list of factories in Saran district which belonged to the Bihar Indigo Planters Association:[77]

TABLE 5

Serial No.	*Name of the factory*	*Outworks*	*Thana*	*Remarks*
1	2	3	4	5
1	Bansopali[78]		Siwan	
2	Baharauli		Masharak	
3	Barhoga[79]		Basantpur	
		1 Chitauli	"	
		2 Dhobaulia	"	
		3 Basaon	"	
4	Chetan Parsa		Parsa	
5	Chakia (1864)		Siwan	
		1 Jagadishpur (1865)	"	
6	Maniara[80]		Mirganj	
		1 Sipaiya	"	
		2 Tirverawa	Gopalganj	

1	2	3	4	5
		3 Ghunapatti	"	
7	Partabpur		Siwan	
		1 Ratansia	"	The factory was actually in Gorakhpur.
		2 Bankat[81]	"	
8	Ramkola[82]		Masharak	
		1 Marhowrah	Parsa	
		2 Ghorha	Masharak	
9	Sitalpur[83]		Sonpur	
		1 Murah	Parsa	
10	Jogapur[84]		Siwan	
		1 Kahala	Gopalganj	
		2 Chauki	Siwan	
		3 Madhopur	"	
		4 Kabulla	Basantpur	
11	Gopalpur		"	
12	Rampur		"	
13	Rajpatti[85]		Gopalganj	
		1 Pakri	Masharak	
		2 Pipra	"	
14	Zamapur		Siwan	
15	Gaighat		"	
		1 Harpur	Durauli	
16	Sadwa		Gopalganj	
		1 Shahpur	"	
		2 Sonbarsa	"	
		3 Bhaisahi	"	
17	Kehumia			The factory was in Gorakhpur but the land was partly in Saran (Mirganj) and partly in Gorakhpur.
18	Harpur		Chapra	

There were also indigo factories which did not belong to the Bihar Indigo Planters Association.

1	2	3	4	5
19	Bansghat[86]		Gopalganj	It ceased to belong
		1 Bhamo	"	to the Bihar Indigo
		2 Dekauli	"	Planters Association
				in 1899.
20	Nawada[87]		Parsa	
		1 Hariharpur	"	
21	Arwa[88]		Chapra	The Arwa concern
		1 Dangharn[89]	"	with five outworks
		2 Tajpur	"	never belonged to
		3 Tehti	"	the Bihar Indigo
		4 Aura	"	Planters Association
		5 Paigambarpur	"	
		6 Urna		
		7 Jalalpur		
		8 Chaitanparsa		
22	Bala		Basantpur	
23	Nagwa		"	
24	Garkha		Chapra	It was closed.
25	Tircalpur		Durauli	
26	Gaur			In fact the
				factory was in
				Gorakhpur but
				the indigo land
				was in Mirganj.
27	Saflabad		Gopalganj	It was closed.
28	Jaitpur		Manjhi	
		1 Banwar	"	
		2 Mubarakpur	"	
29	Kindupatti[90]			The factory was in
				Gorakhpur but
				the land was in
				Mirganj.
30	Mohammadpur		Gopalganj	It was an indigo
				factory owned
				by a native.
31	Ramghar		Manjhi	
		1 Baghar	"	
32	Sahagra		Darauli	It was closed.

1	2	3	4	5
33	Seunagar		Gopalganj	
34	Hajipura		Siwan	It was owned by a native.
35	Goomar		Derauli	It was owned by a native.

Besides the factories listed above there were some other factories. They were located at Baikunthpur, Domath,[91] Muniarah,[92] Jamunpur,[93] Jatepur[94] and Seerepore.[95] Thus there were 31 indigo factories with about 42 outworks in Saran district. At the time of the previous settlement operation, i.e. between 1893, and 1901, 45,513 acres of land was under indigo cultivation. When the revision of the survey (1915-1921) was going on the area under indigo cultivation was 7,904 acres only.[96] Thus the area to net cropped area under indigo cultivation comes to 3.5 per cent,[97] as per the statement furnished in the *Survey and Settlement Report* of Purnia district, while the Saran *Survey and Settlement Report, 1893-1901* puts it at 3.54 per cent. [98]

BHAGALPUR

Formerly indigo was extensively cultivated in Bhagalpur district, particularly in the north. This industry was gradually given up. During the survey and settlement operation, 1902-10, only five factories were manufacturing indigo.[99] Two factories, i.e. Narayanpur and Pathargarh, were located in the north of the district and the remaining three were located at Sangrampur, Kahalgaon and Salempur in the south of the district. Sangrampur was in Munger district, just on the border of Bhagalpur, but some of the indigo manufactured by this factory was grown in Bhagalpur.

Besides these five factories, there were 34 indigo factories formerly cultivating and manufacturing indigo. These factories were located at Bhatina, Chandipur, Singheshwar, Rajpur, Mampur, Nathpur, Dhaipur, Simraha, Lalitpur, Katia, Pipra, Bajhama, Hulas, Bhaiso, Babhni, Baijnathpur, Teria, Chaura, Murwala, Bishunpur, Dhangama, Bhawanipur, Gobargarha, Parmanandpur, Latona, Kashnagar, Nardah, Chausa, Belo, Tulsia,

Khunti, Imampatti,Kharagpur and Akbarpur.[100] At Latona and Bangaon also indigo was cultivated but these did not manufacture indigo. Thus taken together there were 43 factories in Bhagalpur district. Most of these were established by the Europeans between 1830 and 1860. A few of these were also built by the local zamindars. For example, Marwala faetory belonged to the Panchgachia *Babus*, while Gobarghara and Dhangama to the Raja of Banaili and Salempur to Shri Deep Narayan Singh.[101]

PURNIA

Indigo plantation was in a flourishing condition in this district during the eighteenth and nineteenth centuries. A.W. Johnson, one of the last remnants of indigo planters in Purnia, recalls that his own great-grandfather, who was a indigo planter, came into the district in the seventeenth century. Possibly Nilganj was the first place where indigo industry was erected in 1775.[102] In the nineteenth century there existed 92 factories but by 1908 their number was reduced to 21 factories.[103] Although indigo cultivation occupied only one per cent of the total cropped area in Purnia district,[104] its cultivation in the first half of the nineteenth century was very intensive. In Hunter s *Statistical Account*, a list of 60 factories has been provided which cultivated in all an average of 81,000 *bighas* of land per year for the ten years previous to 1875.[105] During the period when the survey and settlement operation was going on only 19 factories existed in this district. The most important *thanas* where indigo was cultivated were Dhamdaha, Korha and Saifganj. Sultanpur which was one of the largest concerns in the first half of the nineteenth century ceased to cultivate and manufacture indigo in the first half of the twentieth century. In view of the paucity of records it is difficult to provide a complete list of all the indigo factories in Purnia district. An attempt is, however, being made to furnish the number of factories and the names of the planters. These are as follows:

TABLE 6

Serial No.	*Name of the factory*	*Name of the planter*	*Outworks*	*Pargana*
1	2	3	4	5
1	Nilganj (1775)	Coustard		South of. Purnia
2	Kolasi[106]			Katihar. 1400 acres of land
3	Munshai	C.A. Shillingford		Kumaripur
			1 Kirpur	
4	Miannagar	G.Burnell		Kankol
			1 Byna	
			2 Kaliganj	
			3 Mahadebpur	
5	Pirganj	H.Cruise		Haveli Purnia
6	Sultanpur	A.J.Forbes		
			1 Amona	
			2 Rohikpur	
			3 Jalalgarh	
			4 Forbesabad	
			5 Rampur	
			6 Maisakul	
			7 Khopda	
7	Bhaugaon	Rai Lakshmipat Singh		Tajpur
8	Gonddwara	H. Cane	Dharampur	
			1 Kora	
			2 Nisendra	
			3 Dumar	
			4 Debipur	
			5 Jauria	
			6 Bopira	
			7 Khawaspur	
			8 Kabar	
			9 Gornia	
9	Nilganj	R.S.Ryne		Dharampur Haveli Purnia
			1 Kaja	
			2 Khaga	

1	2	3	4	5
			3 Putilwa	
			4 Banbagh	
			5 Bishunpur	
			6 Mirzapur	
			7 Sirsi	
			8 Mansaua	
10	Sahara	J.L.Shillingford		Dharampur
			1 Hansaili	
			2 Koashi	
11	Kolasi	G.W.Shilingford		Kolasi
			1 Katiyar	Dharampur
			2 Sambalpur	Haveli
12	Mahendrapur	F.Cruise		"
			1 Nathaur	
			2 Sauhesballia	
			3 Dinapur	
13	Dharara	E.D.Sauza		Dharampur
14	Kaltai[107]			Lakshmipur (Bhagalpur)
			1 Burgawan	Purnia
			2 Phusiyan	"
15	Barraria[109]	M.Allister		Dharampur
			1 Maikant	
			2 Maharajganj	
			3 Parmanandpur	
			4 Gokulnagar	
16	Nathpur	Gangaldahi[110]		South Dharampur Bhagalpur
17	Bawara	R.Walker		Kankjol
			1 Dilawari	
			2 Sibganj	
			3 Jotram Rai	
18	Gidwas	Rai Lakshmipat Singh		Haveli Purnia
19	Deoria	Bentley		"
20	Lalpur	Miss Gouldhuke		"

Taken together the total number of indigo concerns comes to 64 as against 92 factories as recorded in the *Bihar District Gazetteer* of Purnia. Generally the owners of the factories were Europeans except a few zamindars whose factories were confined to the eastern skirts of the district. The land was usually taken by the planter on lease from the Maharaja of Darbhanga. The soil was less productive as compared to the soil of the other parts of North Bihar. Therefore the rates of advance paid to the tenants varied from 8 *annas* to Rs 2 per *bigha* of 2400 square cubits or *haths*. The common variety of indigo seed was the *Sumatrana* type which was obtained from Kanpur in the United Provinces. In about 1904 a new variety of indigo seed was introduced from Java which came originally from Natal. The Java variety of seed was really an improved type because it obtained 20 *seers* of finished indigo per acre as against 8 *seers* per acre obtained from Sumantra variety of indigo seed. It was possible that modern machinery was used.

MUNGER

As compared to Tirhut division, and Champaran and Saran districts indigo cultivation in Munger was so negligible that it did not even draw the attention of the government. The Acting Magistrate of Munger wrote to the Government of Bengal in 1830 that the area under indigo being very limited there were only a few clashes.[111] In 1878, the officer in-charge of the Begusarai subdivision in which all the chief factories were located furnished information regarding indigo cultivation in Munger district.[112] According to W.W.Hunter there were factories at Manjhaul, Begusarai, Bhagwanpur, Begumsarai and Daulatpur.[113] But based on Hunter's *Statistical Account* and the *District Gazetteers* of Munger (1960 Patna) the following 35 factories with outworks existed in Munger district as given below:

TABLE 6A

Serial No.	*Name of the factory*	*Outworks*	*Remarks*
1	2	3	4
1.	Begusarai		Begusarai district
		Teghara	Barauni Block
		Barauni	"
		Nawada	Teghara Block
		Jhamatia	Bechhabara Block
2.	Bhagwanpur		Bhagwanpur Block
		Agapur	"
		Surajpura	"
		Kirtaul (Kiratpur)	"
3.	Harrakh		Begusarai Block
		Masnadpur (Maksaspur)	"
		Mahna	Barauni Block
		Dhabauli	Begusarai Block
		Mati Hasir	(?)
4.	Manjhaul		Begusarai Block
		Bishunpur	"
		Birpur	Barauni Block
		Garhpura	Bakhari Block
5.	Sisauni		Begusarai Block
		Bandwar	"
		Gamharia	Bakhari Block
		Kamalpur	"
6.	Nayagaon		Matihani Block
7.	Sadanandpur		Balia Block
		Hitanpur (Hetampur)	"
		Samastipur	Sahebpur Kamal Block
		Meghaul	Khudabandpur Block
8.	Daulatpur		"
		Ramnagar	Begusarai Block
9.	Manglagarh (Jaimanglagarh)		Cheriya Bariarpur Block
		Malipur	Bakhari Block
		Govindpur	Bachhabara Block

1	2	3	4
10.	Munger		Munger District (old)
		Digaon	Tarapur Block
		Sangrampur	Kharagpur Block

In the districts of Patna, Gaya and Shahabad also the number of indigo concerns were very few. The Commissioner of Patna informed the Government of Bengal that indigo disputes rarely took place in the district as the planters were very few in number.[114] Equally negligible was the indigo cultivation in the district of Gaya. The tour diary of W.C. Costley, Deputy Magistrate of Sargathy, recorded "there was an old indigo factory at Soojee Khap".[115] In Shahabad district indigo was cultivated in different *mauzas* but there is no record of an indigo industry. Details regarding indigo cultivation in Shahabad district based on the *Board of Revenue* are furnished in the table below.[117] These *mauzas* were confiscated from the possession of Babu Bir Kunwar Singh after the 1857 revolt and given to the planters.

TABLE 7

Statement showing the mauzas taken under lease in the names of the European planters and their servants living in Shahabad.

Serial No.	*Name of the pargana*	*Name of the mauza*	*Name of the planter*	*Servants*
1	Chynepoor	1. Sherpur	M.W. Walker	
		2. Eusopur & Co		
		3. Ranjeetpur & Co		
		4. Medha		
		5. Belleeon & Co		
		6. Lowan		
2	Chausah	1. Khetpara	M. Fulton	40
3	Bhojpur	1. Majhauria & Co	"	40
4	Bhojpur	1. Jhunwar & Co	Combs	
5	Bhojpur	1. Dumari & Co	Allan	
6	Danwar	1. Naghikas & Co	R. Clanvor	
7	Chainpur	1. Jhobah	Well & W. Ward	

Serial No.	*Name of the pargana*	*Name of the mauza*	*Name of the planter*	*Servants*
8	Chausa	1. Pipra & Co	M.W. Ward	
9	Beehian	1. Sahpur & Co	Gibbon	
10	Arra	1. Goondees & Co 2. Surroyee	Lethhridge	
11	Arra	1. Tendowah	"	
12	Arra	1. Nurpur & Co	M.Z. Gusper	
13	Sasaram	1. Bikram & Co	Atkins	
14	Sasaram	1. Seereebaun	W. Bruce	

Thus the total number of factories[118] with their outworks in then existing districts of Bihar is as follows:

TABLE 8

Serial No.	*Name of the district*	*Number of the factories*	*Number of outworks*	*Total*
1	Muzaffarpur	32	48	80
2	Darbhanga	28	36	64
3	Champaran	21	53	74
4	Saran	31	42	73
5	Bhagalpur	43	--	43
6	Purnia	20	44	64
7	Munger	10	20	30
8	Gaya	1	--	1
9	Santhal Parganas	1	--	1
		187	243	430

Thus out of 2,702 concerns at work in India[119] in 1892, 430 factories existed in Bihar. The average exports from India were fifteen million pounds valued then at nearly fifty lakhs of rupees.

As may be seen from Table 8 indigo cultivation was much more intensive in North Bihar than in South Bihar. In North Bihar, i.e. Muzaffarpur, Darbhanga, Champaran and Saran districts, the soil was more fertile and irrigation was not essential for indigo cultivation, although "a very class cultivation with drill sowing was practised".[120] In these districts soil was alluvial and therefore a simple system of cultivation with broadcast sowing was enough. In South Bihar (i.e. Patna, Gaya and Shahabad), on the other hand, irrigation from the tanks, wells and canals was found necessary for the cultivation of indigo.

The earliest attempt to estimate the area of land under indigo in Bengal was made by the late Dr H. Mc Cann. His figures were compiled from the reports of the local officials furnished in connection with the formation of the Economic Museum. He arrived at the conclusion that in 1877-78 there were 6,37,956 (subsequently quoted as round figures as 700,000) acres of land was under indigo. Another estimate furnished in the *Statistical Atlas* recorded the area in 1884-85 as approximately 1,3000,000 acres. If the same method is applied in testing these figures given above, in Bengal the area under production in 1877-78 would be Bihar 297,716 acres and Lower Bengal 340,240 acres. According to George Watt per acre yield in Lower Bengal was 12 lb while in Bihar per acre yield was 20 lb.[121] Although the Bengal dye had rivals in Madras, Guatemala, Java and Manila, it had an ascendancy over the qualities of the produce of every other country. Its average produce was 1,20,000 *maunds* a year.[122] Official values of some principal exports for the period 1860-61 and 1870-71 indicate that indigo fetched Rs 1.89 (1860-61) value in crores and its ratio to the value of total commodity exports was 5.7 per cent. While its value increased to Rs 3.19 crores in 1870-71 the ratio to the value of total commodity exports remained the same, i.e. 5.7 per cent.[123] While its value increased to Rs3.19 crores in 1870-71 the ratio to the value of total commodity exports remained the same, i.e. 5.7 per cent.[124] Except raw cotton and rice indigo excelled other items of export such as raw jute, raw silk, raw wool, seeds, oil, sugar, coffee, tea and saltpetre. Although the exact area under indigo in all the eight districts of Bihar is not known, an attempt is being made to show how indigo cultivation has progressed.

MUZAFFARPUR

The progress of indigo cultivation on European methods or "San Domingo methods" in this district is as follows:

TABLE 9

Years for which figures were available	*Areas*		*Out-turn*
	Bighas	*Acres*	
1794	767.14 *katha*	670 .	Not known
1804	586..	512 .	Not known
1882-83	65,000	56,741	14,000
1883-84	69,700	60,848 .116	15,200
1884-85	76,960	37,181	19,200
1885-86	80,000	69,752	19,200
1886-87	99,959	87,258	20,786

The indigo factories had proprietary interest in just under one per cent. Out of the district the permanent tenure and under-tenure holding interest was 15.3 per cent. The planters in their capacity as superior landlords held 17.59 per cent of the district area, but their landed interests were permanent and secure in just over two per cent only.[125]

In Darbhanga district the area under indigo cultivation was nearly 1,00,000 acres.[126] Till the end of the nineteenth century Darbhanga had the largest concern in India. Pandaul with its outworks comprised an area of 300 sq.miles. During the survey and settlement operation in Darbhanga 52,136 acres or 3 per cent of the cultivated area was under indigo.[127] By 1904 the number of factories had fallen because of the discovery of Badische artificial dye in Germany (1897) and therefore only 34,000 acres of land was found sown with indigo crop. Of the whole indigo area more than three-fifths of the total indigo area was in Samastipur subdivision.[128] Since the Darbhanga *raj* was much more powerful than the planters the latter had relatively limited secure rights in this district. This does not mean that the Darbhanga Raja was opposed to indigo cultivation in his estate. In 1899 the term of lease to Messrs Thomas & Co to cultivate indigo land in Purnia was not renewed in view of the resistance of the peasantry there. The Darbhanga Raja took possession of the land. He demanded an enhancement of rent as well as the continuation of indigo cultivation but the raiyats refused in a body to comply with his demand.[129] Only in Samastipur subdivision the planters cultivated directly no less than 30,700 acres of land or 94 per cent of the total area.[130]

The average area sown with indigo in Champaran district in the late 1890s by the concerns belonging to the Indigo Planters Association amounted to 87,827 *bighas* or 76,666.8 acres. The quantity of land found during the survey and settlement operation was 75,758 acres, viz 7.96 per cent. Of the total area of 2,079,815 acres and cultivated area of 1,447,668 acres, 95,970 acres were under indigo cultivation[131] (ie 6.63 per cent). The area under indigo showed an upward trend till 1904-05 after which a downward trend set in, especially because of the introduction of German synthetic dye (1897) in the international market.

The area under indigo cultivation in Saran district during the last decade of the nineteenth century was 45,513 acres while during the survey and settlement operation (revision, 1915-21) the area was found to be only 7,904 acres.[132] Thus indigo was sown in 3.5 per cent of the net cropped area in this district.[133] According to Hamilton Buchanan's estimate in 1810, 24,000 acres of land in Purnia district was sown with indigo. According to Hunter's *Statistical Account* in the period from 1865 to 1875 an average of 81,000 *bighas* of land per year was sown with indigo.[134] During the survey and settlement operation indigo covered 20,752 acres in Purnia district[135] (ie 1 per cent of the total cropped area) and the bulk of it was found in *thanas* Dhamdaha, Korha and Saifganj. In Bhagalpur district only 5,267 acres of land (ie 0.03 per cent of the total cropped area) was sown with indigo.[136] In Munger indigo was cultivated only by five factories. In north Munger the area under indigo cultivation covered 2.5 per cent of the net cropped area.[137]

Thus the growth of commercial agriculture by the Europeans was an important feature of Bihar during the nineteenth century. It is significant that indigo was being produced in response to the external demand and profits from this trade was remitted to England while there were famines in Bihar and indigo production meant reduced area under other food crops required by the starving natives. Out of 30 famine years in India[138] Bihar was affected by 6 famines and scarcities (1769-70, 1783-84, 1853-55, 1873-74, 1888-89 and 1891-92) of which five occurred in Saran district[139] (1769-70, 1783, 1866, 1873-74 and 1879). In such a situation the cultivation of indigo even in some tracts of fertile *bheeth* land was injurious to the tenantry of Bihar. It is true that planters undertook some relief works in course of the recurring famines in Bihar but since the huge profit from indigo was not invested here, "forced commercialization" of indigo made no difference to the poverty of Bihar. Out of 17 million people affected by the famine in India (1875-76) 8 million people were in North Bengal and Bihar.

INDIGO CULTIVATION AND MANAGEMENT OF *KOTHIS* IN BIHAR

There were three main systems of indigo cultivation in Bihar known as *zeerat*, *assamiwar* and *khuski*. In the *zeerat* system of cultivation the entire land was under the direct occupation of the factory, whether held by the proprietor, tenure-holder or under raiyat. Under this system land was cultivated by the factory at its own expense with hired labour. Over one-fourth of the area under indigo came under this category. Due to careful cultivation the maximum profit was earned under this system.[140] In Darbhanga district a substantial area was directly cultivated. It was estimated that "the amount of indigo not grown direct by the factories could not exceed 10 per cent of the total".[141] In Muzaffarpur district 61 per cent of the indigo area was held under this system.[142] Under it the cost of cultivating one *bigha* of indigo was Rs 6.40 paise (old paise).[143]

Under the *assamiwar* system of cultivation indigo was grown by the tenants of factories at a fixed rate per *bigha*. *Assamiwar* denoted a state of things in which a raiyat had to enter into an agreement with the planter to grow indigo on a portion of his holding. *Raiyati* and *tinkathia* were other terms applied to this system. The raiyat was paid for at the rate of Rs 13 to Rs 14 per *bigha* in Muzaffarpur district.[144] The raiyat had to prepare the land, sow it with indigo and reap the harvest as and when the season started. When the crop was ready it was carted by the factory. The amount advanced to the raiyat, generally Rs 2 or Rs 3, was adjusted against the rent payable by him to the factory. *Satta* was executed by the raiyat before he was given an advance.[145] In Champaran district also the same system prevailed. The price paid to the raiyat was Rs 11 per *bigha* for the full crop; in case of failure of crop for no fault of the raiyat, the latter received as *bijmar* a minimum of Rs. 5 - 5 *annas* (one rupee was equalent to 16 annas or 64 paise). Successive sowing of indigo adversely affected the fertility of a piece of land and under the *satta* system the raiyat was liable to pay damages (generally Rs 50 to Rs 60 per *bigha*) in the event of willful negligence in producing the stipulated crop.[146] In view of the successive use of land after indigo cultivation it was necessary for the planter to arrange for exchange of land called *badlain*. This was the practice in all the districts.

Under the *khushki* system the raiyat voluntarily undertook to grow indigo without any agreement. This system was in vogue in Muzaffarpur, Darbhanga and Saran districts, but not in Champaran. In Tirhut division *khushki* system was applied to *sattas* executed by the raiyats of estates not in lease to the factory.[147] The rate of remuneration for indigo cultivation under this system was much higher than under the *satta* system. An advance of Rs 20 to Rs 30 per *bigha* was given to the raiyat at a nominal rate of interest in Muzaffarpur district.[148] In Saran district where the system was very much in vogue, the factory supplied seed and the carts. The dues were paid weekly but there was no advance of any kind.[149]

Besides these three main systems we come across a system known as *kurtauli* (*shikmi*). Under this system the factory took land from a raiyat and grew indigo with its own labour. The rent of the sublet land was deducted from the rent due from the raiyat to the planter as landlord. Thus factory was a mere under-raiyat. This system was more common in Motihari district than elsewhere.[150]

The average rate in Tirhut division where the *bigha* was about 4225 sq. yards, was from Rs 8.50 to Rs 9 including rent. In Saran district the *bigha* was the same as in Tirhut, and the average rate was from Rs 7 to Rs 9. In Champaran district where the *bigha* comprised 7225 sq. yards, the usual rate of payment per *bigha* was about Rs 13. Here the rent was generally included in the price paid to the raiyat. This was the practice in Saran district also.[151]

Thus under all the systems of indigo cultivation the raiyat was tied to the factory and he was not "free" to cultivate a crop of his choice other than indigo, notwithstanding J.P. Grant's wishful thinking in this regard. The government was, on the other hand, glad to note that the "independent cultivation by the planters flourished best in Bihar" under the systems mentioned above.[152] Since the raiyats were poor and illiterate, the planters employed them for work at irregular intervals. Since *satta* and contracts were legally valid for 20 years in the case of the death of the contracting raiyats, their successors inherited the obligation to cultivate indigo. It is true that unlike the zamindars the planters introduced the system of cash advance; this was intended to control production and benefit the planters themselves. The low price of the yield and the perpetual indebtedness of the raiyats ensured their bondage and depressing economic condition.

At the top of the management was a manager who was methodical, shrewd and businesslike. He possessed the quality of securing and executing contracts with the raiyats. He was required to supply water for the manufacture of the dye and therefore he possessed an influence, direct or indirect, over the neighbouring cultivators in order to gurantee a regular supply of green plant.[153] A factory was commonly called the concern or *kothi* which contained a few vats, tools and appliances already under indigenous use and a staff of loyal employees who were required to carry out their various duties effectively and promptly. The persons regularly employed in a factory numbered 25 to 40 but at the manufacturing time their number rose to 200 and even 300. The natives employees were paid from Rs 10 to Rs 30 per month and the subordinate servants from Rs 4 to Rs 6 per month. The carpenter-sawyers and bricklayers were paid from Rs 5 to Rs 8 per month while the coolies from Rs 4 to Rs 6 per month. A factory at Gaya employed 9 persons who were known as *mukhtar* (Rs 12 per month), *karinda* (Rs 8 per month), *jamadar* (Rs 6 per month), *mori mate* (Rs 4.50 per month), *nil maha mate* (Rs 4 per month), *nil maha* (Rs 4 per month), *pechawa* (Rs 4 per month), *chulhakas* (Rs 4 per month) and a *ziladar* (Rs 3 per month). Thus the total amount spent by a Gaya factory for one month came to Rs 49.50 only.[154] In Purnia district the cost of cultivation including seed, manufacturing, establishment and all other charges and contingencies came to Rs 150 per factory maund on an average.[155] But this figure furnished by George Watt, ie Rs 150 for the production of one factory maund of indigo does not tally with the figure furnished in the *Survey and Settlement Report* in the same district. According to this report the "average total cost of making one maund of indigo may be taken as Rs 90" while the price then obtained averaged Rs 200 per maund.[156] Thus the profit was more than fifty per cent.

According to George Watt nearly Rs 1,20,000 were required under various items of expenditure such as establishment, cattle, salaries of three European managers and the total working charge for the same year was about Rs 4,20,000. The actual yield, however, was 1,150 maunds thus bringing a profit of Rs 2,30,000. These figures prove beyond dispute the enormous profit made out of the indigo business. In Bihar one maund of indigo could be produced at an outlay of Rs 130 to Rs 150 per maund. One head factory with two or three outworks cultivating about 5000 *bighas* of land used to employ only 63 persons for the whole year.[157]

Thus the management of the indigo factories was clearly and exclusively profit-oriented. It did not improve the efficiency of the traditional system of agriculture. The capital and skill were confined to the semi-manufacturing processes.

It is true that indigo plantation was a capitalist enterprise where the means of production were owned by the planter but the system did not have other features of capitalism. According to the capitalist theory, labour is largely free and its participation in the production process is based on voluntarily entered contract. It is time we consider the issue whether or not indigo cultivation contributed to the development of capitalism in this country and how far this affected the overall situation in Bihar. The theory put forward by the advocates of colonial historians and supported, among others, by a number of scholars [158] does not appear to be tenable if we go into the actual details of the situation. This was evidently not the case in indigo cultivation in Bihar. Here the cultivators were tied or bound to factories under the imposed and enforced systems (like *assamiwar*, *zeerat*, *khushki* and *kurtaili*) by the colonial government and duly recognised in courts of law. Indigo has no local market or internal competition leading to better accumulation of surplus and its investment inside the country; nor did the benefits from plantation accrue to the cultivators and workers who remained very poor, illiterate, dependent and indebted either to the planters or *mahajans* or zamindars.

Technological improvements and their application in various fields had played a significant role in the development of capitalism in Europe. But indigo cultivation in Bihar was largely based on indigenous feudal mode of production where implements used were old and outmoded and the system found place for a large number of hangers-on of the beneficiary owners who had developed an exploitative relationship with the cultivators where the latter had virtually no say; collaboration with and support by alien rule gave them (planters) overwhelming strength to entrench themselves and their unjust economic order.

Of course some planters of Purnia and Champaran made use of new machines, implements and technology in their indigo concerns for improving the quality of the dye. But mere use of machinery did not go hand in hand with the development of machinery and the use of skilled labourers and artisans as was done in the western capitalist countries where these factors served at one and the same time as instruments of raising productivity.[159] But in the case of colonial India in general, and plantation work in particular, unskilled agricultural labourers were employed on a very low wage. It not only hampered the growth of capitalism but also resulted in the exploitation of labourers and the peasantry. Even the *zeerat* system of farming as practised by the planters in the production of indigo was not allowed to grow fast; the planters always preferred the *assamiwar* system of cultivation to *zeerat* system.

No doubt the Saran canals were constructed between 1877 and 1880 at the instance of the indigo planters but their overall impact was minimal. Even less substantive change occured in farming technology in the nineteenth and twentieth centuries. The *hal* (a wooden plough with an iron shoe) remained the main agricultural implement with virtually no change in agricultural technology or farming techniques.[160] The introduction of railways and modernisation of surface transport helped to accumulate the desired raw materials and grain for shipment to other countries. The fiscal base of the *raj* still rested on the muddy fields of the indigo growing peasants in Bengal and Bihar.

Mc Alpin [161] finds positive effects of the commercial agriculture; and Fisher [162] argues that the expansion of indigo was not at the expense of agricultural production while B.B. Chaudhuri asserts that the growth of commercial agriculture heightened tensions in the agrarian society by strengthening the hands of the landholders.[163] An analysis of the data as referred to in this chapter suggests that the forced commercialisation and the forced integration of the Indian economy into an international capitalist framework led to the underdevelopment of productive forces in the country and also led to the underdevelopment of the capitalist classes, [164] especially when the surplus generated in indigo cultivation was invested elsewhere. Thus there is a truth in the statement that in colonial India the British had been able to "forcibly convert part of the Hindoo self-sustaining communities into mere farms producing opium, cotton, indigo, hemp and other raw materials in exchange for British stuffs".[165]

REFERENCES

1 The method employed for extracting the finished indigo from the green plant is very ancient; the manufacture was performed by hand. But in modern times machinery was used for extracting finished indigo by the Europeans and therefore it is called European methods.

2 C.J. Stevenson Moore, *Final Report on the Survey and Settlement Operation in the Muzaffarpur District, 1892-1899* (Patna, 1922), para 867, p. 336.

3 Ibid., para 868, p. 337. Out of eleven Europeans, five were engaged in indigo business. Their names were James Gentil, C.W.S. Schuman, James Gallen (a native Portuguese), John Miller and Francis Rose. James Gallen forcibly established a factory in the *jagir* of Raja Raj Ballab of Tirhut.

4 Minden Wilson has provided all the details of these factories including the years when these were started. See Minden Wilson, *History of Bihar Indigo Factories, Reminiscences of Bihar - Tirhut and its inhabitants of the past - History of Bihar Light Horse Volunteers* (Calcutta, 1908). According to him Daudpur factory was built in 1798 and its outworks, Arringpur in 1829, Musahari in 1822 and Chhajan in 1822. Ibid., p. 12.

5 Ibid., p. 44. Although no records are found, native tradition believed that Zeigler built the Saraiya factory. He was a planter in about James Gibbon's time and had Sitalpur factory in Saran (now Chapra) district. In 1847-48 or thereabouts Edward Studd was the Manager of the factory. In 1908 it

belonged to the Maharaja of Darbhanga. The first *mokkaarie patta* indicates the year 1802 when twenty-five *bighas* of land in the *mauza Karara Dakhli* Rohna, Sarkar Hajipur, was taken from Chaudhary Bhairo Datt of Basaulpur. In 1811 Boldvaite got another fifteen *bighas* of *bhith* land from Devaladhari Misra. C. Bell was managing the factory in 1907.

6 C.J. Stevenson Moore, *Final Report on the Survey and Settlement Operation in the Muzzafarpur District, 1892-99*, op.cit., para 872, p. 338.

7 Ibid., para 873, pp. 338-39. The old Muzaffarpur district includes the present districts of Vaishali and Sitamarhi.

8 Minden Wilson, op.cit., p. 1. It was built in 1886-87 as a defence against interloping. It was located in Dholi *dehat* (village Bela Sadan). W.S. Mackenzie, a planter, formed the village with the intention of building a factory against Teg Ali, an interloper. After having sold the Jitwarpur concern Agrail was bought by Messrs Hudson, Lamb and others.

9 Minden Wilson, op.cit., p. 3. It was built in 1794. Earlier it belonged to Raja Mustafa Khan. Bhagwanpur was built in 1846; Bellahi in 1861. Minden Wilson writes that there were three other factories at Sukreah, Baijnathpur (1846) and Lakshampur (1871). But these factories were later abandoned

10 Ibid., p.3. Bhataulia was built by an interloper. It became an outwork of Shahpur Mircha concern. Rustamganj was built in 1892; Ramdaspur in 1882. In Inaitnagar also there was an indigo factory.

11 Ibid., pp.2-3. Bhikhanpur was built in 1818. The lease to build the factory was given by Syed Mir Muhammad. Permission to build the factory was given by the East India Company in which the Company authorized the indigo concern to hold fifty *bighas* of land. Earlier it was an outwork of Kanti concern and belonged to Noel and Company. Its outworks Bochacha and Sahajpur were built in 1872 and 1860 respectively.

12 Although the *mokkaarie* is dated back to 1822, the Chhatwaria was purchased by the Tirhut Indigo Association of London, which sold it to Tirhut Indigo Company. Its outwork Shahpur Mircha used to grow all kinds of crops as it was turned into a farmhouse. Chhatwaria was managed from Shahpur Mircha in and around 1847.

13 Ibid., p. 8. Kanti factory was the oldest concern built in 1778 by Alexander Noel. From 1816 to 1825 it was the head factory under which there were factories at Belsand, Motipur, Amoah, Tatereah, Bhikhanpur, Peepra and Seeraha (in Champaran district). Raghai was built in about 1778; Lautan in 1884; Nariar in 1887. The bungalow which stands even now was built by Cahill or George Taylor. Taylor was fond of horses. Near Kanti there is a village known as Panapur where the planters used to assemble for picnic party.

14 Ibid., pp.18-19. Dholi factory was built in 1796. Its outwork Birauli was built in 1825 and Sarbnaha in 1890.

15 Ibid., pp. 15-18. Before indigo, saltpetre was a paying industry in Deoria. An indigo factory was established here in 1780 by John Flinch. The indigo produced in Deoria was noted for its beautiful colour and therefore it was the costliest in Bihar. From the beginning of the industry till 1880 there were 243 planters who managed the factory. All the names of the planters are given in Minden Wilson, *History of Bihar Indigo Factories*, op.cit.

16 Ibid., p.11. It was first a sugar factory. An indigo factory was built in 1804. R.Ronald, a planter was murdered by the mutineers at Deogarhi in 1857.

17 Ibid., p.32. Karnaul was known to the natives as Sahebganj. It was built in 1803. Its outwork Monine was built in 1836; Tajpur in 1862 and Gaura in 1884.

18 Ibid., p.35. In Motipur there was a sugar factory. In 1816 it was made a group of indigo factories owned by Noel & Company.

19 Rajkhand was also known to the natives as Aurai.

20 Ibid., p.40. Runisaidpur factory was built in 1862-63.

21 Ibid., p.45. Singhia factory was built in 1791. It was known to the natives as Lalganj. The Dutch East India Company first established the indigo factory on 29 July 1791. Earlier a saltpetre factory was started here by the Dutch East India Company. It was one of the first factories occupied by the Europeans in Tirhut.

22 Ibid., pp. 41-42. Shahpur Mircha factory was built in 1799. In 1856-57 it was purchased jointly by Kali Prasad and James Smith. In 1895 its propriertor was Babu Jadunandan Sahai who was the adopted son of the late Babu Gajraj Sahai. A

fine hospital was founded in 1895 in Baghi. It was known as "Gujraj Hospital". An average of 10,000 patients were treated annually.

23 *Final report on the Survey and Settlement Operation in the Muzaffarpur district 1892-1899* (Patna, 1922), para 874, p.339.

24 Minden Wilson, op.cit., p.27. The Jaitpur factory was built by H.E. Abbot in 1872-73. Its outworks were Teekaha, Nirghai, Pakri and Gadai built respectively in 1875-76, 1880 and 1884.

25 Minden Wilson, op.cit., p.8.

26 Ibid.

27 *Final Report on the Survey and Settlement Operation in the district of Muzaffarpur*, op.cit., para 876, p. 341.

28 J.H. Karr, *Final Report on the Survey and Settlement Operation in Darbhanga District, 1896-1903* (Calcutta, 1904), para 484, p.136.

29 Ibid., para 489, p. 137.

30 Quoted in Stephen Hanninghain, *A Great Estate and its Landlords in Colonial India, Darbhanga, 1860-1942* (Oxford University Press, New Delhi, 1990), p.44.

31 Ibid., para 484, p.135.

32 Minden Wilson, op.cit., pp.50-51. Jainagar, Narhar and Kamtaul belonged to the Maharaja of Darbhanga. Jainagar factory was built in about 1847. Earlier it was a sugar factory.

33 Minden Wilson, op.cit., p.29. Kewan was also called Bachaur. It was under the Pandual concern.

34 Minden Wilson, op.cit., p.51. It was built some time in the 1830s.

35 Ibid., p.54. Raiyam was an outwork of the Pandual concern.

36 Ibid., p.1. Benipur factory was built in about 1834.

37 Ibid., p.24. It was built in 1844.

38 Ibid., p.22. Perhaps this factory was built in 1845 .

39 Ibid., p.1. It was built in about 1861-62.

40 Ibid., p.23. No exact year is known, but it appears to have been built in the 1830s.

41 Ibid., p.12. It was built in about 1850.

42 Ibid., p.33. It was built in about 1862.

43 Ibid., p.28. It was built in 1795-96 by Noel and Company.

44 Ibid., p.24.

45 Ibid., p.21. Formerly it was an outwork of Daulatpur. It was bought by the planter from Babu Parmeshary Narayan Singh of Narhan. It was established in about 1860.

46 Ibid., p.34. The *Mehtas,* who were the bankers of Muzaffarpur, acted as interlopers and built it in the Dalsingsarai *dehat.* But the planter of Dalsingsarai did not like the construction of the factory as there was some dispu e relating to the boundary. No exact year is known when it was established, but it was not a very old factory.

47 Ibid., p.40. This factory was built in 1790 by Joseph Finch, the head of the Finch family.

48 Ibid., p.19. This factory was built in 1825. It was an old factory.

49 Ibid., p.40. This was built in 1890.

50 Girish Mishra, *Agrarian Relations of Permanent Settlement: A Case Study of Champaran* (New Delhi, 1978), p.98. If we take into account the *Report on the Survey Settlement Operation in the Champaran District, 1892-1899*, the number of outworks came to be 53 and not 48 as stated by Mishra.

51 C.J. Stevenson Moore, *Final Report on the Survey Settlement Operation in the Champaran District, 1892-1899* (Calcutta, 1900), para 527, p. 147. Also see Girish Mishra, op.cit., pp.98-99.

52 This factory was built by Stewart in about 1820.

53 Minden Wilson, op.cit., p.72. Jagaulia factory was built in 1848, Mahuawa in 1881-82, Gondaha in 1882-83, and Rasulpur in 1892-93.

54 Minden Wilson, op.cit., p.74-75. This factory was built in 1884.

55 Minden Wilson, op.cit., p.87-88. Lalsaraya is only 24 miles from Sugauli where a regiment of Native Cavalry was stationed. Officers attached to the regiment often visited Lalsaraya. This factory was built as an outwork of Terkaulia in about 1822. During the Revolt of 1857 the 12th Irregular Cavalry mutineed and killed Colonel Holmes, his wife, the doctor and his wife. Only his child was saved by an *ayah* (maidservant). The factory was then managed by L. Cosserat. After the Mutiny was suppressed, he was made an honorary magistrate. The person who killed Colonel Holmes was arrested in Sugauli and then hanged.

56 Minden Wilson, op.cit., p.76.

57 Girish Mishra, op.cit., p.99. Exact year of its establishment is not known, but it was built some time before 1870.

58 Girish Mishra, op.cit., p.99. It was established in 1863.

59 Minden Wilson, op.cit., p.76. See also Girish Mishra, op.cit., p.99. The Motihari factory was established by C. Moran in 1817, Puranhia in 1859, Bhelwa in 1861, Haraj in 1863 and Chailaha in 1890.

60 Minden Wilson, op.cit., p.76. This factory was built in 1864-65. Girish Mishra does not mention Pokhari.

61 Minden Wilson, op.cit., p.78. Pipra factory was first built by the Dutch but the year is not known. Later it was established by Dr Gibb in 1807. Its outwork Madhuban was built in 1885, Jagiraha in 1885, Dinamath in 1812 and Dhabaulia in 1880. The indigo produced in Pipra was of a very high quality. It was used as the standard test for comparison in London.

62 Minden Wilson, op.cit., p.79. The Rajpur factory was built in 1801 by Jeffry Flinch. Its outwork Hussaini was established in 1856, Pakri in 1887 and Jamunapur in 1894.

63 Minden Wilson, op.cit., p.78. The Parsa factory was built some time in the 1860s. The years in which these two outworks were established are not known.

64 Minden Wilson, op.cit., p.79. The Sathi factory was established by Sir W.B. Hudson but the exact year of its establishment is not known. It was managed by Carlton in about 1874.

65 Minden Wilson, op.cit., p.80. This factory was established in 1807. According to Minden Wilson there were five other outworks in addition to Parewa. Girish Mishra does not mention any of them (op.cit., p.99). Sir W.B. Hudson had purchased Siraha concern in 1889 for over eight lakhs. Hudson sold Tellara factory to Bloomfield and J. Smith. Bloomfield was later murdered on 13 February 1907 by the raiyats in the indigo disturbance that occurred in Champaran. Girish Mishra has mentioned the name as "Seerah" and not Siraha (op.cit.).

66 Girish Mishra, op.cit., p.99. This factory was built in 1853-54.

67 Minden Wilson, op.cit., p.82. Probably Tarkaulia factory was built in about 1816.

68 Minden Wilson does not mention the year in which this factory was established.

69 Minden Wilson, op.cit., p.75. This factory was built in 1884. For some time it was an outwork of Lohera.

70 Minden Wilson, op.cit., pp. 75-76. The Hardia factory was established in 1862. Till 1885 it was an outwork of Murla. It is only three miles from the Nepal frontier.

71 Minden Wilson, op.cit., pp. 75-76. No exact year is known about the establishment of this factory. For some time it was an outwork of the Seeraha concern. It was bought by Robert Bloomfield and J.H. Smith in 1892.

72 *Final Report on the Survey and Settlement Operation in the District of Muzaffarpur, 1892-1899*, op.cit., para 876, p. 341.

73 Ibid., p.341.

74 Girish Mishra, op.cit., p.100.

75 *Final Report on the Survey and Settlement Operation in the District of Saran, 1893-1901* (hereafter *Saran Survey and Settlement Report*), para 611, p. 173.

76 Ibid., para 612, p. 173.

77 Ibid., para 613, p. 173.

78 Minden Wilson, op.cit., p.97. According to him Bansopally was an outwork of Jogapur. It was built in 1864.

79 According to Minden Wilson (op.cit., pp.93-94) Balla Barhoga was established by W. James in 1854. A bungalow in Balla Barhoga was set on fire by the rebels in 1857. The planters had to escape in the exciting days of the Revolt of 1857.

80 Minden Wilson, op.cit., p.100. Maniara was built in 1867 Sipaiya in 1824-25 and Tirverawa or Triveni in 1887-88. All these factories were known as the Sadowah concern which was established in 1819.

81 Minden Wilson, op.cit., p.98. Bankat was an old shut-down factory and was reopened as an outwork in about 1857-58. In 1904-05 it was converted into a sugar factory.

82 Minden Wilson, op.cit., p.100. This factory was established in 1836. Its outwork Ghorha was built in 1878. Ramkola was built by one of the Wilsons who was Irish. They lived in

Saran since they came to India. W. Wilson went to Calcutta to sell his indigo in 1870-71.

83 Minden Wilson, op.cit., p.102. This factory was built in 1801.

84 Minden Wilson, op.cit., p.97. This factory was built in 1863. Its outwork Chauki was built in 1868. Madhopur was bought from a native in 1885. Kahalla was managed till 1878 by W.Smith.

85 Minden Wilson, op.cit., p.99. This factory was built in 1836 by Wilson. Later on it was closed.

86 Minden Wilson, op.cit., p.92. This factory was built by W.Wilson in 1869 and was closed down by 1908. It ceased to belong to the Bihar Indigo Planters Association in 1899.

87 Minden Wilson, op,cit., p.96-97. Once Nawada was amalgamated with Hariharpur by Laurie. It was closed in 1902-03.

88 Minden Wilson, op.cit., p.89. The exact year in which the Arwa concern was established is not known. According to Minden Wilson these factories were built before 1830. In the 1850s Kazi Ramzan Ali was its owner, and he had many European managers. Kazi Ramzan Ali was the person who was the most trusted by the government. He mentions that Urna, Jallalpur and Chaitanparsa (now Chetparsa) were the outworks of the Arwa concern.

89 In the *Saran Survey and Settlement Report*, p. 174, Dangharn has been mentioned as one of the outworks of the Arwa concern but in Minden Wilson, op.cit., p.89, it has been spelt as Dungaraha.

90 Table 5 shows that there were 35 factories, out of which factories at Serial Nos 7, 17, 26 and 29 were located in Gorakhpur but the indigo land was in the Saran district, mostly in Mirganj *thana*.

91 Minden Wilson, op.cit., pp.89-103.

92 Minden Wilson, op.cit. This factory was established in 1867.

93 Minden Wilson, op.cit., p.102. There was an indigo factory there, but the exact date when it was built is not known.

94 Ibid., p.102.

95 Ibid., p.101. Seerepur was also called Amakpur or Ambikapur. The proprietor of this concern was Indra Pratap Shahi, Maharaja of Hathwa. It appears to have been built by Malcolm Mac Donald. It was at a place called Dularpur, nine

miles from Chakia. Mac Donald's services were requisitioned by the Maharaja of Hathwa to build a factory for him. Indigo cultivation was started with 250 *bighas* of land. Next year 2,900 *bighas* of land was brought under cultivation and 700 maunds of indigo produced. In the early 1880s this was a fine concern, but it was closed by the Raja as an indigo concern. The Brahmins advised the Raja that no son would be born to him as long as he cultivated indigo. Seerepur was then made a farm only.

96 *Final Report on the Survey and Settlement Operation* (Revision) in the district of Saran, 1915-1921 (Patna, 1923), para 15, p.8, Phanindra Nath Gupta. Also see *Saran Survey Settlement Report, 1893-1901*, para 616, p. 175.

97 *Purnia Survey and Settlement Report*, para 315, p. 103.

98 *Saran Survey and Settlement Report,1893-1901*, para 616, p.175.

99 *Report on the Survey and Settlement Operation in the district of Bhagalpur, 1902-10*, para 205, p. 110.

100 Ibid., para 204, p. 110.

101 Ibid., p. 110.

102 Bihar *District Gazetteers*, Purnia, (Patna, 1968), p.229. Also see George Watt, *A Dictionary of Economic Products of India*, Vol.IV, p.393 and W.W. Hunter, *Statistical Account of Bengal*, Vol.XV (Reprint, 1976), pp.367-68. But Amiya Kumar Bagchi tells us that "probably the first person to start indigo manufacture in Bengal proper under Company's patronage, after "San Domingo method' was John Prinsep". He established a factory at Nilganj near Barasat (in 24 Parganas district of Bengal) in July 1797. See his book, *The Evolution of the State Bank of India*, op.cit., p.123.

103 Bihar *District Gazetteers*, Purnia, op.cit., p.229.

104 *Final Report on the Survey and Settlement Operation in the district of Purnia*, op.cit., para 326, p. 106.

105 Ibid., p.104. Of the main indigo concerns along with their outworks the total number of factories comes to 61 as shown in Table 6. Out of 61 concerns Gidwas in *pargana* Haveli Purnia and Bhaugaon in Tajpur *pargana* belonged to Rai Lakshmipat Singh, a local zamindar.

106 W. W. Hunter, *A Statistical Account of Bengal*, Vol.XV, Munger and Saran, op. cit., pp. 367-68, 370-77. The average

price which indigo fetched from 1862 to 1872 was £24 per factory maund. The average outturn was 280 factory maunds.

107 Ibid., p. 371.

108 *Bihar District Gazetteers*, Purnia, op.cit., p. 228. In view of the crisis created by the introduction of a synthetic dye in 1897 the research in indigo cultivation was started to compete with the German dye in the international markets.

109 Ibid., p. 371. This factory was closed in 1875.

110 Ibid., p. 371. The main concern was in Bhagalpur but the factory was located in Purnia.

111 *Judicial Criminal Proceedings*, No.182, 1 June 1830, from the Acting Magistrate of Munger to the Government of Bengal, 13 February 1830.

112 W.W. Hunter, op.cit., p. 138.

113 Ibid., pp. 138-39.

114 *Judicial Proceedings*, No.85, 2 October 1856, from the Commissioner of Patna to the Junior Secretary to the Government of Bengal, para 3, 13 September 1856.

115 P.C.Roy Chaudhury, *Gaya Old Records*, Vol.79, correspondence, Gaya, from 6 January, 1866 to January 1867 (Patna, 1958).

116 K.K. Datta, *History of the Freedom Movement in Bihar* Vol.I, Government of Bihar (Patna, 1957), p.169. Datta himself visited the place and found the ruins.

117 *The Board of Revenue*, No.25, 29 November 1833. From C.Mechenzia, Acting Collector, Shahabad (Saran Commissioner's office, 15 September 1833) to the Commissioner of Saran, 30 August 1833. Since the area of land has been given in *bigha*, *katha* and *dhur*, it is difficult to calculate.

118 The table is based on figures available in various *Survey and Settlement Reports*, *Industries in Bihar* (Minden Wilson), Hunter's *A Statistical Account of Bengal* and papers of the *Judicial Proceedings*. In Patna district, there were a few factories but sites of their location have not been indicated in the sources. In Sahahabad there was no indigo factory as such but in 7 *parganas* of the district, there were 14 *mauzas* where indigo was cultivated. Although the years in which these factories were established are not found in many cases,

these factories were set up during the period from late eighteenth century to the end of the nineteenth century. According to an official account of 1830 (Henry Shakespear, Judicial Secretary to the Government of Bengal), there were then about 1000 indigo factories in the Bengal Presidency, quoted in K.K. Datta, *Freedom Movement in Bihar*, Vol.I (Patna, 1957), p. 169.

119 *Nineteenth Century Studies* (Trade and Commerce), No. 8, October 1974, p. 495; an article entitled "Present State of Indian Manufactures" by M.G. Ranade has been reproduced in the Journal.

120 George Watt, *A Dictionary of the Economic Products of India*, Vol IV (Second Reprint, 1972), p.399.

121 Ibid., p.42.

122 *Nineteenth Century Studies* (Trade and Commerce), No. 8, October 1974, p. 424.

123 Sabyasachi Bhattacharyya, *Financial Foundations of the British Raj*. (Indian Institute of Advanced Study, Simla, 1971), Table No. 7.1, p.302.

124 *Muzaffarpur Survey and Settlement Report*, op.cit., para 875, p. 340. Areas indicated in the *Survey and Settlement Report* appear to be wrong. In fact, it comes to 67,196 acres.

125 *Muzaffarpur Survey and Settlement Operation*, op.cit., para 876, p. 341.

126 L.S.S.O'Malley, *District Gazetteers of Darbhanga* (1907), its extract on the indigo industry has been reproduced in the *Bihar District Gazetteers*,Darbhanga, Appendix IX, para 760.

127 Ibid.

128 J.H. Karr, *Final Report on the Survey and Settlement Operation in the District of Darbhanga* (Calcutta, 1904), para 487, p. 136.

129 *Bihar District Gazetteers*, Purnia, op.cit., p.229.

130 Ibid., para 489, p. 137.

131 C.J. Stevenson Moore, *Final Report on the Survey and Settlement Operation in the District of Champaran*, para 528, p. 148. Also see Girish Mishra, *Agrarian Problems of Permanent Settlement: A Case Study of Champaran* (New Delhi, 1978), pp. 102-3. The area under indigo in Champaran from 1892-93 to 1931-32 is given yearwise. It also contains a table (pp. 100-1) showing the output turn yearwise along with the value.

132 *Final Report on the Survey and Settlement Operation (Revision) in the District of Saran, 1915-1921*, Phanindra Nath Gupta, para 15, p.8.

133 *Final Report on the Survey and Settlement Operation in the District of Purnia*, para 315, p.103.

134 Ibid., para 319, p.104.

135 Ibid., para 319, p.103.

136 *Final Report on the Survey and Settlement Operation in the District of Bhagalpur, 1902-1910*, P.W.Murphy, para 205, p.110.

137 *Final Report on the Survey and Settlement Operation in the District of Purnia*, op.cit., para 315, p.103.

138 Quoted in V.C.P. Chaudhary, ed, *Unclassified Class Oppression under the crown: An Archival Probe*, (Rahul Press, Patna, 1991), pp.4-7.

139 Anand A. Yang, *The Limited Raj, Agrarian Relations in Colonial India, Saran District, 1793-1920*, (OUP, New Delhi, 1989), p.36.

140 *Final Report on the Survey and Settlement Operation in the District of Champaran*, op.cit., para 337, p.152.

141 *District Gazetteers of Darbhanga* (1907), L.S.S.O'Malley, its extract on Indigo industry has been reproduced in the *Bihar District Gazetteers, Darbhanga*, Appendix IX, p.767.

142 *Final Report on the Survey and Settlement Operation in the District of Muzaffarpur, 1892-1922*, C.J.Stevenson Moore, para 885, p. 345.

143 Ibid., para 885, p.345. One *bigha* of land in Muzaffarpur was equivalent to 4226 sq.yards. The estimate of cost for one *bigha* of indigo cultivation was supplied to the Settlement Officer by C.M.Macpherson of the Tewara concern.

144 *Final Report on the Survey and Settlement Operation in the District of Muzaffarpur*, op.cit., para 886, p.346.

145 The *satta* in Champaran and contract in Muzaffarpur districts which were executed by the raiyat for indigo cultivation are given in Appendices I and II.

146 *Final Report on the Survey and Settlement Operation, Champaran*, op.cit., para 538, p.152.

147 *Final Report on the Survey and Settlement Operation in the District of Champaran*, op.cit., para 540, p. 152. Also see Girish Mishra, op.cit., p.115.

148 *Final Report on the Survey and Settlement Operation in the District of Muzaffarpur*, op.cit., para 887, p.347.
149 Ibid., para 887, p.347.
150 *Final Report on the Survey and Settlement Operation in the District of Champaran*, op.cit., para 541, pp.152-53.
151 George Watt, op.cit., Vol. IV, p. 42.
152 D.H.Buchanan, *Development of Capitalist Enterprise in India* (New York, 1934), p. 51.
153 George Watt, op.cit., Vol. IV, para 242, p.427.
154 Ibid., para 283, p. 439.
155 Ibid., para 282, p.38.
156 *Final Report on the Survey and Settlement Operation in the District of Purnia*, para 321, p. 105.
157 *Final Report on the Survey and Settlement Operation in the District of Muzaffarpur*, op.cit., para 891, p. 348. One seer of indigo from 10 maunds of plant was a good average produce in Muzaffarpur district.
158 The most important of these scholars are P.E.Roberts, *History of British India under the Company and Crown*, completed by T.G.P.Spear (Oxford University Press, London, 1952); P.Woodruff (Mason), *The Men who Ruled India*, Vol. I; P.Griffiths, *The British Impact of India*, (London, 1952); G.Bearce, *British Attitude Towards India, 1784-1858*, (London, 1945) and J.P.T. Bury, ed, *New Cambridge Modern History*, Vol. X, Zenith of European Power. Even the *Cambridge Economic History Of India* Vol. 2, 1757-1970, ed, Dharma Kumar (Cambridge University Press, 1982) shows an ambivalent attitude towards indigo cultivation and its impact on agrarian economy and peasantry. It states "the cultivation of cash crops did play some positive role in the traditional peasant economy. The cultivation, *except perhaps that of indigo during certain period* (emphasis mine) was not based on coercion alone", p.327.
159 Amiya Kumar Bagchi, "Reflections on the Nature of the Indian Bourgeoisie" in *Social Scientist*, Nos 214-15, New Delhi, 1991, p.7.
160 Anand A.Yang, *The Limited Raj, Agrarian Relations in Colonial India*, Saran, op.cit., p.40.
161 McAlpin Michelle Burge quoted in Anand A.Yang, ibid., p.39.

162 C.M.Fisher, *Indigo Plantation and Agrarian Society in North Bihar in the Nineteenth and Early Twentieth Centuries,* unpublished Ph.D dissertation, Cambridge University, Cambridge, 1976, pp.121-24.

163 B.B. Chaudhuri quoted in Anand A.Yang, op.cit., p. 39.

164 Amiya Kumar Bagchi, "Reflections on the Nature of the Indian Bourgeoisie", op.cit., p.13.

165 Karl Marx quoted by Irfan Habib in an article "Process of Accumulation in Pre-colonial and Colonial India", *The Indian Historical Review,* July 1984-January 1985, Vol. XI, Nos1-2, p. 78. Running into twenty-five pages it is one of the best articles ever written on the subject.

CHAPTER III

Zamindars, Planters and Raiyats: A Study in Agrarian Relations

From the beginning of the nineteenth century the raiyats were opposed to indigo cultivation in Bihar as its production, especially during the famines, hampered the sowing of foodgrains. In such a situation the planters generally obtained the goodwill of the raiyats through the influence of the landed proprietors who often borrowed money from the planters.[1] The zamindars generally gave villages as farms to the planters, who paid them higher rent in cash more promptly than the raiyats and the native *thikadars*. The planters were glad to have zamindars on their side as it provided an opportunity to influence the raiyats in getting the land cultivated for indigo. In this way the villages were held in the name of the *munshi* or head servant of the factory, who entered into a bond with the planters to ensure his good faith. Whenever the raiyats violated the contract to sow indigo, the landed proprietors used their influence and asked them to fulfil their engagement.[2]

Although the interests of the zamindars of Bihar (Patna district) were affected in the sense that land came under the use and control of the planter, they candidly remarked: "to the best of their belief they had no prejudice of the indigo planters established in their district". A native "gentleman" (zamindar) thought of the planters as "honourable and upright men".[3] The Magistrate of Bihar (Patna) observed that a large portion of the landed proprietors had benefited by the diffusion of capital, the extension of indigo cultivation and the enhancement of rent which followed a small body of planters taking up this business.[4] In Munger district the planters conciliated the landholders and the cultivators and obtained their goodwill and cooperation by lenient enforcement of engagements.[5] The practice in general was to take the lease of a whole village or *taluk* from the *maliks*. The planters very often made large advances to the *maliks* before taking the *thika* of the village. Sometimes half of the aggregate amount for the whole term was paid to the *maliks*.[6] Although the planter obtained a *patta* of a large piece of land, he was unable to sow indigo on a *biswah* of it without making further agreements with the actual cultivators.[7] It clearly indicates how the zamindars sold the land to the planters which was, in fact, occupied by the cultivators in Munger district. In Purnia district the Gondwara concern covering a large part of Korha and Dhamdaha *thanas* was leased to Thomas and Co. in the late 1880s, although the Darbhanga *raj* had declared that no indigo would be grown there.[8] Thus till 1839 the attitude of the zamindars to the planters remained favourable. The situation changed for a short term when some differences cropped up and there was an amount of bickering between the planters and the zamindars in 1839 when the planters of Tirhut, Saran and Munger made a representation to the Government of India in which it was alleged that the Magistrate of Tirhut sided with the views of the zamindars.[9] An order was passed by the Sessions Judge of Tirhut açcording to which no *assamie* agreement without the consent of the *malik* was valid. A proclamation to this effect was made by the Magistrate of Tirhut by beating of drums all over the district. The planters objected to making such a proclamation and pleaded that they should not be put under the power of the zamindars or *maliks* as it would amount to non-fulfilment of indigo contract by the raiyats. In order to prove their point the planters produced several witnesses to show how a raiyat was threatened by the zamindar that if he sowed the land with indigo without the consent of the *malik*, he would be fined a sum of Rs 200 and would be jailed.[10] In Tirhut alone there were 38 complaints by the *maliks* and raiyats against the planters.[11] Most of these complaints were related to the disputes between the planters and the *maliks*. Since there were so many *maliks* in one estate, the matter was complicated by the interference of the zamindars. There were 48,757 revenue paying estates in North Bihar, ie Purnia (1,712), Saran (5,655), Champaran (1,267), Muzaffarpur (21,416), Darbhanga (14,340) and North Munger only (4,367).[12]

In the 1840s also we come across a few cases where the zamindars showed their hostility towards the planters. They regarded the growing influence of the planters over the raiyats as interference with their feudal rights.[13] This antagonism between the zamindars and the planters gave rise to the establishment of the *lattials*[14] (a band of men armed with clubs, etc.).

But the anti-planter stand of the zamindars did not mean any sympathy for the cultivators. J. Reily makes a classic observation regarding the oppression perpetuated by the zamindars. This statement was occasioned by the government's query regarding whether the zamindars should be invested with the powers of the magistrate. According to J. Reily the idea of investing the zamindars with the powers of the Magistrate was wrong both in theory and practice. He gave an example of Europe where the feudal system of authority was abolished and the power was given to a duly elected and undivided government. The idea of giving additional power to the zamindars surprised him. He described how the zamindari system of managing the estates allowed the *amlah* to extort the raiyats. Whenever the raiyat refused the demand of the *amla* his property was distrained, ploughing oxen were taken, cattle were carried off from the house of the raiyat, especially when the sowing season had set in. At the same time the *patwari* sued the raiyats in the court for non-payment of rent on time. The raiyat was kidnapped, sent away to some other parts of the estates where he was imprisoned or placed under close surveillance. When the raiyat's relations made enquiries about his whereabouts, he was declared *goom* by the *daroga* who was often bribed by the *amla*. Whatever little land the raiyat possessed was seized by the zamindar by managing an *istifa* from him. In view of the enormous power and influence enjoyed by the zamindar, J. Reily suggested to the Government of Bengal not to invest them with the power of a magistrate because they already possessed more than adequate power to oppress the raiyats. Such a measure initiated and later adopted by the government was like a "pigmy pitted against the government. It would be arming the giant with additional weapons against the dwarf".[15] This was a practice adopted by the zamindars and it continued throughout the province till the abolition of the zamindari system in 1952.

The anti-planter stand of the zamindars of Bihar was only short-lived and, by and large, both collaborated in the exploitation of the raiyats. According to Act XI of 1836, the planters were deprived of their special privileges and were brought under the jurisdiction of the *mufassil* civil court. The European community strongly protested and held rallies against this Act and dubbed it as a "Black Act". In their opposition to the government they sought the support of a few natives in Bengal. Of all people Raja Rammohan Roy conveyed his appreciation of the good work of the planters to the British Government. He wrote: "I have travelled through the districts of Bengal, Bihar and Orissa and have also observed the living condition of the people. I am of the opinion that the standards of life of the people who reside near indigo factories are better than the people who stay away".[16]

At a mass meeting of the Europeans held in Calcutta, Dwarkanath Tagore, the grandfather of the great poet Rabindranath Tagore supported the Europeans and expressed the indebtedness of Indians to the non-official Europeans for their prosperity and progressive views.[17]

The position of the zamindar was further strengthened by the Landholders and Commercial Association. In a letter to the Government of Bengal the Association asserted, "the land within the limits of the perpetual settlement was in no case, and in no sense, the land of the ryot; but that in every sense, and to the fullest extent; the land and the actual property in the soil were vested solely in the representatives of the original landholders, zamindars and others with whom the perpetual settlement was made".[18] It reminded the Government of Bengal that even the *khoodkast* raiyats were declared by the government (Section 60 of Regulation 8 of 1793, and by the 10th Section of Regulation 51 of 1795) to have merely a right "not to be dispossessed so long as they continue to pay the stipulated market rate". The Assistant Magistrate of Madhubani tried to interfere with the power of the zamindar in an indigo dispute between the planter and the raiyat. He also passed an order. But his order was withdrawn by the Magistrate of Tirhut as the Magistrate of Madhubani was not authorized to interfere with the exercise of any of his ordinary right by a landholder merely because such exercise required vigilance on the part of the police.[19] All such orders and patronages were extended to the zamindars in order to conciliate them to the side of the indigo planters so as to enable the latter to do indigo business peacefully.

Although the Maharani of Bettia[20] had reservations regarding the planters in Champaran district, the estate was mortgaged to them because of the financial stringency. There were thirty factories at that time in the district cultivating 37, 183 *bighas* with indigo. The rent paid to the zamindars (Rs 20,000) was in excess of the rent received from the raiyat. But the *thikadars* enhanced the rent and paid less than what they collected from the raiyat. In this way the estate was financially ruined and the raiyats were impoverished. The raiyats (Shaik Madar Bux and others) of Tuppas, Dawlta and Sonaul who alleged that ever since the Bettia estate was mortgaged to the planters 14 new factories were established there.[21]

The Bettia estate was in a state of deep financial crisis. The Raja was addicted to drinking and was careless in his worldly affairs. It was alleged that under the influence of alcohol he gave villages to the factory at a nominal rate.[22] It was at this stage that the planters offered higher rent to the Raja. They were even ready to make large cash advances for all farms that they received. Ultimately five *Mahals* were leased to the Europeans, although the cultivators were producing foodgrains in the plots.[23] The Raja was induced to appoint Captain Gale as Manager of Bettia estate. After some time Captain Gale was replaced by T. Gibbon whose first duty was to ensure financial equilibrium. Gulliland House (London) consented to float a loan of 95 lakhs on the sole condition of substantial European security. To satisfy this condition and cover the interest on loan, permanent leases of villages were granted to the indigo planters and thus the factories were placed in their hands on a secure basis.[24] Besides, the zamindars whose authority and influence were required to induce the raiyats to carry on indigo cultivation, there were headmen in the villages. For the cultivation of indigo much depended on their inclination, wishes and orders. They were also induced by the planters. Thus the zamindars of Champaran were benefited by the system of indigo cultivation although they did not increase the productivity of the land. Rather they squandered the surplus in debauchery.[26]

Some of the raiyats in Champaran withheld the payment of rent to the planters. In such a situation a *hukumnama* was issued by the Raja of Bettia on 9 October 1867 and the *gumasta* and *patwari* were asked to instruct the raiyats (*assamees*) to pay rent to the planters and thereby maintain the *dastur* of the factory.[27] Many *assamees* started depositing rent in the Champaran Collectorate directly without bothering to pay it to the planters. Again the Raia of Bettia was requested by the government to sign a *rubokari* in order to conciliate the raiyats to the side of the government and the planter. The *rubokari* was first prepared and signed by the Commissioner of Patna, R. P. Jenkins, and this was okayed by the Raja. The Raja directed the *karpardas* to make the *assamees* understand the issue and behave properly with the planters. While protesting against the proclamation of *rubokari* by the Raja, the raiyats complained that they had already been sold to the planter for money.[28] The renewal of seven years' lease given to the planters depended upon the whims of the Raja who had no objection to renewing the lease to the planters. The cases referred to the Small Causes Court at Motihari clearly indicate that a planter (a gentleman) had collected Rs 40,000 from the raiyats and paid Rs 52,000 to the zamindar thus incurring a loss of Rs 12,000 per annum to be earned out of indigo plantation.[29] Thus the numerous examples clearly demonstrate the favourable attitude of the Raja towards the planters and the alien government.

Similar was the attitude of the zamindars of Tirhut towards the planters. The premiums paid by the planters for taking leases were very lucrative and offered great inducement to the landowners. It was known to the government that no raiyats in the villages would willingly cultivate indigo unless they were asked by the zamindars and the *thikadars* to do so. The Secretary to the Government of Bengal wrote to the Secretary to the Government of India that the raiyats of Tirhut had traditional respect for their landlords and the *thikadars* and therefore reconciling the zamindars to the planters was necessary for the cultivation of indigo.[30] The Secretary to the Government of Bengal wrote:

"The zamindars in Tirhut are therefore on the planters' side, and their influence is so great that, as long as this is the case, I do not believe that there will ever be any widespread repudiation of indigo contracts or refusal to grow indigo... but no general combination against indigo cultivation will take place in Tirhut as long as the planters are backed by the influence of zamindars...".[31]

Even the Governor-General in Council observed that although the system of indigo cultivation was ruinous to the raiyats, it was highly profitable to the zamindars.[32] In Muzaffarpur district the *maliks* sublet the land to the factories in order to collect enhanced rates. In this way the zamindars were interested in getting as much money as they could extort from the *thikadars*. It was customary for the zamindars to demand higher rent on the renewal of every lease. The new *thikadars* made such demands of the zamindars either by raising the rent payable by the raiyats or by adding wasteland to their holdings. Thus the greedy zamindars needed the planters as much as the planters needed the *thikadars*. Such was the position of the zamindars in Muzaffarpur and Champaran districts.

In Darbhanga district also the embarrassed proprietors turned to indigo factories for loans. Even the proprietors who were well off wanted to avoid the trouble in managing the land-holdings. They handed over their holdings to the tenure-holders who paid the full rent punctually and managed the estates efficiently. Thus loan was the primary consideration for the grant of tenure to the planters and the tenure-holders.[33] In fact the planters had been well represented among the rent-farmers: for example, 58 of 219 farms of which the lease expired in 1868-69 were re-let to the indigo planters. Most of the managers and assistant managers of the Darbhanga *raj* were former planters.[34] The native zamindars and landlords also owned a few factories, but due to the financial difficulties most of the factories were sold to the European planters.

The Arrowal concern (Saran district) was owned by Kazi Rahmat Ali with Madhopur as its outworks. Since Kazi Rahmat Ali did not repay the loan to his creditor, his concern was put under the Civil Court in 1864-65.[35] The Behrauli concern belonged to Ram Charan Das of Pusa. It was also sold to H. Curtis in about 1860. The proprietor of the Seereepore concern (Saran) was Indra Pratap Shahi (1874-94), the Maharaja of Hathua. It was a flourishing factory in the 1880s, but it was closed by the Raja on the advice of a brahmin that no son would be born to him as long as he cultivated indigo.[36] So far as his attitude to the planters was concerned, he appreciated them and said that "they managed the raiyats much better than the native *thikadars* did".[37] He also found it advantageous to entrust the planters with the lease of distant villages in which there were no substantial raiyats to co-opt as intermediaries. Raja Chand of Kishanpur (Purnia) had a factory in *thana* Dhamdaha. In Bhagalpur district there were factories established by the Babus of Panchgachhia, Gobargarha and Phangama. The Marwala factory belonged to the Panchgachhia

Babus, while Gobargarha and Dhangama belonged to the Raja of Baneli and Salimpur to Dip Narayan Singh.[38]

The disputes between the planters and the raiyats reached a point of no return in the Pandaul concern. The Darbhanga Maharaja was requested by the raiyats to intervene in the matter, but he maintained "neutrality". Similar was the attitude of the zamindars in Champaran district where they looked upon themselves as absolute owners of the soil. The raiyats also did not dispute this. They could demand any amount of rent from the raiyats.

Thus the Rajas, Maharajas, Rai Bahadurs, Raja Bahadurs and Khan Bahadurs of the indigo growing areas of Bihar were favourable to the *Raj* in general and the planters in particular. The Maharaja of Hathua (Saran) helped the Company in suppressing the Kol Insurrection (1831-33) of Chotanagpur and the Santhal Insurrection (1855). Kumar Harendra Kishore received the titles for his "loyalty to the government" while the Banaili Raja was conspicuous by "his devotion to the government". Besides family titles, Rajendra Pratap Shahi got reward for his father's loyalty to the *Raj*. A perpetual rent-free *jagir* and a number of confiscated villages in the district of Shahabad yielding an annual income of Rs 20,000 was given to him. He himself rendered support to the government in the Mutiny. Later, Krishna Pratap Shahi of the same family also received the title of Maharaja Bahadur from the government on 31 December 1874. The Governor himself was present at the time of the installation ceremony. This Raja was one of the founders of the Bihar Land Holders' Society which was sympathetic to the planters' cause. The Darbanga Maharaja was not lagging behind in extending his patronage to the *Raj*. He was busy in planning a programme to celebrate the Diamond Jubilee in the memory of Her Majesty's "glorious reign".[39]

The planters adopted the policy of appeasing the zamindars by paying them higher rent. Once appeased it was possible for the planters to contract for thousands of *bighas* of land for indigo cultivation.

The colonisers such the French, the Spanish, the Portuguese and the English, took to indigo cultivation. European skill and capital soon placed the indigo enterprise on a sound footing which completely destroyed the indigenous trade.[40] The British

West Indian colonists found that coffee, sugar and other products were more remunerative and at the same time the severance of America from Great Britain (1775-83) left the British dyers at the mercy of the foreign countries for their supplies of indigo. The article of indigo occupied so distinguished a rank in the list of Asiatic products that even the sons and daughters of highly placed officials began to do business in indigo trade. It was occasioned by its demand in the European countries particularly after the American War of Independence when the American market was closed. The slave revolts in the West Indies disrupted the production of indigo there and compelled the English to search for avenues for the production of indigo elsewhere. Indigo was found more profitable than sugar and therefore the cultivation of sugar was gradually replaced by indigo. It was found out by the East India Company that indigo could be grown in the alluvial soil of Bengal and Bihar. Many experienced planters, most of them slave-drivers in the West Indies, were brought to India for the cultivation of indigo. The first effort to revive the indigo industry proceeds from a small French factory at Chandannagar on the Hoogly but very little was done there. In order to save the British manufacturers from dependence on French and Spanish colonists for dye, the East India Company resolved to take active steps for indigo cultivation in the selected districts of Bengal and Bihar. The officers of the Company were permitted to trade in the article and the home remittance was made for many years.

The Company made its first contract with Prinsep who conceived that India might supply sugar, cotton and indigo to Europe. The Company, on the other hand, agreed to extend financial as well as other arrangements till 1788.[41] But when the situation was reviewed by the Company it was found that loss had been incurred. At the same time another planter, J. P. Scott, produced indigo that gave profit. To overcome loss every encouragement was given to improve and make cheap the process of indigo manufacture so that it could compete in quality in the international market. Ultimately the British planters succeeded in their venture to eliminate from competition the French and the Spanish.[42] The political supremacy achieved by the Company in India also helped the indigo planters in Bihar and Bengal to get their foothold while the Spanish and the French did not achieve this goal.

Once established the planters desired that the Company should prohibit the establishment of new factories within certain limited distances of those already in existence. The Company desired that the new enterprise might be undertaken with prudence. It also restrained its servants from issuing any advance, but the planters ignored it and starting advancing money in order to attract the poor cultivators to their side. Macaulay was opposed to it in principle as he believed that zamindars exercised their power with more justice or humanity than the planters.[43] Advance offered by the planter at the season of the cultivators' greatest impecuniousness was a bribe which a few raiyats could refuse. But it was in the interest of the planter to secure a maximum amount of indebtedness on the part of the neighbouring raiyat.

Nearly forty years passed with tacit official support or encouragement given to the planters. Indigo attracted the public attention in 1859 when the Bengal indigo disturbances took place.

The enactment of the law in 1835 empowered the planters to enforce the indigo contract. According to this law the planters could criminally prosecute the raiyats if they failed to cultivate indigo and the latter were not shown even the slightest consideration.[44] The planters became friendly with the government officials and powerful in the aftermath of this legislation that the cultivators were completely at their mercy. But complaints of forced cultivation of an unprofitable crop on the one hand, and of want of protection against dishonest cultivators on the other became rife. Ultimately a commission was appointed by Act XI of 1860 to inquire into the whole subject. The report of the Indigo Commission revealed faults on both the sides. The Act gave powers to the Magistrate to enforce the completion of the contract to grow indigo where advances had been made by the planters. But such contracts were found to have been obtained by fraud, force or unlawful intimidation to the raiyats. In 1868 this special Indigo Contract Act was, however, repealed.

Although a series of difficulties arose at Pandaul in Darbhanga district and at Bettia in Motihari disstrict, and the raiyats lodged complaints and filed petitions to the government, yet no commission was appointed. It was only in 1876-77 that an elaborate enquiry was instituted by the Bengal Government into the complaints. But the planters' efforts to provide some relief to the cultivators in course of famines satisfied the government and hence the government did not appoint any commission.

The abrogation by the government of export duties as also tax on the green plant greatly favoured the planters and the indigo trade. Prior to 1875 an export duty of Rs 3 a maund had been levied but from 1875 onwards it became Rs 3 a maund on manufactured indigo and Rs 3 a ton on indigo leaves. On 25 February 1880 the duty was entirely abolished.[45] Tirhut was described as the most productive indigo area and the only tract in which native manufacturers had not succeeded in establishing themselves in competition with Europeans.

The fortunes of the planters depended more upon their immediate relationship with the local government officials, zamindars and raiyats than it did upon government policy.[46] They benefited from the presence in the *mufassil* of the East India commercial residents and business agents who were provided with large amounts of capital to purchase local products for the Company's investment. Commercial residents assisted the private indigo planters with loans. But the office of the Commercial Resident was discontinued in 1834 and the planters lost a valuable ally in the *mufassil*. The Board of Trade also encouraged and supported the planters while the Judicial Department kept a careful watch on their abuses. The relationship between the planters and the district officers varied with the individuals concerned. It depended on the social status of the individual planter, his background and bank account. To a lonely Magistrate the house of a wealthy planter was a paradise in comparison to the neglected, rambling and crowded houses of the zamindars.[47]

Although in criminal matters the planters were exempted from the jurisdiction of any court below that of a District Magistrate, in civil matters they were under the jurisdiction of all *mufassil* courts. The three lower courts (*munsifs, sadar amins* and principal *sadar amins*) were predominantly staffed by the Indians (Bengalees). In prosecuting minor cases against the raiyats and small landholders, the planters left the court work to their agents and factory servants. Since the courts were notorious for their corruption, minor court officials were easily bribed by the planters. The raiyats invariably suffered and the administration could not be considered judicious or fair. Minden Wilson has given a description of the corruption practised by a *daroga* when the latter was approached to intervene in a dispute between the zamindar and a planter.[48]

Prior to 1829 the land was controlled by the zamindars and the landlords and not by the planters. In this situation the main concern of the planters was to increase their power over the raiyats through the expediency of holding leases in the names of their factory servants (*benami*) and after 1829 in their own names. The power of the planters was greatly increased in 1837 when the government enacted that any subject of the Crown could acquire and hold land in perpetuity. It gave an opportunity to the planters to increase the *zeerat* system of cultivation in Bihar. The planters began to spend their resources on acquiring *zamindaris* through purchases. They started converting the raiyats' small holdings into *zeerat* and deprived them of their titles to the individual holdings. It adversely affected the raiyats in the sense that it became difficult for them to establish their titles after the expiry of the lease.

The planters held land under almost every type of tenure, from *zamindari* down to sub-tenantry of raiyats. Indeed the planters' right to land was limited by the peculiarity of the land tenure systems in India, particularly in Tirhut. They were declared proprietors of the land which in effect was already under the possession of raiyats. They were allowed to lease their land and collect rent but not to dictate what crops were to be cultivated. The planters used their power and influence over the zamindars and the government machinery in the situation.

After the Revolt of 1857 in Bihar the planters became more powerful than before as they helped the Company to restore its rule. In these circumstances it became difficult for the raiyats to escape the obligation of cultivating indigo. The indigo disturbances in Lower Bengal in 1859 compelled the planters to invest their capital in Bihar. As a result of their active participation on the side of the Company, the planters were made honorary magistrates and given representation on the boards and committees formed by the government. These new privileges enabled them to act with impunity.

In Darbhanga district a very large area was directly cultivated by the planters themselves. The factories in the Samastipur subdivision directly cultivated 94 per cent of the cultivable area.[49] In Champaran district the indigo concerns exercised the right of landlords in nearly half of the district either as proprietors or tenure-holders. [50] Since the planters had become landlords in so much of area in Champaran, they were relieved of haggling with the pretty proprietors and cultivators to which their less fortunate fellow-planters had to submit in Saran and Tirhut.[51]

The origins of most of the disputes which occurred in Bihar in the first half of the nineteenth century could be attributed to the native servants of the factories, who were the means of communication between the indigo planters and the raiyats. It was a strange inconsistency in the conduct of the planters that they did not trust the natives and give any advance to them without *satta* and contract. They, however, implicitly reposed their confidence in their native servants.[52]

In 1839 the planters of Tirhut, Saran and Munger made a joint representation to F. J. Haliday, Secretary to the Government of Bengal and asked for a specific regulation against those raiyats who did not fulfill their legal engagements.[53] Their representation included a lien on the land, complaint against cart-drivers and the withdrawal of an order by the Magistrate of Tirhut according to which the *malik's* consent was necessary for making contracts with the raiyats. They expressed their anxiety for the commercial prosperity of the mother country if the capital invested by them (Rs 60 lakhs) in the blocks was not protected by the government. They wanted the government to protect their interests as the prosperity of the districts also depended upon it.[54] Fifteen cases were brought before the Judge of Tirhut between 1855 and 1856. Most of these cases were related to taking up farms from some co-shares of a joint estate. [55]The planters levelled 48 charges against the raiyats under Regulation 1830 in Purnia district, but all of them were dismissed. Planters as a body were well organised in the 1860s and they strongly refuted the charges levelled against them in the Indigo Commission Report of 1860.[56] They were very critical of J. P. Grant whom they accused of creating confusion and nothing else. The enquiry conducted into the affairs of the planters of Lower Bengal created an element of fear among them. But the planters of Bihar were unnerved by it. Being aware of the repercussions of the enquiry Messrs Gisborne and Co. sent a circular to the planters of Tirhut asking them to increase the rate of indigo payable to the raiyats.[57] But this piece of advice was ignored by the planters.

The planters did not hesitate to resort to force. In Pandaul (Darbhanga district) the planter Gale forcibly occupied the *assaminwar* land. He was supported by the local officials of the government. With such backing too much of land was taken and converted into *zeerat* and cart-drivers and labourers were insufficiently paid.[58] In a petition the raiyats complained that nine factories had been established there and thousands of *bighas* of *bheeth* land was sown with indigo. The planter of Pandaul *kothi* (factory) had taken away their bullocks and ploughs. When the raiyats refused to sow indigo, they were kept in the *Moorgi Khana* and this hurt their religious sentiments. Besides, the raiyats were subjected to assault and law suits on false charges.[59] The planters of Champaran were more ruthless and oppressive than their counterparts elsewhere in Bihar. Since the occupancy rights were not clearly established, the planter got a chance to evict the raiyats easily. In their complaints to the Government of Bengal the raiyats referred to the cruelties they were being subjected to by the planters. Although the *thikadars* promised to protect them against the planters, the raiyats were forced by two planters -- Messrs Balpia and Hulwant -- to sow indigo in four *kathas* a *bigha* at a rental of Rs 20 and 8 annas annually, while the cash they earned was Rs 18 annually.[60]

In another village (Bajaria) the planters appropriated all land for the cultivation of indigo. All the paddy fields had been forcibly sown with indigo and cattle seized for cultivating indigo.[61] The planters instituted false cases against the raiyats and chiefly used factory servants as witnesses. They succeeded in putting in jail many raiyats in Motihari with the help of the Assistant Magistrate of Motihari.[62] Constant harassment of the raiyats by the underlings of the factories was admitted even by the Collector of Champaran. The raiyats' appeal for protection was largely ineffective because of the planter's influence on the local administration.[63] A petition of the inhabitants of several villages of Motihari subdivision illustrates the plight of the raiyats: "We applied to our zamindar, the Raja of Bettia, but to no purpose, as he had already sold us to the planters for money. We applied to the High Court, but it seems it was to no purpose too. In vain we cry and make our grievances known to the Magisterial Officer of the district. A deaf ear is always turned to our piteous cries and in hundreds of instances we are turned out even from the presence of this gracious Magistrate's Court of Justice, when the hard-hearted tyranny of the planters became insufferable to us".[64]

They complained that 90 per cent of the raiyats of Motihari had marks of whips on their backs which the planters and their men had inflicted upon them. Because of this torture many raiyats fled to Nepal Terai. Given below is a table showing the list of 18 villages in Motihari, the number of villagers who fled to Nepal and of those who stayed back.

TABLE I

Serial No.	*Name of the village*	*No. of inhabitants*	*No. fled to Nepal*	*No. left behind*
1	Manikhpur	91	61	30
2	Jhokora	141	101	40
3	Marooa	41	10	31
4	Laukoria	73	31	42
5	Dholkura	68	41	27
6	Fulbaria	121	84	37
7	Seerisia	64	50	14
8	Dubaulia	51	40	11
9	Lakhanpur	52	40	12
10	Gokhula	28	21	7
11	Doowaill	45	12	33
12	Muttiah	90	45	45
13	Lohiar	92	51	41
14	Buromotipur	60	10	50
15	Jakotia	150	50	100
16	Choraungha	74	25	49
17	Jessoielee	91	50	41
18	Gumoria	72	43	29
		1404	765	639

Note: In terms of percentage, 54.48 percent of the raiyats fled to the Nepal Terai due to the oppression of the planters in 1868.

The situation was more or less similar in Saran district. Established during the regime of the Company Bahadur the planters were generally "the true-born white men of Britain".[66] Discrimination of the poor raiyats against the planter-zamindar collusion in the mercantilist and post-mercantilist phases of Indian history was a common phenomena. Although desertions of raiyats were caused by many factors, the oppression perpetuated by the planters was the most important factor. In 1984, twenty-seven raiyats, mostly small tenancy holders, deserted seventeen villages in which the Maniara indigo factory had plantations. Again, as many as eighty-three raiyats fled between 1889 and 1892 from a number of villages that Hathwa Raj had leased to the Maniara factory; the Hathwa Raj was a partner with the planters in the profits of the indigo industry. Planters were not merely "rent collectors". Rather they were the actual *maliks* in practice. In Champaran district they even exercised the zamindari rights. It did not matter to them what he paid for a village or for the renewal of a lease for indigo land. Despite speculation and fluctuations in its trade indigo remained a highly profitable enterprise.

To say that the Hathwa Raj had a great deal of "power over the rest of local society" as asserted by Anand A. Yang[67] does not seem tenable. The *Raj* was the Supreme Commander at the top, sustained by the zamindars, *thikadars*, money-lenders, landlords and planters at the village level, local support being essential for the continuance of the colonial rule in India. The zamindars, an ally of the *Raj*, considered the planter an important ally because the latter had "the ear of the official". Minden Wilson, a planter in Muzaffarpur, testified that the support of the zamindars was crucial in determining the willingness of the raiyats to sow indigo.

The migration or "absconding" of the raiyats to Nepal or any other place was neither "voluntary", "seasonal" or "induced by push" or "pull" factors or by ecological "pressure" as stated by Anand A.Yang.[68] No doubt the migration of raiyats was also caused by the famines and oppression of the landlords and the *thikadars* but in the case of Champaran, and to some extent Saran, migration or "absconding" took place because the raiyats could not fulfil the planter's demands on their land and labour. The raiyats were not in a position to resist the oppression through violent methods as the planters enjoyed two forms of power: one deriving from the zamindars and the other from the local administration. Although the planters were in need of labour for the indigo industry, their urgent desire for land was fulfilled. The estate and the planters both profited from desertion because the indigo factories often assumed responsibility for the holdings of absconders after paying an enhanced rate of rent to the greedy zamindars. Thus the collusion between the parasitic zamindars, the enterprising planters and the "benevolent raj" worked satisfactorily to the neglect of productive forces ,ie the raiyats.

Some of the planters were aware that the terms under which indigo was grown should be made more remunerative to the cultivators but they were unable to act independently because of the fear that the planters as body would oppose it. In some cases the owners resided in England and their managers had no authority to alter the rates.

Sir Ashlay Eden, the Lieutenant-Governor of Bengal, noted that in 1877 a number of crimes were committed in the indigo districts of Saran, Champaran and Tirhut. The government officials were asked to give their opinion regarding the unsatisfactory relations between the planters and the raiyats. But he was not in favour of appointing a commission as demanded by the raiyats. The reason was that as in Bengal this might embolden the raiyats further and ultimately induce them to give up indigo cultivation altogether. He, however, suggested that the defects should be rectified. Ultimately a meeting of the planters was convened on 2 April 1877 at Planters Club, Muzaffarpur, which was largely attended. The object of the meeting was to form an association and to take into consideration any matters brought before it in order to protect the planting community.[69] The meeting was attended by 29 "gentlemen" representing various concerns. The first meeting favoured the *Khushki* system of cultivation but the matter was dropped. On 21 June 1877 a general body meeting took place formally and it was resolved that the association be named as Indigo Planters Association. It started its work with Thomas Fraser and George Toomey as honorary secretaries. The formation of the Association had the official backing of the Governor (His Excellency). The committees formed by the Association took up the work and looked into the complaints of the raiyats. But the complaints made directly to the individual planters were not entertained and thus the grievances remained unredressed.[70]

The Small Causes Court was established in Motihari in 1864 in order to look into the complaints regarding indigo cultivation but it was being misused by the planters. Lawrence wrote to Henry Maine that he had no confidence in the establishment of the Small Causes Court. He feared that the planters will be too much for the raiyats. He believed that it would amount to "putting a weapon into the hands of the planter".[71]

It would be wrong to assume that planters wanted the capitalist development of agriculture by introducing the *zeerat* system of cultivation in Bihar. Temple wrote to Salisbury: "I have heard indigo planters themselves say that many indigo concerns will not survive the introduction of improvements like railways which will cause wages to rise and the independence of the peasant to grow. All this introduces special complications into economic questions in Tirhut. The case of Saran was stronger still in the same direction".[72]

It clearly illustrates that the planters did not like the progress of the country; not did they appreciate the transition from landlordism to capitalism. In social matters too their attitude was pre-modern. The Hindu zamindars of Bihar made an issue of cow-protection. The Bihar Indigo Planters Association took up the issue and wrote to Lord Elgin under pressure from the zamindars that cow-slaughter should be stopped. The *Sudhakar* wrote that some beef-eaters pleaded for the protection of the cows as demanded by the Hindu zamindars because the planters held indigo lands under them. The planters sent this memorial with the object of pleasing the Hindu zamindars.[73] The planters (*bara sahibs* as they were called) behaved like typical landlords. They gladly accepted *salamis* (gifts) from the *amla*. The *amla* on the other hand had the authority to take *dastoori* from the raiyats.

The basic identity of interests of the planters, the zamindars and the government comes out clearly from the evidence available for Bihar in the second half of the nineteenth century. While the planters were interested in the profit, the zamindars in rent and the government in remittance -- all of them at the cost of the raiyats and the common masses -- collaboration among them was an essence of their inter-relationship. It is true that differences occasionally cropped up among them, their relation to developments sometimes diverged and each one was concerned most about his own interests. They made adjustments among themselves through mutual give and take and also made occasional concessions to the raiyats under pressure of public opinion in favour of the oppressed.

Buchanan's hypothesis regarding the introduction of "a new capitalist development" and change in the context of Bihar appears rather bold and untenable.[74] Landlordism was the dominant fact of agrarian life in Bihar which neither the planters nor the government could afford to ignore. There were 48,757 estates in North Bihar towards the end of the nineteenth century and none of them was abolished; rather these were protected and pampered.[75] The net result was that these estates not only leased indigo land to the planters but they remained strong and ardent allies of colonial rule.

To suggest that *zeerat* and *sikmi* systems of cultivation gave rise to the development of capitalism in agriculture hardly bears scrutiny. The route to capitalist development in agriculture did not lie through the *zeerat* system. The leases given to the planters had to be renewed by the zamindars and therefore the planters themselves were not the zamindars in any sense of the term. They could not dictate terms to the cultivators as the zamindars did. Unlike the zamindars they did not have the authority to direct the raiyats to produce only a crop of their choice. Theoretically not being owners of the soil, they had to renew contracts and *satta*. But once the *satta* was renewed they became virtually the *maliks* of the land.

The planters did not clash with the zamindars for the "decomposition" of the feudal landed property required for the formation of industrial capital. Industrial capitalism could have developed in the nineteenth century if the *zamindari* system in Bihar had been abolished and surplus retained and used for indigenous growth, but this was not the concern of the three major beneficiaries of the system -- the zamindars, the planters and the government. Mere cash payment by the planters did not enable the raiyats to sever their bonds with the zamindars and planters and act independently in their own interest. The development of peasantry and sharp differentiation within its ranks cannot be discerned and therefore social relations of production remained far from being transformed in Bihar. The continuance of vestiges of feudal forces is reflected in *abwabs*, *salami* and other extortions in Bihar. Though we notice various categories of raiyats like occupancy raiyats and non-occupancy raiyats, etc., their petitions to the government do not reflect the growth of a class consciousness among them as a body, which could look with optimism to the future and join hands with any forces working for the country's growth along modern capitalist lines.

REFERENCES

1 *Judicial Criminal Proceedings* No.167, 1 June 1830, from Acting Magistrate of Tirhut, E.S.Campbell to the Government of Bengal, 22 January 1830, para 6.
2 Ibid., para 7.
3 *Judicial Criminal Proceedings* No.174, .1 June 1830, from G.I.Morries, Officiating Magistrate of Bihar, 30 January 1830, to the Government of Bengal.
4 Ibid., para 7.
5 Ibid., para 2.
6 Ibid., para 5.
7 *Board of Revenue*, 29 November 1833, No.25, from the Acting Collector, Munger (8 May 1833) to E.Lee Warner, Commissioner of Revenue for 12th Division, Munger.
8 *Final Report on the Survey and Settlement Operation in the district of Purnia*, para 320, p.104. Here there was a dispute between Darbhanga Raj and Raja Chand of Kishanpur. The Raja of Kishanpur feared that the rent-free land would be taken by the Darbhanga Raja and excess land assessed at a high rate. So he became sympathetic to indigo cultivation.
9 *Judicial Criminal Proceedings*, No. 26, 27 December 1839, from Messrs Machinan and H.Hill (representatives of the Indigo Planters of Tirhut, Saran and Munger) to F.J.Halliday, Secretary to the Government of Bengal, Judicial Department, Fort William, para 7. In a meeting held at Muzaffarpur on 22 December 1839 the planters of Tirhut, Saran and Munger resolved to send a "respectful" petition to the Government of India.
10 An affidavit dated 24 April 1839 signed by Tribhuban Koiry was put up before the Magistrate of Tirhut. Tribhuban

testified to the threat by a zamindar, although the Magistrate did not take cognizance of it.

11 *Judicial Proceedings* No.71, 2 October 1856 from the Commissioner, Bhagalpur to the Government of Bengal, 30 August 1856.

12 *Final Report on the Survey and Settlement Operation in the district of Purnia*, para 347, p.112.

13 *Minden Wilson, History of Bihar Indigo Factories* (Calcutta, 1908), p.VII, preface.

14 These *lattials* were also called factory men in Bihar who were used for beating, whipping and suppressing the raiyats. Both in Bengal and Bihar they were generally men of the lowest strata who were unable to support themselves and their families. They gladly took this opportunity of employing themselves in any capacity however deterimental it might be to their future interests. In this way thousands of them, in the hope of supporting themselves and their families, had met with a violent death particularly in Bengal and their wives and children were seen weeping in the streets of Calcutta.

15 *Judicial Proceedings* No.244, January 1861, from J.Reily to W.S.Seton Karr, Official Secretary to the Government of Bengal, No. 225, 22 December 1860. According to J.Reily it was the first error of the government to invest the zamindars with the powers of the magistrate. But his suggestion did not suit the imperial government which was in search of a powerful ally - the zamindars.

16 *Nil Darpan* or the *Indigo Planting Mirror,* translation from the Bengali by a native (Dinbandhu Mitra) (Calcutta, 1861), Introduction by the Editor, p. VIII, Introduction.

17 Ibid., In fact Raja Rammohun Ray, Rishi Bankim and other zamindars were dependent mainly on land and the support of the landed magnate to the planters was of greater significance. Since the government support to the planters was confined to cities only, it was essential for the planters to seek the support of the local chiefs, zamindars and *maliks* who exercised real authority in their own way with the help of *lathials* or factory men. In the 1830s, 40s and 50s there was no efficient and prompt postal system, no telegraph, no railroads in large parts of the countryside which could provide security to the planter. The police stations were also

far away from the villages. Hence the help of the rural chief was of immense importance to the planter.

18 *Judicial Proceedings,* June 1864, from J. Reckwith, Secretary to the Landholders and Commercial Association to the Officiating Secretary to the Government of Bengal, No. 55, 3 May 1864.

19 *Judicial Proceedings,* No. 49, February 1867. Memorandum by A. T. Maclean, Officiating Magistrate of Tirhut, 23 January 1867.

20 The Maharani of Bettia estate was alleged to have employed three persons named Pullak Singh, Bakhtiar Tiwary and Gajadhar Mishra (*Meseer*). These persons were very influential and they instigated the troubles in Bettia against the planter.

21 *Judicial Proceedings,* No. 49, February 1867, from G. T. Metcalf, Officiating Magistrate of Champaran to R. P. Jenkins, Officiating Magistrate of Patna Division, 15 December 1867.

22 Ibid. A petition of Shaik Madar Bux and others was sent to the Lieutenant Governor of Bengal in which the condition of the raiyats living in the villages leased to the planters was described.

23 Ibid., para 5.

24 *Bihar District Gazetteers,* Champaran (Patna, 1960), p. 268. See also Girish Mishra, *Agrarian Problems of Permanent Settlement: A Case Study of Champaran* (New Delhi, 1878), pp. 94-110.

25 Ibid., Letter from V.T. Metcalf, Officiating Magistrate and Collector of Champaran to R. P. Jenkins, Officiating Commissioner of Patna Division, 24 January 1868, para 5.

26 Ibid., para 56.

27 Ibid., *Judicial Proceedings,* No. 209, October 1868, They were *paikast assamee* of the villages of Chyllia who refused to pay rent to the planters.

28 Ibid., p. 221. In a petition submitted to the Secretary to the Government of Bengal (24 March 1868) by the inhabitants of several villages of Motihari subdivision, the raiyats registered their protests.

29 Ibid., No. 225, from H. Bell, Officiating Judge of the Court of the Small Causes, Motihari to the Secretary, Government of Bengal, No. 14, 24 April 1868.

30 *Home Department* No. 5581, 17 October 1868, Fort William, from H.L.Dampier, Officiating Secretary to the Government of Bengal to the Secretary, Government of India.

31 Ibid.

32 *Judicial Proceedings* No. 37, May 1869, from A. P. Howell, Officiating Secretary to the Government of India, Home Department, to the Secretary to the Government of Bengal, No. 5072, Fort William, para 14, 31 December 1868.

33 *Final Report on the Survey and Settlement Operation in the district of Darbhanga*, J. H. Karr, para 492, p. 137.

34 Stephen Henningham, *A Great Estate and its Landlords in Colonial India, Darbhanga, 1860-1942* (OUP, New Delhi, 1990), p. 42.

35 Minden Wilson, *History of Bihar Indigo Factories* (Calcutta, 1908), p. 91.

36 Ibid., p. 102.

37 Anand A. Yang, *The Limited Raj, Agrarian Relations in Colonial India Saran district, 1793-1920* (OUP, New Delhi, 1989), p. 133.

38 *Final Report on the Survey and Settlement Operation in the district of Bhagalpur, 1902-1910*, P.W. Murphy, para 285, p. 204.

39 *The Bihar Times*, 30 April 1879, quoted in V.C.P. Chaudhary, *Imperial Honeymoon with Indian Aristocracy*, (K. P. Jayaswal Research Institute, Patna, 1980), p. 450. F.J. Halliday even bestowed judicial and executive appointments as a reward for loyal services to the *Raj* during the rebellion of 1857. It may also be mentioned that the Governor General in Council had earlier decided the precedence according to which Raja Bhoop was the first followed by the Maharaja of Doomraon, the Maharaja of Bettia, the Maharaja of Tikari and the Maharaja of Deomoongarh.

40 George Watt, *Dictionary of the Economic Products of India*, Vol. IV, p. 393.

41 George Watt, op.cit., pp. 393-94.

42 Ibid.

43 Ibid., p. 397.

44 Ibid., pp. 396-97.

45 Ibid., p. 399.

46 Blair B. Kling, *The Blue Mutiny, The Indigo Disturbances in Bengal 1859-1862 Philadelophia, 1966*, p. 48.

47 Ibid., p. 50.

48 Minden Wilson, *History of Bihar Indigo Factories* (Calcutta, 1908), pp. 142-43, Appendix III.

49 Appendix IX *Indigo cultivation*, p. 764, reproduced in *Bihar District Gazetteers*, Darbhanga, P. C. Roy Choudhury. Also see *Final Report on the Survey and Settlement Operation in the district of Darbhanga*, op.cit.

50 *Final report on the Survey and Settlement Operation in the district of Champaran, 1892-99*, para 530, p. 149.

51 *Bihar District Gazetteers*, Champaran, P. C. Roy Choudhury, Patna, 1960, p. 268.

52 *Judicial Criminal Proceedings*, 1 June 1830, No. 167, para 3, from the Acting Magistrate of Tirhut to the Government of Bengal, 22 January 1830.

53 Ibid., No. 26, paras I & II, 27 December 1839.

54 Ibid., para 18.

55 *Judicial Proceedings*, No. 92, 2 October 1856.

56 There were five members of the Commission which consisted of (1) Seton Karr, the Secretary to the Lieutenent Governor, (2) Temple, a civilian, versed in official business, (3) Furgusson, a merchant in Calcutta having great experience in the commerce and manufacture of indigo, (4) the Rev. Mr Sale, a missionary and (5) Baboo C. M. Chatterjee, a native, who held several subordinate offices under the Government of Bengal. The enquiry contains more than 1000 printed pages. The opinion of the enquiry was divided. It was assented to only by Rev. Sale and Baboo C. M. Chatterjee. It was in all its important parts dissented from by Temple, the Secretary to the Indian Finance Minister. It was protested against *in toto* by Furgusson. The Landowners and Commercial Association of British India also sent a copy of the *Memorial* to the Secretary of State for India in answer to the *Minute* of the Lieutenant-Governor of Bengal on Indigo contracts and the answers therto. It was also very critical of the *Minute* of J. P. Grant.

57 *Judicial Proceedings*, No. 386, July 1861 from Messrs Gisborne and Co. to certain managers of indigo concerns in Tirhut, 12 July 1861.

58 *Judicial Proceedings,* No. 53, February 1867 from A. T. Maclean, Collector of Patna to the Commissioner of Patna, 4 February 1867.
59 Ibid., No. 129.
60 *Judicial Proceedings,* No. 75 (Bettia), May 1868, petition of the raiyats to the Government of Bengal (undated).
61 *Judicial Proceedings,* No. 34, July 1868. This petition of 5 December 1867 was sent to the government by Mahashaya Singh, Daulat Singh, Gopal Rai, Chattar Mahto, Ganesh Mahto, Bhigali Mahera, Chatter Rai, Jothi Goaia, Began Ojha and Randhi Rai.
62 Ibid., No. 211, petition of Shaik Madar Bux and others to the Lieutenant-Governor of Bengal, 28 January 1868.
63 *Home Department* No. 50, 6 January 1868. It was a petition of the raiyats sent to the Governor-General in Council.
64 Ibid., No. 221.
65 Ibid.
66 Amiya Kumar Bagchi, *The Evolution of the State Bank of India, The Roots* 1806-1876, Part II: Diversity and Regrouping, 1860-1876 (Oxford University Press, Bombay, 1987), p. 164.
67 Anand A. Yang, pp. 132, 133, 134, 138.
68 Ibid., pp. 181-84.
69 Minden Wilson, op. cit., p. 58.
70 Ibid., pp. 58-59. Most of the planters from Saran, Champaran and Tirhut used to assemble at the Planters Club, Muzaffarpur, on almost all Saturdays and Sundays. It became meetings ground for the planters and the government officials.
71 Lawrence Papers, Reel 5, extract from Lawrence's letter to Henry Maine, 4 April 1864 reproduced in R. B. Chaudhary, *British Agrarian Policy in Eastern India, Bengal & Bihar 1859-80* (Patna, 1980), Appendix F, p. 188.
72 Ibid., Appendix P, p. 205.
73 *Report on the Native Newspapers of Bengal,* para 41, Sudhakar, 2 March 1894.
74 D. H. Buchanan, *The Development of Capitalist Enterprise in India* (New York, 1934), p. 27.
75 *Final Report on the Survey and Settlement Operation in the district of Purnia,* op. cit., para 347, p. 112.

CHAPTER IV

Impact of Plantation on Tenantry and Labour

Indigo cultivation in Bihar neither converted a medieval raiyat into a prosperous farmer in "prosperous India" nor did it produce an organised and disciplined labour force; rather it created uncertainty, insecurity and oppression leading to his eviction from the landholdings. Whether the raiyat took his advance with reluctance or cheerfulness, he was never a "free man". Rural indebtedness increased enormously and the raiyat had to sell his small holdings either to the *mahajans* or to the zamindars. The tenantry of Bihar in 1833 was scarcely better than in 1783. His condition was even worse on account of forced labour exacted by unscrupulous indigo planters and the parasitic zamindars. Sandwiched between the zamindar and the planter, the poor raiyat was utterly helpless.[1]

The official records also confirm that the cultivation of indigo in Muzaffarpur district was very unpopular with the raiyat.[2] When the raiyats were subjected to oppression by the zamindars, they had to transfer their holdings to the factory. But when oppression of the zamindars was relatively less, the raiyats' attachment to land grew and its price went up. Seeing the difference the raiyats naturally felt unhappy at the growth in indigo cultivation.[3] Though the raiyats were fixed and stable, they were unable to pay off the rent on time because of abject poverty. Besides, they were coerced by the *thikadars* and other underlings who made them cultivate indigo at the most seasonable time, however inconvenient this might be to them. The price paid for indigo was not remunerative enough to the raiyats to sustain their families. Being illiterate they did not understand the accounts which were mixed with rent.[4] After the adjustment of land rent and the deficit of the previous years, advance was made to the raiyats. But it was so negligible that the maintenance of the raiyats family was rather difficult. They were so poor and the social usage made so many demands on them that they were regularly forced to borrow money from the *mahajans* and landlords. Thus the debt proved useful to the planters which gave them an opportunity to control the raiyats.[5]

Because of their subjugation by the planters, *mahajans* and the landlords, ignorant and illiterate tenants were in a hopeless condition, and independent thinking or action on the part of raiyats were out of question, especially in the absence of the capitalist class. For the raiyats indigo was much less advantageous than other crops. Towards the end of the nineteenth century the price paid for indigo was Rs 13-8-0 per *bigha*. The average rent rate in four *thanas* of Muzaffarpur district where indigo was grown was about Rs 3-5-0 (Rupees three five *annas*) per acre. After deducting this the raiyats received Rs 11 per acre as profit. Out of this he had to spent Rs 5 on indigo cultivation. The net profit was therefore Rs 6 only.[6] This meagre sum was not enough to sustain a joint family of a raiyat, especially when the price of grain had increased enormously due to famines. Thus the payment of cash whether as advance or otherwise did not materially change the structure of the peasantry, rather it pauperised him further. Sometimes the debt of the *mahajan* or landlord was much more than Rs 6 earned out of indigo cultivation.

If the relative price of indigo, *rabi* (wheat) and barley is kept in view, the role of indigo cultivation as an important factor of his poverty becomes obvious. It is well known that indigo was mainly grown on land that could otherwise have been sown with *rabi* and other food crops. The profit earned in two crops, viz wheat and barley, was not less than Rs 12-9-0 (Twelve rupees nine *annas*) and Rs 9-9-0 per acre (Nine rupees nine *annas*) respectively inclusive of the rent. Thus excluding the rent the net profit was Rs 8-9-0 or Rs 5-9-0. Besides this net profit, the *rabi* and barley produced husk required for the cattle. Exclusive of husk a raiyat earned a net profit of Rs 2-9-0 (Rupees two nine *annas*) per acre more than indigo. In the cultivation of barley however 7 *annas* was less profitable than indigo.[7] Since the soil of Tirhut was alluvial and fertile, it did not require frequent irrigation for the production of *rabi* and barley. Indigo required occasional irrigation. George Watt tells us that although irrigation was not necessarily required for the cultivation of indigo in Tirhut, the raiyats did it. Producing two crops a year on this land was quite possible but indigo cultivation foreclosed that option. Thus, the raiyats incurred considerable loss by cultivating indigo except in years of drought.

Equally adverse was the impact of indigo cultivation on the tenants of Darbhanga district. As compared to other districts of North Bihar, indigo was directly cultivated here by the factories themselves. Under the *zeerat* system of cultivation which was in vogue in the district till the end of the nineteenth century, the raiyats' small holdings were converted into farms. When the raiyats got back this land after the expiry of the lease, refixing of the boundaries of their land was quite difficult and it involved considerable litigation among the raiyats themselves. The *thika* leases were most common of all. The *thikadars* promised raiyats protection from the planters but no effort was made by them to fulfil their promise. In this situation the planters forcibly evicted the tenants from their holdings and sowed indigo in the disputed land. The case of Govind Jha illustrates that the land forcibly sown with indigo by H.L.Gale, the Manager of the Pandaul concern, was not the *zeerat* land. It belonged to the individual cultivators under the *jot* of Govind Jha who did not pay the rent.[8] Two cases were filed by the raiyats but they failed to prove that their land was in the *jot* of Govind Jha. The planter, on the other hand, proved that he held the land as a raiyat under one Devi Prasad *thikadar*.[9]

Official records such as the *Final Report on the Survey and Settlement Operation in the district of Darabhanga* and *District Gazetteers* (1907) try to project the view that the planters were relatively less oppressive than the landlords who were in the habit of frequently enhancing the rent.[10] But the non-official sources such as the native newspapers and memoirs prove beyond doubt that the condition of the raiyats under the planters was pitiable. The fact is that both of them were equally oppressive in their relations with the raiyats.

The *Som Prakash* on 7 April 1876 reported that the planters had made Ratanpur, Sasaulla, Sivapore, Barahi and neighbouring villages in Darbhanga district a scene of desolation. The inhabitants had left their ancestral homes and sought refuge in the province of the Gorkhas.[11]

The tenants had hardly recovered from the distress of the recent famines when the oppression of the planters pressed heavily on them. Upper Bihar was laid waste and devastated by the oppression of the late Manager of the Darbhaga estate. Gedde's report on the Darbhanga estate was not made public and

Mac Donnell's report did not contain anything regarding the oppression of the planters. The extortion by the landlords was very heavy. Out of each rupee earned by a tenant the zamindar took more than half and very little was left to the tenant to feed and clothe his family. The tenants did not have permanent right to the land which belonged to the zamindar and the condition of the tenant was no better than that of common labourers in many respects. The labourers at least got remuneration for their work while the tenants did not.[12] The peasants were relatively better off under the Mughals than under the planters' *Raj*. It has been proved that although the King was the owner of the soil, he did not claim the right to evict the peasant occupant from his holding so long as he continued to cultivate the land and pay the land revenue.[13] The sale of estates or land was regarded as a social disgrace only to recourse to as a last resort in Darbhanga district in particular and Bihar in general. Hence the proprietors did not want to part with their rights unless they were forced to do so. Secondly, with the rise of the value of land the practice of granting permanent leases had almost died out. Factories were therefore dependent on temporary leases for acquiring interest in the villages for indigo cultivation. This gave rise to the *thika* system. Such leases were granted to the planters by the landlords as security for loan. Financially embarrassed proprietors therefore often granted leases to the planters. They also did not like the management of the estates due to land disputes between the raiyats and themselves. In such circumstances the estates were leased to the factories for 5 to 20 years.[14] Whenever the estates were leased to the planters, the tenants attached to these were practically kept on lease to the factories. Thus the planters became the masters of the raiyats and dictated their own terms and conditions to them. This reminds us of a classic case of feudalism in early medieval India and also of the serfdom in Russia before 1861.

Since the sowing of indigo coincided with the reaping of food crops (*mahye*), the tenantry were oblidged to give up their own agricultural occupations and work for the factory. The tenants had to prepare the soil for indigc first, then attend to his own agricultural work. In 1876 the Manager of the factory in Tirhut had framed a new rule that no tenant would be allowed to reap his own crops before the indigo fields were prepared for sowing.[15] As a result of this rule the ripe crops (*bhadai* crops were *makka, kodo, marua, urdi,* etc.) of the tenants were wasted on the fields. The raiyats were also subjected to physical torture. For some reason or the other if a person failed to attend to the indigo fields at the break of the day, the factory peons dragged him out before the Manager *Sahib* where he was not only caned but also fined at the Manager *Sahib's* discretion. The fine realised from the raiyats varied from four *annas* to five rupees. In order to pay the fine the raiyats had to sell their utensils and sometimes their clothes.[16] Like the zamindars the planters also held regular "court" for the hearing about indigo as well as other complaints.[17] The judgement delivered by the planters in the cases between the raiyats themselves was more effectively carried out than in those of the zamindars.[18]

The correspondent of the *Amrit Bazar Patrika* reported that a *Sahib* of a factory made an effort to whip some respectable females and ordered a servant of the factory to take off their clothes.[19] Due to famines the raiyats were not in a position to pay the whole rent to the planter on an appointed date as fixed by the *Sahib.* In that case cattle were attached and brought to the factory and were afterwards sold to realise the arrears. If the cattle of the raiyat were found grazing in the indigo fields, fines varying from 4 *annas* to 1 rupee were imposed and realised from the tenants (for every goat from 4 to 8 *annas*; for every cow, buffalo, ass, horse or hog one rupee).[20] Realising fines from the raiyats for grazing their goats in the indigo fields in Paru *thana* of Muzaffarpur district was regarded so oppressive that a folk song (*holi*) maintained: *bhaile nilaha ke raj ab kaise jibu ge bakaria* (O my dear goat! the planter's *raj* has come about; how shall we survive?).[21]

The *Sadharani* of 18 November 1877 reported that the plight of the masses was reflected in their movements from villages in Tirhut to the districts of Bengal where they outnumbered others as domestic servants (87.1 per cent of the total domestic servants, viz 14 *annas* in a rupee, in Calcutta were either Biharis or Maithils).[22] They would not have left Bihar if subsistence was possible at home. The *Amrit Bazar Patrika* of 13 September carried a story about the partisan attitude of a Magistrate of Munger, Magarath and the Lieutenant-Governor of Bengal towards the planters who had been adversely commented upon by the High Court.[23] Since the story correctly represented the prevailing situation, it was a common talk those days in the offices. A government officer, who maintained his anonymity, candidly asserted that Magarath had often acted as an honorary agent of the planter. He had allowed his position to be used by the planters for obtaining indigo land. The Subdivisional Officer of Hajipur reported that those planters who oppressed their tenants in land disputes did not enlist themselves as members of the Bihar Indigo Planters Association.[24] The *Medini* of 2 April, 1882 reported that 50 *bighas* of alluvial land in village Mahapur, located on the southern side of the Kosi river, was forcibly sown with indigo at the night; the piece of land had been prepared by the raiyats for the cultivation of *teel*.[25] Describing the general condition of the raiyats the *Sanjivini* of 19 April 1884 reported that "men were sold at Tirhut. A few months ago a mother sold her child for 8 rupees".[26] Besides the oppressive acts of the planters, a kind of slavery prevailed in Tirhut. If a man/woman borrowed money from a moneylender, he/she had to serve him as a slave until the debt was repaid. Such persons had to leave their own houses and live in the moneylender's house or in some place assigned by him. They had to obey their masters. References to debt slavery are plenty in ancient legal texts.

Irrespective of the social hierarchy indigo was cultivated by all castes in Tirhut. Broadly speaking, the people of Tirhut should be divided into three categories. The Kayasthas, the substantial agriculturists (among whom were several *maliks* and zamindars) and the poor peasantry. The peasants were the cultivators of the soil and the labouring classes in general and among them were Brahmins, Babhuns (Bhumihar Brahmins) and men of all castes. Thus the caste-based "prejudices against the cultivation of indigo" as stated by John Augustus Voelcker does not seem to be correct in the case of Bihar.[27] Some of the Brahmins were cultivators, while a majority of them lived by begging.[28] No Kayasthas were found among the labouring classes, which mostly consisted of *Dhanuks, Kurmis, Goalas, Dusadhs, Chamars* and other low castes. Sections in the first three castes, viz Brahmins, Babhuns and Kayasthas, were relatively well-off but their number was very small. The mass of the people were poor and suffered most at the hands of the planters in Tirhut.

The material condition of the raiyats in Saran district was in no way better than anywhere else in Bihar. The proprietors had no hesitation in granting temporary leases to the factories. Since the principal amount of rent was not paid to the planters under the *zarpeshgi* lease, the latter continued to enjoy the tenure of the land. Thus the tenants attached to the land had to remain under the complete control of the planters.[29]

The *panchkathia* or *tinkathia* system of indigo cultivation was injurious to the raiyats. Though efforts were made to restore land to the original raiyats after the expiry of the lease, in many cases the raiyats lost the right to the land.[30] When the land or the village was returned to the proprietors after the expiry of the lease, it was very difficult to restore tenants' rights to the land in the absence of any map or record. The obliteration of field boundaries which was used by the factory deprived the raiyats of their right to individual holdings. Besides, the land was often brought under intensive cultivation by the factory and so it lost its fertility for years to come. In this case the land was let out by the proprietor to some other raiyats for a year or two at a very high rent.[31]

As elsewhere in the indigo growing districts of Bihar, the *satta* system of indigo cultivation adversely affected the raiyats in Saran district. The most obvious disadvantage was that indigo was not so remunerative as ordinary food crops.[32] The raiyat was paid at the rate of Rs 13-8-0 per *bigha* and the expenses incurred on indigo cultivation in one acre were not less than Rs 5 and therefore the net profit was less than Rs 10 inclusive of the rent. While indigo was grown once a year on a piece of land the food crops could have been grown twice a year. Except *kodo* all other crops such as maize, barley, wheat and gram returned better output than indigo. In addition to the loss of two food crops a year the raiyats were subjected to the supervision and control of various factory servants who harassed and oppressed them.

As compared to the raiyats of Muzaffarpur and Darbhanga districts, the raiyats of Saran were relatively better off because they got an advance from the planters without any interest or at a much lower rate of interest than would have been charged by an ordinary *mahajan*.[33] Some factories in Saran were also willing and ready to help the raiyats who got into trouble. Many criminal cases and much of litigation were avoided by the judicious settlement or kindly advice rendered to the raiyats by the planters. As the factory was the landlord, the landlords could not exact various kinds of *salamis* and *abwabs* from the raiyats as in Champaran. But indigo cultivation was not as much remunerative as that of ordinary crops. Possibly because the raiyats in Saran fared better at the hands of the planters than their counterparts in Tirhut and Champaran, no systematic movement against the planters was launched in Saran. All this does not mean that the situation in Saran was ideal. Intensive cultivation of indigo in the district exhausted the fertility of the soil which became useless for further cultivation of food crops. Such land was kept barren for 3 to 4 years so that it could regain fertility. Though harassment by the landlords was avoided, the raiyats were subjected to the annoying visits of the factory's *amlas*.[34] It was found that sections of Brahmins, Babhuns, Rajputs and other high castes held the best land in the villages while the low caste men such as *Koeri, Kurmi* and *Chamar* held the inferior land. These high caste proprietors leased the best land to the planters and therefore the ordinary cultivators were left with inferior land. It proved a hindrance to the production of food crops during the famines.

The plight of raiyats in Champaran was definitely the worst. Indigo had become such an important crop in the district that in 1899-1900 it accounted for 95,970 acres (6.63 per cent of the total cropped area).[35] The southern *thanas* of Champaran had uplands where indigo cultivation was very extensive. In nearly half of the district the planters exercised the rights of the landlords.[36] Unlike in other districts in Bihar, the raiyats of Champaran were "tenants-at-will". They could be evicted from their holdings by the landlords and the planters any time. Since the Bettia raj with its jurisdiction over the largest number of raiyats had been mortgaged to the planters due to financial difficulties, they were freely oppressed by the planters. The *Samay* of 7 September 1894 reported that the condition of the common man was so pathetic that a woman was seen wandering in the bazaar in order to find a customer who might purchase her son and daughter.[37] The daughter was actually disposed off to a woman of the town for only five *paise*.

It has been asserted in some official records[38] that since indigo engaged only a small part of the cultivated area, its impact could only be marginal as it did not affect the raiyats. But a careful look at the situation shows that the reality was much worse than what appeared on the surface. The land taken from the raiyat for indigo cultivation was usually retained by the planters for 3 to 5 years after which it became useless for indigo cultivation. The planters then took over another piece of the best land (*bheeth*) belonging to the raiyat. This had been explicitly stipulated in some of the agreements. In this process the entire holdings of small tenants were engaged in indigo cultivation. Thus what was left with the raiyats was not something that could be made the best use of for themselves and thus the general condition was seriously affected.[39]

It was admitted by the Judge of S.D. *Adalat* that the great difficulty arose from the excessive poverty of the tenants and the excessive wealth gained by the planters through the labour of the raiyats. He found it uncommon and not usual with the production of any other item. To relieve the tenants of their stark misery, he suggested reduction in the planter's profit. He attributed mischief chiefly to *contract* which was sometimes unwritten and vague leaving scope for unrestrained exploitation. After once entering into the *contract* the raiyat was in fact reduced to the status of a slave or bonded labour.[40]

Since the raiyat was tied to a planter for indigo cultivation, his mobility was curtailed and his freedom to deal with other planters in his own interest was undermined. The situation left no scope for him to earn more and make up the deficit.

John Beames[41] in his memoirs cited the case of Forlong, an indigo planter of Tirhut, who pompously lived in Muzaffarpur in the Maharaja's palace and was typical of a whole host of lavishly living planters of his time. A magistrate of the district was a person of no consequence at all to them.

Beams was told by the Commissioner of Patna, Dalrymple, that the government officials in Champaran preferred to let the planters have their own way. They avoided any social estrangement and quarrelling with the planters. The planters resented and did not allow any interference with their despotic hold over the raiyats. They looked upon a person unwilling to cultivate indigo as "a rebel and a dangerous character".[42] Refusal by any one to take the ploughs to the planters entailed confinement with family in the planter's house. Beatings and fines were the normal lot of recalcitrant raiyats.

The planter and the *thikadar* exercised "semi-feudal power" over the raiyats through collaboration.[43] Their superior skill, capital, resourcefulness and liaison with district officers made their power over the ignorant and illiterate raiyats felt. As landlords they accumulated substantial wealth through all means, fair or foul.

The planters were in the habit of retiring to their mother country with "inflated fortunes" after either selling their factories and leaving their charge to junior partners or paid servants. New incumbents were naturally eager "to pay off the borrowed money" with which they had bought their shares and to make their own fortune. The raiyats became victims of fresh extortions whenever there was such a change in the ownership of factories and establishments. The Collector of Muzaffarpur informed the Commissioner of Patna Division that the majority of newcomers were very young. Immersed in their pleasures and enjoyment they bothered little for the raiyats.[44] John Beames, one of the few conscientious district officers of Champaran, drew a stark picture of the over-all situation and recorded that the majority of the planters were "rough, uneducated men, hard drinkers, loose livers and destitute of sympathy for the natives".[45]

The *Hitavadi* of 7 February reported that a Brahmin was in desperate need to see the Maharani of Bettia for help in curbing the oppression by the planters. But he was prevented from doing so by the callous attendants at the "Court" who refused to inform the Maharani of his need and keenness. Driven to despair the man wounded himself in the belly and was found in a precarious condition. This shows that even the Brahmin preferred death to a life which was full of agony and injustice.[46] The *Hindi Bangavasi* of 13 April 1896 also underlined the high-handedness of the planters which had driven the raiyats of Ramnagar to leave their ancestral homes and migrate to Nepal to escape the ill-treatment at the hands of planters. Eighteen villages in Motihari were deserted as the raiyats fled to Nepal (54.48 per cent of the villagers migrated to the "Gorkha" land).[47] To make it impossible for the raiyats to prove their occupancy rights the planters were reported to have snatched *thakbast* and other documents. In such a situation it was difficult for the raiyats to resist the cultivation of indigo and sugar and to sow their land with food crops.[48] Even the landlords were not spared by the planters who forcibly sowed indigo in all their land. The landlords were however in a fix and unable to decide whether to stay or to leave.[49] The planters were bold enough to send the Court of Wards men to the interior apartment of the Maharani and these rogues used obscene language against her; false cases were also instituted against the private servants of the Maharani.[50]

By 1908 the relations between the planters and the raiyats became severely strained as the latter openly began to defy the planters to grow indigo and sugar. This was publicised by the *Howrah Hitaishi* of 7 November 1908. The government apprehended serious agrarian troubles and a punitive force was requisitioned and deputed to Champaran. The Subdivisional Officer of Bettia issued warrants of arrest against 200 leading raiyats for no other offence than refusing to sow indigo on the terms dictated by the planters. Some of the *lathials\kothials* even thrashed a woman to death.[51] The united action of the planters and the local officials had made life very difficult for the raiyats of 35 villages. Their representative Sital Ray was arrested. Narrating the plight of the raiyats, the *Amrit Bazar Patrika* of 7 November 1908 observed that at the best of times, the common agriculturists led a hand to mouth life.[52] Since a large number of raiyats were shut up in the *hajat*, their families were undergoing every kind of hardship. Even influential people were unable to stand security for Sital Ray for the fear of the planters. Following this incident the raiyats of Mallahia factory left their homes apprehending arrest. It was reported from Muzaffarpur that ten raiyats belonging to different villages in the Bettia subdivision had been wounded and brought to Muzaffarpur hospital. The bodies of the victims bore wounds caused by spears and *lathis*. The wounded raiyats reported that some *kothials* tried to forcibly plough their land with indigo to which they objected. Fifty raiyats of Sanichari factory were also injured. The injured included Jakki Kowar, Prayag Teli, Sew Saran, Desa Koeri, Raji Koeri and Bhikhali Teli. Instead of protecting the raiyats the punitive force stationed there began to coerce them to sow indigo and sugar.

A complete story of the miseries of the raiyats of Champaran could not be possible until the impact of these *abwabs* and cesses is studied in detail. The planters realised *abwabs*/cesses from the raiyats although these do not find a place in the Tenancy Act of 1885. The number of such *abwabs*/cesses was around 52 as calculated by late Dr Ram Manohar Lohia.[54] Among other cesses/*abwabs* were the following: *Amahi* -- it was a kind of cess imposed by the planters on the raiyats at the rate of one rupee per year for mango crop. *Amahi* had to be paid even if the mango crop failed. *Kandhahi* -- it was a cess imposed on the raiyats for cultivating sweet potatoes. *Panikharcha* (irrigation tax) -- it was a tax collected by the planters for supplying water through canals for irrigation; whether water was supplied or not the tax was collected. The maintenance of the embankment cost was Rs 300 only per year but the tax realised from the raiyats amounted to Rs 9,000. The Settlement Officer confirmed that *panikharcha* was even levied in villages in which there was no irrigation.[55] *Bethmahi* -- it was a cess at the rate of Rs 3 per plough imposed on those raiyats who were unable to furnish ploughs to the planters. *Bapahi-Putahi* -- it was a kind of death tax imposed after the death of the raiyat and realised from his son. *Marwach* -- it was a kind of tax at the rate of 4 *annas* to one rupee which was realised at the time of the marriage of a girl. *Sagaura* -- it was a tax of Rs 5 which was realised at the time of a marriage of a widow. *Kolhu-awan* -- it was a tax taken from every oil and sugar cane mill (*kolhu* where *gur* was prepared). *Chulahi-awan* -- it was a tax taken at the rate of Re 1 for boiling turmeric. *Batchhapi* -- it was a kind of a tax realised from sellers of oil and milk for every pail at the rate of Re 1. *Bichai* -- a tax realised from the sellers of the grain at the rate of Rs 2. *Hathiahi, Motorahi* and *Nawahi* -- it was a tax imposed on the raiyats for the purchase of an elephant, a motor, a horse and a boat. *Ghawahi* -- it was a tax which was realised from the raiyats by the planters for the expenses incurred on the sore of the *Sahib* (planter). *Phaquahi, Dasahari, Chaitnaumi, Dawatpuja,* etc. -- these taxes were collected on the celebrations of festivals. *Amadi Salami* -- one rupee was paid by the raiyat before saluting a planter. *Dasturi* -- it was a kind of tax which was paid to the *amlas* of the factories. *Mahapatri* -- it was a cess exacted for the worship by the Indian priests of English planters. *Raj-ank* -- it was a kind of tax realised by the planters in their assumed capacity of a king.

With so many cesses routinely expected from the raiyats their plight was indeed unbearable. Interestingly we find a man, a manager of the Belwa factory who himself was a *zabardast* (powerful) planter telling the Committee that since the *thikadars* were squeezed by the planters, they should also squeeze the raiyats.[56] The sky was therefore the limit of extortions in the planters' *Raj.* When indigo cultivation decreased in the late nineteenth century and the early twentieth century the planters started the *hunda* system under which the raiyats were asked to pay to the planters a specified amount in a piece of land and the amount itself depended on the sweet will of the planters.

Girish Mishra has furnished rich statistical data on indigo cultivation in Champaran. He however feels that "the peasants did not get full advantage from indigo cultivation because of the existing tenurial arrangements".[57] This generalisation is not substantially borne out by actual evidence. For example, though tenurial arrangements were somewhat better in Muzaffarpur, Darbhanga and Saran districts, the raiyats did not benefit from indigo cultivation and were literally squeezed in practice. Tenurial arrangements in themselves therefore could not have protected the raiyats in Champaran. Moreover "tenurial arrangement" was not a deterrent to the improvement of Champaran as stated by Mishra. But the fact is that in the whole of the permanently settled areas of Bihar the condition of the under-raiyats or *bataidars* was more or less the same. They remained tenants-at-will; they could be *de facto* occupancy raiyats but they could not transfer their holdings as there was no record to prove occupancy right. It was due to this that the whole of Bihar remained one of the poorest, most backward and feudal regions in the country.[58]

By 1908 the indigo trouble turned into an agrarian unrest and a violent clash took place. Government officials in collusion with the planters started harassing the tenants. It was reported that Brahma Deo Dubey, Ram Pratap Tiwari, Satyanarayan Tiwari, Radhe Tiwari and Jokhan Mahto attached to Norton factory were to be prosecuted. They were called by the *Sahib* of the factory in his bungalow and were asked to pay a *salami* of Rs 500 or Rs 1,000 each, if they were to escape from being sent to jail.[59]

Not only was the installation of punitive force (military police) in the villages of Shikarpur *thana* justified by the Lieutenant Governor of Bengal, the Subdivisional officer of

Shikarpur also issued a notice through the *sirdar* or *patwari* to a Brahmin, Baldeo Tiwari, asking him to supply *rasad* (provisions) to the military police stationed there.[60] The provisions required for the *Subedar* Major per day were 2 fowls,1/2 *seer* of milk, 4 eggs, 1/2 *seer* of potatoes, one *powah* of first class rice, two *chittaks* of *ghee*, two *chittaks* of onions, 1/2 *chittak* of salt, 1/2 *seer* of flour, 5 *seers* of fuel wood and 6 pounds of beef. Baldeo Tiwari was asked to supply the following provisions to each one of forty sepoys per day: 1/2 *seer* of flour, 1/2 *seer* of rice, 1 *powah* of *dal* (pulses), 1/2 *chittak* of condiments, 2 *chittaks* of sugar, 1 *chittak* of tobacco (for smoking and also to use with betel leaves), 1 *powah* of meat, 1 *powah* of *ghee*, 1/2 *chittak* of mustard oil, a cooking pot, 1 *powah* of gram and 3 *seers* of fuel wood. This supply of provisions continued for a week. The hardships caused to Baldeo Tiwari and the villagers at a time when there was famine can easily be imagined.

To ask a Brahmin in the first decade of the twentieth century to supply not only chicken but also beef meant deliberate and deep hurting of religious sentiments. Thus, the planters' dealings with the raiyats in Champaran is undoubtedly a dark spot in the history of agrarian relations in colonial India.

In Bhagalpur district indigo was sown in produce-rent paying land. The whole of indigo was taken by the landlord who paid to the raiyats for half of it.[61] The raiyats were asked by the landlords to say that they held the land on produce rent although they were occupancy raiyats. The planters acquired proprietary rights in the small area where the factories acquired the indigo land through temporary leases from the proprietors of villages in which they wished to grow indigo.[62] Indigo cultivation in Bhagalpur affected the Santhals in Tappa Madhuban most seriously. Although Tappa Madhuban had been reclaimed by the Santhals through hard labour, they were dispossessed by the *Babhuns* (Bhumihar Brahmins) and the Rajputs.[63] *Babhuns* and Rajputs working as peons on a salary of Rs 2 to 3 per month in Kahalgaon indigo factory lent money to the Santhals at exorbitant rates and eventually expropriated them.

The total area of land under the proprietors in Purnia was 49,844 acres. This was only 2.2 per cent of the total occupied area. Of this the maximum area was in Korha and Dhamdaha where Gondwara concern was located. The land retained by the factories on lease was not settled with the raiyats because Darbhanga raj had been working indigo on its own account.[64] The net profit per annum made out of indigo cultivation by the planters amounted to Rs 1,22,274.[65] Indigo was cultivated in 321 acres in Ahmedabad and 187 acres in Karimullahpur by the raiyats. But Hennessy, the planter, wanted it to be made *bakast* land. He pleaded that the cultivators were really hired labourers and not tenants.[66] The planters' plea was upheld and it therefore shows how easy it was to evict the raiyats from their holdings.

In the first half of the nineteenth century indigo cultivation in Purnia district was very intensive and the net cropped area under indigo was much higher than one per cent. The contract obliged the raiyats to grow indigo in an area varying from 4 to 5 *kathas* to 1/2 *bigha*. Once the raiyat received the advance (usually one rupee per *bigha*) he could not sell the yield to any other factory[67] even if the latter would have paid him more. The raiyat was required to get the land ready on proper time; to sow it with indigo when land was ready; to weed the land at the proper time with the help of the servants of the factory; to cut the plant when it was ready and also to maintain a certain quality in the production of indigo. Besides, sometimes the raiyat had to plough the field twelve times. He was required to weed out all grass from the indigo fields.[68] All such labour put in by the raiyats caused harassment to them as the price paid for indigo was too inadequate to meet his requirements, especially at the time of famines. According to the Attested Accounts about 2,00,000 (two lakhs) people had perished due to famine in 1870.[69] A *Faujdar* of Purnia, Mohamad Ala Khan, reported that "hardly a day passes without thirty or forty people dying.... Seed grain has been sold for food, cattle and agricultural utensils, children offered for sale, and no buyers".[70] Mohamad Ala Khan however admitted that since he was a government officer he maintained "blindness to distress" and "deafness to lamentation" in the interest of the *Sirkar Bahadur*. In this situation indigo cultivation even in one per cent of net cropped area was detrimental to the lives of the people.

The official records and other papers such as the *Reports on the Survey and Settlement Operations* in Muzaffarpur, Darbhanga, Champaran and Saran districts, the *Imperial Gazetteers* and the *Judicial Proceedings*, Bengal, try to assert that indigo cultivation was beneficial to the labourers as it gave them employment in the factories and also saved them from starvation deaths during the famines. Before the data are analysed let us look up what these sources speak about the labourers.

Macnaghten, Secretary to the Indigo Planters Association, stated that the indigo concerns in Muzaffarpur district employed an average of 35,000 labourers per day throughout the year.[71] The total figure for the whole year has been calculated at 12,775,000 labourers. According to him the factories belonging to the Bihar Indigo Planters Association had indigo in 74,214 acres. It came to 172 labourers employed in indigo cultivation per acre. Therefore in every 100 acres of cultivated land indigo provided labour to 967 labourers as against 5,513 labourers employed in the remaining area of 94.38 per cent under food crops. Macnaghten thus concludes that though indigo occupied only 5.62 per cent of the net cropped area in Muzaffarpur district, it provided labour to 15 per cent of the labourers He, however, admits that the wages paid to the labourers by the factories were lower than those generally prevailing, ie two *annas* an adult male and one *anna* a boy per day.[72]

It had been estimated that the total labour force employed in indigo cultivation in Saran district was equivalent to nearly 8 million units per day in one year.[73] The daily average wage was two *annas*. The persons employed in the industry included skilled artisans, carpenters, blacksmiths, masons and the like. The total yearly bill of the Saran factories was just little short of rupees ten lakhs and thus it was found beneficial to the labourers of Saran district.[74] In the case of Darbhanga district it has been asserted that the cultivation of none of the ordinary food crops gave employment to so much labour force as indigo.[75] Similarly it had been asserted that the benefits of the indigo industry to the labouring population in Champaran district were still more marked as these were the classes in greatest need of support.[76] Further, it had been estimated that the average number of labourers employed in Champaran per day by indigo factories was 33,000 and more than half of the labour force got employment in the cold weather months when these classes were most liable to destitution.

The data on labour employment furnished in all the *Survey and Settlement Reports* of the districts of North Bihar give the impression that industries created an organised labour force in Bihar. But an examination of the rich statistical details on the employment of labour in industry suggests that the wages given to the labourers were very low, ie two *annas* a male adult per day and one *anna* a boy in Muzaffarpur district, two *annas* in Saran district and very low wage in Champaran. It has been admitted that the wages paid to the labourers in Muzaffarpur district by factories were lower than those generally prevailing.[77] Besides, whatever little wage was given to the labourers the *amlas* took a part of whatever meagre wage was received. Factories exploited the famine situation prevailing in Bihar by employing labourers casually on daily wages. Only a handful of skilled labourers were retained throughout the year. Female labourers got only half of what their male counterparts earned.

A discussion on wage rates reveals that the low wage pocket comprised the whole of the south, the United Provinces and Bihar at the end of the nineteenth century.[78] The labourers did not and could not improve their living conditions as the "real wages" were too meagre to sustain the family. They would have migrated to other provinces where the wage rate was higher but their mobility was restricted due to lack of transport facilities in the nineteenth century. No hours were fixed for the agricultural labourers working in indigo factories. They had to work from dawn to dusk and if they collapsed through exhaustion or weakness they were severely beaten and confined to the *kothis*. The factories which did not belong to the Bihar Planters Association had not maintained any norms in payment of wages. The government had not framed any rule to oblige the factories to pay a specified wage. The first Act regarding the employment of children in the factories came into being in 1881, according to which 9 hours per day were fixed for the children between 7 and 9 years of age. The Act of 1891 made little change. Until 1911 men, women and children continued to work twelve to fifteen hours.[79] In fact there was no legislative protection to the labourers although "a large number of labour force was recruited on indigo plantations through agents who exploited the poor by unscrupulous means".[80]

Thus from the middle of the nineteenth century to the first decade of the twentieth century neither the "radical utilitarian theory of peasant proprietorship" nor the "Victorian liberalism with laissez-faire" emerged and succeeded in giving protection to the raiyats of Bihar. The development of agriculture in Bihar was rather deformed by the interaction between the pre-capitalist zamindars and the profit-oriented planters under British colonial domination. India under colonial rule could not save the interests of its own people. The amount of net profit made by the indigo planters was much larger than what had been paid to the raiyats and the labourers. Besides extraction of surplus from the raiyats and the labourers, *salamis, nazranas abwabs* and a number of other cesses realised from them enabled the planters to amass enormous wealth. Sometimes the amount realised on these items exceeded the amount realised as rent. For example, in 1911 the raiyats of the five villages of Champaran (Ramnagar estate) paid Rs 9,737 as land revenue as against Rs 11,204 as *abwabs*.[81] Although rural indebtedness was more or less a universal phenomenon in Bihar, the indigo cultivation contributed to the growth of rural indebtedness as it was unremunerative to the raiyats. The volume of "rural indebtedness was usually larger in the regions affected by commercial farming than in those where the economy was largely subsistence based".[82]

Gandhiji aptly, unerringly and even somewhat generously remarked to the government:

"... *tinkathia* has bound the raiyat like the coil of a serpent from which whether it be legal or not the raiyats have ever striven to get free and from which the government had hitherto made unsuccessful attempts to free them".[83]

REFERENCES

1 Ram Narain Sinha, *Bihar Tenantry (1783-1883)* (New Delhi, 1968), p. 148.

2 *Final Report on the Survey and Settlement Operation in the district of Muzaffarpur, 1892-1899*, C. J. Stevenson Moore, Patna, 1922, para 886, p. 346.

3 Ibid.

4 Ibid.

5 D. H. Buchanan, *The Development of Capitalist Enterprise in India* (New York, 1934), p. 43.

6 Ibid. Before the contract system was introduced in Muzaffarpur district a raiyat had to cultivate 4 or 5 *kathas* or *bighas* with indigo. The cost of stamp for executing the contract was usually paid by the raiyats.

7 Ibid.

8 *Judicial Proceedings,* No. 49, February 1867. The correspondence between the Assistant Magistrate of Madhubani, the Officiating Magistrate of Tirhut and the Commissioner of Patna speaks of the disputes. It clearly shows that the holdings of the raiyats of Mauza Ekwari, Pargana Bhour, were forcibly taken and sowed with indigo in the teeth of opposition by them. By converting the *raiyati* land into *zeerat* 9 new factories were established.

9 Ibid., No. 91, from D. M. Barbour, Assistant Magistrate of Madhubani to the Officiating Magistrate of Tirhut, 16 February 1867.

10 *The Indigo Industry,* Extract on Indigo Industry from the *District Gazetteers* of Darbhanga (1907), L.S.S. O'Malley, from pp. 97-108 reproduced in the *Bihar District Gazetteers,* Darbhanga, P.C. Roy Chaudhury, Patna, 1964, Appendix IX, pp. 767-68.

11 *Report on the Native Newspapers of Bengal,* April 1876, *Som Prakash,* 7 April 1876.

12 Ibid.

13 See for details Irfan Habib, "The Social Distribution of landed Property in Pre-British India: A Historical Survey" in R. S. Sharma and V. Jha, ed, *Historical Probings in Memory of D.D. Kosambi* (New Delhi, 1974), pp. 263-316.

14 *The Indigo Industry,* Extract on Indigo Industry from the *District Gazetteers* of Darbhanga (1907), L.S.S. O'Malley, reproduced in the *Bihar District Gazetteers,* Darbhanga, Appendix, p. 764.

15 *Report on the Native Newspapers of Bengal, 1876, Amrit Bazar Patrika.* The correspondent who reported the story was a tenant and had worked in an indigo factory in Tirhut district. He was unable to bear any longer the oppression of the Manager of the factory. When he joined this newspaper, he personally visited a large number of factories in Tirhut, Saran and Champaran and filed a story.

16 Ibid.

17 D. H. Buchanan, *The Development of Capitalist Enterprise in India* (New York, 1930), p. 44.

18 An interview with late Rajendra Prasad Sharma of Vishnupur Saraiya (Muzaffarpur) on 20 May 1986. He was himself a zamindar. He testified that during the first half of this century, say around 1905, the planters of Deoria Kothi were very powerful. They also held regular court and sorted out many differences among the raiyats. According to him one of the planters kept a beautiful Muslim girl as his keep in the Kothi for many years but the zamindars and the raiyats did not dare oppose him as they feared the influence and power of the planter.

19 Ibid. The correspondent was going east to Muzaffarpur when he watched the scene in which women were humiliated.

20 Ibid.

21 An interview with Pandit Shiva Kumar Sharma on 20 May 1986. Pandit Sharma is a retired Professor of Sanskrit, Sanskrit College, Muzaffarpur. He hails from Fatehabad village in Paru *thana* of Muzaffarpur where indigo cultivation was carried on under the *zeerat* system.

22 *Report on the Native Newspapers of Bengal*, para 12, *Sadharani*, 18 November 1877.

23 Ibid., para 9, *Amrit Bazar Patrika*, 13 September 1880.

24 Ibid., para 9. It may be noted that there was a demand by the press that the report of O'Donnell should be made public. But Sir Ashley Eden, the Lieutenant Governor of Bengal (often branded as a friend of the raiyats in official papers) did not disclose the report of the officer which contained the oppressive acts of the planters. According to him the report was prepared by an "inexperienced and subordinate officer".

25 *Report on the Native Newspapers of Bengal*, para 2, *Medini*, 2 April 1882.

26 Ibid., para 63, *Sanjivini*, 19 April 1884.

27 *Report on the Improvement of Indian Agriculture*, John Agustus Voelcker (Reprint, New Delhi, 1886), Chapter III, pp. 20-23.

28 *Report on the Native Newspapers of Bengal, Sahachar*, 3 July 1876.

29 *Final Report on the Survey and Settlement Operation in the district of Saran, 1893-1901*, Calcutta, 1903, para 631, p. 179.

30 Ibid., para 632, p. 179. Macnammara, the planter of Ramkola factory and Mackonzie of Rajpatti factory tried to secure the

restoration of original rights to the raiyats. But they did not succeed fully in their efforts to restore the rights of the raiyats to their original lands.

31 Ibid.

32 Ibid., para 637, p. 181.

33 Ibid., para 637, p. 183.

34 Ibid., p. 284.

35 Girish Mishra, *Agrarian Problems of Permanent Settlement: A Case Study of Champaran* (New Delhi, 1978), p. 102; also see *Report on the Survey and Settlement Operation in the district of Champaran, 1892-99*, C. J. Stevenson Moore, Calcutta, 1900, p. 148.

36 *Final Report on the Survey and Settlement Operation in the district of Champaran, 1892-99*, C. J. Stevenson Moore, para 531, p. 149. Under the term landlords all tenure holders and proprietors were included.

37 *Report on the Native Newspapers of Bengal*, para 32, the *Samay* of 7 September 1894. This news was given to the reporter from Samastipur, but the general condition of the raiyats in other indigo growing districts was no better.

38 *Final Report on the Survey and Settlement Operation in the district of Saran*, op.cit., p. 181.

39 General Administration Report for 1872-73, Patna Commissioner, Letter No. 85, 8 September 1873, from S. C. Bayley, Officiating Commissioner of Patna Division to the Secretary to the Government of Bengal.

40 Judicial Proceedings, Bengal, No. 25, 9 June 1830, Leyeetor's Minute.

41 John Beames, *Memoirs of a Bengal Civilian*, (London, 1961).

42 Ibid., p. 135.

43 *Report of the Committee on the Agrarian Condition in Champaran*, Vol. I, (Patna, 1917), p. 4.

44 Letter from C. F. Worsley, the Magistrate and Collector of Muzaffarpur, No. 884, to the Commissioner of Patna Division, 2 August 1877.

45 John Beames, op.cit., p. 172.

46 *Report on the Native Newspapers of Bengal*, para 46, *Hitavadi*, 7 February 1896.

47 Ibid., para 52, *Hindi Bangavasi*, 13 April 1896.

48 Ibid.

49 Ibid.
50 Ibid., *Sandhya*, 3 October 1908.
51 Ibid., para 13, *Howrah Hitaishi*, 7 November 1908.
52 Ibid., *Amrit Bazar Patrika*, 7 November 1908. Sital Ray was a respectable person who belonged to Mathia village in Champaran. His house was surrounded by the police headed by the Reserve Inspector, Knight.
53 Ibid., para 8, *Hitavadi*, 13 November 1908.
54 Ram Monohar Lohia, *Champaran Mein Zamin Ka Upyog* (in Hindi), (Patna, 1950), pp 12-14. It is a report on the Champaran Farm Enquiry Commission.
55 Revenue Department file, Government of Bihar and Orissa, A deposition from J. A. Sweeney, Settlement Officer, North Bihar to the District Officer, Champaran.
56 *Report of the Committee on the Agrarian Conditions in Champaran*, op.cit., vol. II, p. 86.
57 Girish Mishra, *Agrarian Problems of Permanent Settlement: A Case Study of Champaran*, op.cit., p. 108.
58 D. C. Wadhwa, "Transferability of Raiyati Holdings in Bihar: A Long Journey (1793-1950)" in D.N. Panigrahi, ed," *Studies in History, Economy, Society and Politics* (New Delhi), p. 180.
59 *Report of the Native Newspapers*, para 38, *Bihar Bandhu*, 3 April 1909. An article on the oppression of the indigo planters in Champaran was written by Chandra Kishore Narayan Lall in this newspaper.
60 Ibid., para 8, *Hitavadi*, 13 November 1908.
61 *Final Report on the Survey and Settlement Operation in the district of Bhagalpur, 1902-1910*, P. W. Murphy, para 112, p. 58.
62 Ibid., para 205, p. 110.
63 Ibid., para 11, p. 3.
64 *Final Report on the Survey and Settlement Operation in the district of Purnia*, para 335, p. 109.
65 Ibid., para 370, p. 120.
66 Ibid., para 215, p. 67.
67 W. W. Hunter, *A Statistical Account of Bengal, Munger and Purnia*, Vol. XV (Reprinted in India, 1976), p. 364.
68 Ibid., pp. 364-65.
69 *Final Report on the Survey and Settlement Operation in the district of Purnia*, op.cit., para 368, p. 119.
70 Ibid., para 368, p. 119.

71 *Final Report on the Survey and Settlement Operations in the district of Muzaffarpur, 1892-1899,* op.cit., C. J. Stevenson Moore, para 894, p. 350.

72 Ibid., para 895, p. 350.

73 *Final Report on the Survey and Settlement Operations in the district of Saran, 1893-1901,* op.cit., J. H. Kerr, para 612, p. 183.

74 Ibid.

75 *Final Report on the Survey and Settlement Operations in the district of Darbhanga, 1896-1903,* J. H. Kerr, para 500, p. 140.

76 *Final Report on the Survey and Settlement Operations in the district of Champaran,* C. J. Stevenson Moore, para 546, p. 153.

77 *Final Report on the Survey and Settlement Operations in the district of Muzaffarpur,* op.cit., para 895, p. 350.

78 Kamal Kumar Ghosh, *Agricultural Labourers in India: A Study in the History of their Growth and Economic Condition* (Calcutta, 1969), p. 276.

79 D. H. Buchanan, *The Development of Capitalist Enterprise in India* (New York, 1934), p. 313.

80 A. R. Desai, *Labour Movement in India, Documments: 1918-1920* (Bombay, 1988), blurb page.

81 Ram Manohar Lohia, *Champaran Mein Zamin Ka Upyog,* op.cit., p. 15.

82 Binay Bhushan Chaudhuri. "The Process of Depeasantisation in Bengal and Bihar, 1885-1947", *The Indian Historical Review,* Vol. II, No. 1, New Delhi, 1975, p. 112.

83 *Revenue Department Confidential File,* Commerce, 29 August 1917 (CSAP), M. K. Gandhi, 29 July 1917. It was a confidential note recorded by Gandhiji.

CHAPTER V

Resistance and Peasant Protests

Although there are a number of theoretical and statistical works[1] on the peasant movements and agrarian tensions in modern Bihar, there is hardly any work on the tenants' resistance to the indigo planters in the nineteenth century. A.N.Das who continues to be most sympathetic to the cause of the raiyats and downtrodden sections of the peasantry casually refers in his long introduction (77 pages) to the "indigo riots (sic) of 1867, 1877 and 1907".[2] D.N.Dhanagre, A.R.Desai, Girish Mishra and many others have wilfully or inadvertently ignored the tenants' resistance to the planters in nineteenth century Bihar. B.B.Chaudhuri, a well known authority on agrarian history in eastern India gives an account of the transformation of agrarian economy through the commercialisation of agriculture, but he also does not pay attention to the tenants' resistance against the indigo planters in Bihar.[3] Ram Narain Sinha's *Bihar Tenantry (1783-1833)*, despite its catchy title, is silent about the indigo growing tenants in Bihar.[4] The Subalterns, the self-proclaimed champions of the peasants' autonomy, have also not found the indigo growing raiyats of Bihar important enough to deserve adequate attention. Such underrating of "traditional" peasants' protests against the planters, especially in the nineteenth century when Indian nationalism was born, is not only unfair but creates the wrong impression of their meek and spineless submission to the exploiting English planters. If one goes into the details of the primary sources one finds the raiyats' awareness of the accumulation of profit by the planters. Because of their perception of wealth accumulated in the hands of a few planters, a number of complaints and petitions were presented to the government. These complaints in the form of charters of demands throw light on the agrarian tensions in the indigo growing districts of Bihar in the nineteenth century.

The discontent of the raiyats against the planters was first noticed in 1830 when the Acting Magistrate of Tirhut informed the Government of Bengal that the "natives" were not at all trusted by the planters and the latter paid no attention to the representations made by them.[6] The origins of most of these disputes between the raiyats and the planters were attributed to the native servants of the factory. The breach of contract by the raiyats was often noticed and it was found that the land which was prepared for indigo was sown with foodcrops. In that case a decree imposing the penalty on the raiyats (*maḻik's* raiyats in the records) was managed, though raiyats were generally too poor to pay the penalty. Although there were numerous complaints in Bihar (Bihar in this core text stands for Patna district) only eight *fauzdari* cases were filed by the raiyats of Bihar against the indigo planters. This figure does not include cases registered at the *thana* level.[7] A typical case was a leasing of a village or *taluk* by the *maliks* to the planters on payment of half of the aggregate amount. This compromised the position of the raiyats and the planters were able to strike a deal easily in their own favour.[8] In such cases the planters "bargained" with the raiyats easily in their own favour.

In 1839 the planters of Tirhut, Saran and Munger sent representations to the Secretary to the Government of Bengal asking for a specific regulation to check the violation of indigo contracts by the raiyats. The raiyats did not act upon their engagements and refused to cultivate the indigo land and sowed it with foodcrops. They did not cut the harvest plants on time. Evasion of engagements by the natives even led to the breach of peace. A *faujdari* case was filed against the planter, Maclead of Saraiya factory. Though localised, the protests initiated by the raiyats involved many planters in legal battles. Under such conditions the planters alleged that "neither life nor property" was safe.[9] Those raiyats who involved the planters in litigation and produced witnesses against them in the court were branded as "fraudulents", who could procure witnesses as cheaply as eggs, etc. It is significant of the pervading anti-planter stand of the common masses that even the ploughmen and cart-drivers refused to cooperate with the planters. Disturbed at this development the planters sought a legislative safeguard for their interest in the form of binding the raiyats, ploughmen and cartmen not to injure the planters' interests.[10]

The Santhal Rebellion caused anxiety to the government and it apprehended agrarian disturbances in indigo growing areas of Bihar. It is against this background that the government for the first time entertained the petition from the raiyats of Panchananpur in Bhagalpur district against the indigo planter, Mr Gray of Maldah. The Commissioner of Bhagalpur found that not only the raiyats but also the zamindar was against the planter and the latter was unable to produce any witness on his own behalf. He therefore decided the case against the planter.[11] A consolidated account of how the indigo growing passed in the area of Munger, Bhagalpur, Purnia and Tirhut districts was sent by the Commissioner of Bhagalpur to the Lieutenant Governor. According to this report 2 cases were filed by the raiyats of Bhagalpur against the planters; 2 cases against the planters in Purnia and 38 complaints were registered in Tirhut. Of the 38 cases 23 related to the complaints made by the raiyats against the planters.[12] These cases explain the nature of the disputes between the raiyats and the planters. But since the complaints did not cause any law and order problem, the government did not take them seriously.

The Indigo Disturbances in Jessore and Nadia districts of Bengal caused anxiety to the planters of Bengal, while the planters of Bihar were disturbed over their killings by the people of Bihar in 1857. A number of planters were assaulted, humiliated and even murdered by the rebels of 1857. In this situation Messrs Gisborne and Co., the planters of Bengal, sent a circular letter to the managers of concerns in Tirhut[13] asking them to enhance the rate of indigo price paid to the raiyats. Apprehending that the raiyats in Bihar might become aggressive the planters were advised in their own interest to be somewhat more conciliatory and not mind making some "handsome presents" to make good the losses of the raiyats.

The raiyats of Bihar were agitated because of three reasons: prices paid to them were not remunerative; the time of sowing indigo was the same as that of the foodcrops; and indigo cultivation exhausted the fertility of the soil. The Government's reluctance to accept that the fertility of the soil was seriously eroded due to the indigo cultivation ultimately gave way to the raiyats a firm and unswerving stand. This was a reality and the Tajpur factories conceded that "indigo exhausted the strength of the soil to a very great extent".[14] Left with no alternative the Lieutenant Governor of Bengal observed that the raiyats should be advised to go in for the rotation of crops for retaining the fertility of the soil. He remarked that the raiyats of Bihar should be explained how beneficial was indigo to them and said: "the Bengal ryot was not slow to learn what is and what is not beneficial to him".[15]

Compared to the sporadic complaints and protests of the raiyats of Saran, Tirhut, Munger, Bhagalpur and Purnia in the 1830s against the planters, the tenants' protest in Pandaul (Darbhanga) was more sustained and enduring. The protests here took the form of a movement for three months lasting from January to March 1867.

A number of villages in Madhubani Subdivision united together in a body and refused to grow indigo. They also did not allow the planters to cultivate the indigo lands.[16] Although the Magistrate did not apprehend very serious disturbances, it appeared to him "impossible to foretell what exactly might occur".[17] Keeping in view the law and order situation that might arise, the Magistrate of Tirhut asked the Assistant Magistrate of Madhubani, D.B.Barbour, to remain in the neighbourhood of villages where the latter apprehended disturbances.[18] A notice under Section 62 of the Criminal Procedure Code was also issued to the planter, Gale, to abstain from ploughing *assamiwar* land in some villages. This unusual action of the government made the raiyats feel bold enough to sow their land with food crops.[19] The planter, however, did not reconcile himself to what he believed to be an *ex-parte* decision. The government also came to realise that the raiyats of other indigo concerns might refuse to cultivate the land for indigo. This was considered to be a quite disturbing possibility and therefore the Commissioner of Patna Division asked the Magistrate of Tirhut to settle the cases of disputed possession between the factory and the raiyats.[20] United action of the tenants of Pandaul concern in refusing to cultivate indigo was considered serious enough to warrant appropriate measures from the government.[21] Not only information through proper channels reached the Lieutenant Governor of Bengal, a police force was ordered to be posted in the neighbourhood of the disturbed villages to overawe the local population.[22] The Commissioner of Patna also asked the Magistrate of Tirhut Division to employ additional police force, if required. The Magistrate was asked to proceed "at once" to the spot and take all measures necessary for the preservation of peace. Gale, the planter of the Pandaul concern, on the other hand, insisted on cultivating the *assamiwar* land with indigo despite the warning issued to him not to do so by the Assistant Magistrate of Madhubani. The action of D.M.Barbour, Assistant Magistrate of Madhubani, to prevent a planter from sowing *assamiwar* land was not liked by the Magistrate of Tirhut who called for an explanation from the former.[23] While explaining his position Barbour argued that since he received a number of complaints from the raiyats and ploughmen against the planter, he had to stop forcible cultivation of *assamiwar* land with indigo. Gale, on the other hand, tried to assert his claim to the land; he wanted to retaliate against the raiyats. When the *kothials* of the factory reached the spot, they were warned by a large mob of raiyats to desist from asserting the authority of the planter.[24] Thereupon the Magistrate of Madhubani referred the case to the Judicial Department for a final decision.

Besides filing a petition to the government, a large number of raiyats had gone to Darbhanga to register their grievances against Gale who threatened to evict them from their holdings.[25]

While communicating his decision, D.M.Barbour informed the Magistrate of Tirhut the exact nature of the dispute. He came to know about the truth from Gale himself. According to it there was *zeezbad* land owned by the planter as *zeerat* land. But there was land in every village other than *zeerat* land which was cultivated by the raiyats. In respect of such land the raiyats were not the cultivators of indigo under the *assamiwar* system of cultivation but they were merely hired labourers and getting *mehnatana* (wage) in return of indigo cultivation.[26] Since Barbour was not convinced by the explanation of Gale, the case was referred to a Judge for decision. Unfortunately the raiyats could not establish their right to the land. The Judge pronounced his judgement in favour of the Manager of the factory, Gale. According to the judgement the raiyats Lakshman Paswan and Magho Rawat were sentenced to undergo rigorous imprisonment for one month and one day for having committed trespass.[27] Though the cases were decided by a Judge, one in favour of the planter and the other against him, the raiyats continued their struggle against the planter.[28]

Imprisonment of the raiyats did not have a demoralising effect on them. A body of raiyats from Darbhanga village in the

Terwarra concern sent another petition to the government with a request to interfere in the dispute between the raiyats and the planters, but it did not pay any attention to it. Inspired by the bold step taken by these raiyats the raiyats of Narar adopted a similar attitude in refusing to cultivate indigo.[29]

Frequent visits by government officials in rural areas gave an impression to the raiyats that the government was opposed to indigo cultivation. Although this was not true, this impression emboldened the raiyats of Khutcha factory to decide on "combined opposition" to the planter. They collected a sum of money through voluntary subscriptions on the basis of the number of cattle each of them owned.[30] The government got a hint of this development and considered it serious enough to seek the help of the Darbhanga Raj.

That the movements of resistance were infectious and tended to percolate to new areas is borne out by the fact that the raiyats of several villages of Hathauri factory began to sow *zeerat* land with food crops.[31] Patterson (the planter) and Smith (the manager) personally visited the site to ascertain the situation. They found that Smith's ploughmen and other servants of the factory were warned by the raiyats despite the fact that Patterson had made his identity known to the raiyats.[32] An adequate number of guards were provided to the planter. This incident was confirmed by the Inspector of Police who submitted a report to the local government. According to the report the raiyats of the villages cultivating indigo for Hathouri factory did not allow the servants of the factory to sow indigo even in *zeerat* land.[33]

The tenants of Ekwari Pergana Bhour & Co., zila Tirhut (Darbhanga) were also disgusted with the planters due to their oppression and ill-treatment. They sent a joint petition to the Commissioner of Patna on 27 January 1867.[34] The petition bearing the name of Giridhari Rai and 202 raiyats contained their grievances against the planter. They complained that 14 or 16 miles around Pandaul concern, the planters had built 9 factories in the villages namely, Buhera, Tapsipur, Raiyam, Muhsat, Motipur, Khema, Belawar and Bhugu. Thousand *bighas* of their land which produced *marua, shama, kauni, makai, khurree, guddhur, anus, kodo* barley, wheat, *mung, rahar, masur*, plantain, cotton, *cheena* potato and tobacco had been forcibly brought under indigo cultivation. Their paddy and *bheeth* land was converted into indigo land. They complained that since their grain producing land had been brought under indigo cultivation, they were put to hardship at the time of famine. Their other grievances included forcibly taking away of bullocks and ploughs under the authority and influence of the *thikadars* and the planters, especially during the season when they were required. They also expressed their resentment at the payment of very low wage to the labourers, erection of 14 new *kothis* and forcible eviction of the raiyats from their holdings even after the rent had been paid to the *firangees*. They wanted an inquiry to be instituted against the oppressive planters. But the government did not pay any attention to their petition as no specific charges were levelled against the planter. The Raiyam factory charged Harihar Rai, Tulsi Koiri and Santokh Koiri with having beaten the servant of the factory.[35] The servant of the factory who had tried to prevent the raiyats from preparing the land for foodcrop received blows. This case was decided in favour of the raiyats as they proved that they were the cultivators of the land.

Of all the areas of resistance to the indigo planters in Bihar, Champaran witnessed the most sustained and violent upsurge on this issue. The raiyats of Tuppeh Madholi and Nanore Seronah in the Majhaua Pargana of Motihari subdivision sent a petition to the government of Bengal against the planters. Chief among them were Meer Enaet Karim, Dauli Shah Kalwar and Goolee Burrac (*mauza* Siswah, Ajgureeh), Hari Rawat Kurmi (village Tuppeh Ninora), Har Charan Lal Patwari of Ninora and several others.[36] These raiyats were the inhabitants of the villages mentioned above which were in the *thika* of Lala Tej Pratap Narain of Bhawanipur (pargana Majhaua). Evidently they did not belong to the most affluent or high caste segment of the society. The main grievances of these petitioners against the planter of Seharho were that they had to cultivate four *kathas* a *bigha* with indigo at the rate of Rs 20-8-0 per *bigha* whereas the expenses on indigo cultivation were about Rs 18; Rs 2 or 3 were advanced to them and the balance was promised to be paid afterwards but the same balance was never paid to them even after the fulfillment of the terms of the *satta*. In such a situation the land was sown by the raiyats with *cheena*, barley, sugarcane and cotton. The planter retaliated through destroying the standing food crops of the raiyats by his men. The raiyats' complaints to the Magistrate of

Motihari were not entertained and the factories fined them for refusing to cultivate indigo. Lala Har Charan Lal Patwari was dismissed from the service by the planter for having adopted a sympathetic attitude towards the raiyats. The raiyats naturally felt seriously wronged and made use of the visit of the Commissioner of Patna to Motihari by presenting before him some 20,000 aggrieved persons. They recorded their grievances in most unmistakable terms against the planters. The planter, on the other hand, resented such demonstration and articulation of grievances by the raiyats and became more repressive towards them. The raiyats did not have money to file suits against the planters and pay the fees of the *mokhtars* and pleaders. They however prayed to the Lieutenant-Governor of Bengal to appoint a commission of enquiry failing which they threatened "bloodshed and destruction to property".[37]

Another petition was sent to the Lieutenant Governor of Bengal through Keso Prasad by the raiyats. Important among them were Hari Charan Lal Patwari, Hari Raut, Ram Suhae Mahto, Sheo Charan Mahto, Badur Mahto, Sheikh Husain, Sheikh Dost, Bhola Sahaya, Durga Raut, Sosehi Mahto and Prayag Lal. They clearly represented different local groups at the grassroot levels. In their petition they requested the Lieutenant Governor of Bengal to regulate the rate of the hire for carriage; to fix the rate for the ploughmen and labourers connected with indigo cultivation, and also to regulate the cultivators' prices for indigo. But the Lieutenant Governor informed the raiyats that it was not within his power "to comply with their prayer".[38] This petition was clearly somewhat more radical than the previous one.

Even the raiyats who were prisoners in the jail did not fail to register their grievances against the jail authorities who were in league with the planters. This was occasioned by the discriminatory preference towards relatively better off and more influential raiyats who had been lodged in jail and who were released for use by the planter in his indigo cultivation plant.[39] Chief among the prisoners who sent petitions to the government through their *mokhtar* included Bhikhari Mahto, (inhabitant of Bairia), Jhotee Sahu (Panapur village), Khobhari Mahto (Bowdha village) and Parmeshwar Pandey (Tuppeh village). Although the Lal Saraiya factory was burnt by the factory people themselves, the innocent raiyats were charged with unlawful damage to property and imprisoned.[40]

A petition by Mahashaya Singh, Daulat Singh, Gopal Rai, Chhattar Mahto, Ganesh Mahto, Bhigali Mishra, Chhattar Rai,l Jothi Goala, Began Ojha and Dharnidhar Rai, all raiyats from Bajria village, was sent to His Excellency the Governor-General of India in Council on 5 December 1867.[41] The main grievance of the raiyats was that the planters had almost appropriated all the land in the *mauza* for indigo cultivation. The complaints included low wages and long hours of work for labourers, forcible seizure of cattle and impoverishment of nearly half the peasantry in Champaran due to indigo cultivation. The Collector of Champaran wrongly alleged that a handful of influential raiyats were at the root of the unrest,[42] for the complaints covered other exploited sections and the agitation was more broad based than the authorities were willing to concede.

The refusal to sow indigo by the raiyats of Jokeetia was followed by other villages and in no time it took the shape of a movement. The raiyats of Purandar factory also refused to grow indigo. Instead of indigo they sowed 50 to 60 *bighas* of land with wheat. Village after village began to do so and the villagers were found in groups consulting each other.[43] The Magistrate of Champaran went to Bettia camp and started consulting the raiyat with a view to apprising the Government of Bengal of the latest prevailing situation. He prepared a long memorandum for the purpose. Metcalfe noted that although each raiyat had his individual grievances, on the issue of indigo cultivation they were completely united. He, however, blamed the influential raiyats for instigating the multitude[44] and got the permission of the Lieutenant-Governor to take suitable counter measures.[45]

Eviction from the holdings of the raiyats of Champaran was frequent and it was an emotive issue. A typical case was that of the raiyats of villages Tuppas, Daulta, Sonaulow and Sukhoa who sent a petition maintaining that though they had reclaimed through their toil and perseverance the land which was barren at the time of the Permanent Settlement, they were being evicted from it for its use for indigo cultivation. They were intimidated to utter submission in false cases.[46]

The Commissioner of Patna Division was of the view that the planters' alleged oppression was not the only cause for disturbance and that the raiyats were in fact alert and conscious enough of the enormous profit of the planters and considered themselves entitled to a share in it.[47]

In order to pacify the agitating raiyats the government intended to offer inducements to village headmen whose support was useful in making indigo cultivation smooth and easy.[48] But the plan did not materialise and false rumour spread through messengers and *panchs* deliberately by the raiyats that the government was opposed to indigo cultivation.[49]

The raiyats of Bairia also sent three persons to Calcutta to engage Tweedalo, a pleader, to prepare a case for being sent to the Governor-General in Council. They also made use of a native doctor, Jai Gopal, for preparing their case for despatch to the Lieutenant-Governor of Bengal.[50]

A combination of the powerful groups so formed by the raiyats did not confine its struggle against the planters only; it also posed a serious threat to the landlords. The tenants of 63 villages refused the payment of rent directly to the zamindars' *kachaheri* and deposited it in the Motihari Collectorate.[51] This action of the tenants was occasioned by the landlords' failure to deposit the rent to the government as a result of which the villages had fallen under the jurisdiction of the factory.

The action of the Assistant Magistrate of Bettia added fuel to the fire. Ruddock snatched the wheat seeds from a raiyat who was going to sow indigo land with it. The "seed" had become a symbol for their struggle against the planter.[52] Village after village joined together and a powerful group of raiyats emerged. This "seed" affair was taken as an order for repudiating their engagement to sow indigo. In fact Ruddock's action to snatch the wheat seed from a raiyat was intended to cow down the raiyats but it had just the opposite effect. The "seed" affair in fact led to "popular demonstration". The higher authorities sensed the mood of the raiyats. They disapproved of Ruddock's action and the seed was ultimately restored to the raiyats. The raiyats could not but have enjoyed a sense of success in their struggle.

The prevailing indigo disturbances caused a loss to ten factories in Champaran as was acknowledged by C.T.Metcalfe. These factories were located at Seraha, Peepra, Barah, Rajpur, Titareah, Murilta, Lal Saraiya, Jurkolia, Motihari and Purrah. Metcalfe estimated that a total of 34,100 acres out of 39,870 acres had been sown with indigo and the loss incurred amounted to Rs 19,100.[53] This clearly underlines the vital fact that profits could be turned into losses by a discontented and uncooperative tenantry and labour force.

The tenants' resistance to the planter reached such an extent that Gibbon, the manager of the Bettia estate, gave a verbal order to one Sangam Lal (a servant of the Raja) to go to the villages and exercise his influence to persuade the recalcitrant raiyats to sow indigo. However he was ordered by the Raja not to interfere in it. But when the peace was threatened in the Bettia estate, the Raja was convinced by Gibbon about the seriousness of disturbance. The Raja himself sent his private servant to some of the tenants in order to counteract the disturbances which were spreading all over the estate.[54] Even the *thikadars* had become the victims of the disturbances. According to the *mokhtar* of the *thikadars* the *pahikast assamis* began to refuse payment of rents to the *thikadars*.[55] Ultimately *roobokaree* was sent to the Raja by the government to persuade him to issue a *hukumnama* in order to check the disturbances. The *gumasta* and the *patwaris* were asked by the Raja to convey to the raiyats that payment of rent was obligatory and should in fact be made. But the disturbances did not stop. A petition of the inhabitants of several villages in Motihari Subdivision was sent to the Secretary, Government of Bengal, against the planters. Their complaints included the tyranny of the planters, the misleading rumour spread by the planters that the factories belonged to the government and also the desertion of villages by the indigo cultivating raiyats. They complained that the raiyats who did not leave their ancestral homes were burdened with extra payment to the planters in order to meet the loss they incurred during the disturbances. But the Lieutenant Governor turned down their representation as it was "vague and general".[56]

The Small Cause Court temporarily established at Motihari to deal with the indigo cases exercised its influence to check the movement. H.Bell, Officiating Judge of the Small Cause Court tried his best to settle the dispute amicably, although he remarked that the combination of the raiyats against the planters was "a strike of labour against the capital".[57] In order to overcome the combination of the raiyats, he suggested to the government the appointment of a tribunal consisting of an officer of the government, the employer and the representatives of the workmen.

Although "a large sum of money" was collected from the raiyats for filing suits and drafting and despatching petitions to the government, this did not materialise. The leaders' promise that "if well supported by raiyats" indigo would vanish from the district by 24 March 1868, was not fulfilled. According to R.P. Jenkins, the Commissioner of Patna Division, the raiyats were duped and they lost their faith in their leaders.[58] The tenants accused the leaders of betraying them. Pallak Singh, once a leader of the raiyats against the planters, made modest demand to J.M. Gibbon for a reward in order to check the growing disturbance. But he was not obliged.[59] Madar Bux, once a champion of the raiyats' cause, was seeking employment in the Lal Saraiya factory. Only Enait Karim and a few others remained faithful to the cause of the raiyats. But the raiyats did not feel disheartened as the rate of indigo was raised from Rs 8 or 9 per *bigha* to Rs 12 per *bigha*. The situation appeared to the government as "peaceful" for the time being, although it was "impossible to predict what time may bring forth".[60]

In Muzaffarpur also a few cases of tenants' resistance were noticed by the government. In the indigo concerns of Deen Chapra and Amwa (Belsand *thana*) which belonged to Hicky, indigo contracts had been violated. In some cases the raiyats resorted to violence and sowed the land with *cheena* instead of indigo.[61] The raiyats of Jorangee, two miles south of Surfuddinnagar, made a strong protest to the government against Swaine, the Manager of Atter (Attari) factory.[62]

Apart from the local hostility of the raiyats to the Europeans, the Brahmins of North Bihar showed a sulky and hostile attitude towards the Europeans, which appeared to the government a departure from their usual demeanour in other parts of India and therefore surprising.[63] He expressed his inability to find in it any legitimate or genuine reason for this as the Brahmins and *Babhuns* were the dominant community and the high caste Raja had been lightly taxed. This explains how the local administration expected support from the high caste peasants in the continuation of the planters' *Raj*.

A. Forbes reported from Tajpur to the Commissioner of Patna that there was hatred and evident dislike among the natives for the Europeans due to the oppression committed by the planters to the raiyats.[64] He emphasized that he had not observed such anti-planter hostility even in rural Bengal. He remarked that this hostility in the Tajpur villages was due to the dominance of the *Babhuns* (Bhumihar Brahmins) and the Rajputs.[65] G.Anderson from Kamtaul reported that this place surpassed others in the manifestation of symptoms of dissatisfaction.

J. Crawfurd reported from Rosera to the Collector of Tirhut that the government was intensely disliked. He reported from Tajpur that *Babhuns* were especially aggressive and hostile as they had assaulted the Subdivisional Officer.[66]

Indigo troubles sprang up within the limits of Tilhara factory which resulted in the murder of its manager Mr Bloomfield. It was caused by the refusal of the manager to recognise the transfer of certain holdings. It was followed by a great feeling of uneasiness in the Sathi *dehat* in 1907. Continual meetings of the raiyats began to take place under the leadership of Shaikh Gulab and Sital Rai. The tenants of Sathi and other factories like Parsa, Mallahia, Bairia and Kundia stopped indigo cultivation.[67] A rich *Marwari* named Radhumal and his *gumastas*, who also guided the movement, were arrested on 26 October 1908. Sital Rai was arrested and lodged in *hajat*. In protest against his arrest some four thousand raiyats followed him to Bettia where he was put up in the lock-up. After showing their courage and sympathy these raiyats returned home.[68] The planters, fully supported by the local officials and the *kothials*, did their best to curb the movement. In the name of preserving the peace and maintaining "law and order" the authorities issued a notice to some persons forbidding them to take part in any meeting. The Subdivisional Officer of Bettia issued warrants of arrest to 200 leading raiyats for no offence other than refusing to sow indigo.[69] The *Dainik Chandrika* of 4 November 1908 aptly commented that the change of spirit had affected all classes of people in the country. It reported that a new national awakening was taking place in Bihar and the *zabardast* measures of the government were unable to out an end to the trouble.[70] The *Hitavadi* of 5 November 1908 even demanded that the agrarian tensions and the atrocities committed by the alien should be taken up by the Indian National Congress.[71] The movement became so powerful at the grassroot levels that the government tagged it with the revolutionary movement of the country, although this charge of the government was refuted by the *Hindustan* of 7 November 1908.[72] The fact was that it was a general awakening of the people of Champaran to a sense of their rights and privileges. Although the disturbance was crushed by the alien authorities, the raiyats remained restless.

Pressurized by the movement the government appointed W.R.Gourlay, then Director of Agriculture, to make an official inquiry into the agrarian trouble, although the police administration was opposed to it. After making an enquiry Gourlay submitted his report in April 1909 but his report was kept secret. He brought some boxes from Motihari to Patna. When these boxes were opened, it was found that these contained clods of earth mixed with *rubbi* and indigo plants. After an informal discussion with the representatives of the Indigo Planters Association some concessions were made to the raiyats. The rate of the indigo plants per *bigha* was raised from Rs 12 to Rs 13 and the area under indigo cultivation was reduced from three *kathas* to two *kathas* per *bigha*.[73] But the planters did not fully ratify the agreement. The raiyats again agitated but the disturbance was crushed by the authorities. About 350 persons were convicted and put into prison. The discontent, however, continued, especially after the acquittal of the raiyats connected with the Sathi disturbances. These persons once again became very active in the movement.

In 1911 a large body of agitators assembled at Narkatiaganj railway station to narrate their grievances to King George V, who was on his way back to Nepal. In 1912 the raiyats of Champaran sent their representatives to Calcutta to submit a memorandum containing their grievances against the planters. By then a series of articles appeared in Beharee newspapers in which the whole system of indigo cultivation was opposed. Even then the forcible collection of *abwabs*, cesses and compensation for the loss incurred in indigo cultivation continued. But the raiyats were opposed to the imposition of *abwabs*. They sent a petition to the Lieutenant Governor of Bengal. The raiyats of Pipra and Tarkaulia became very violent in their objection to the decision of the government to enhance rent on non-indigo land. The Survey and Settlement officer had an unpleasant experience. The raiyats were forced to accept the enhanced rent, most unwillingly. Meanwhile the leaders of Bettia had enlisted public support from outside. The press and the public began to openly take interest in the Bettia affair. Raj Kumar Sukul of the village Satwaria under Lawria police station had attended the Provincial Congress at Chapra in 1915 and the Indian National Congress in 1916 at Lucknow.

It was for the first time that the largest number of delegates, mostly peasants, attended the Lucknow Session (1916) of the Indian National Congress. The total number of delegates from Bihar and Orissa was more than 200. Raj Kumar Sukul, a relatively well off peasant, also went to attend the Congress. It was because of his initiative, fully backed by Babu Braj Kishore Prasad and many others that the Indian National Congress adopted the resolution. The resolution reads: "Resolved that the Congress most respectfully urges upon the government the "desirability of appointing a mixed committee of officials' (emphasis mine) to enquire into the causes of agrarian trouble and strained relations between the Indian ryot and the European planter in North Bihar and to suggest remedies therefore".[77]

Though very vague, the resolution was moved by Babu Braj Kishore Prasad of Darbhanga and supported by Shri Raj Kumar Sukul. In fact the Congress did not have any agrarian programme till 1929 [78] and therefore the question of pursuing the resolution did not arise. Braj Kishore Babu, a member of the Bihar Legislative Council from 1912-16, raised the Champaran issue in the Assembly. In reply to the question M. McPherson, Chief Secretary to the Government, clearly admitted on 13 March 1913, the receipt of several petitions signed by the raiyats of Champaran complaining of the relations which existed between them and the landlords.[74] Although McPherson assured that action would be taken in the light of the report received from local officers, he rejected a popular demand for a regular enquiry. Braj Kishore Babu raised the question again in the Council in 1915 and brought to the notice of the government cases of forcible execution of *sharbbeshi* agreements, of assaults and illegal confinements of the raiyats by the planters.[75] As usual the Chief Secretary declared that the matter was being enquired into and that the report of the Settlement Officer was awaited. The demand for an enquiry to look into the affairs of the tenants and planters also made by Braj Kishore Babu at the annual meeting of the Bihar Provincial Political Conference held at Bankipur on 10 April 1914, and then again at Chapra on 3 April 1915.[76] He repeated his demand for an enquiry in 1915 and moved a resolution in Bihar and Orissa Legislative Council. He asked the Lieutenant Governor in Council to appoint a Committee of qualified officials and non-officials to make an immediate enquiry into the causes of the strained relations which existed between the raiyats and the planters. But his motion was defeated by 27 to 4 votes because of the overwhelming official opposition in the Council. Thus the fight for justice through constitutional methods did not prove beneficial to the tenantry of Bihar.

GANDHI, PEASANTS AND CHAMPARAN

Gandhi's Champaran movement has drawn the attention of a large number of scholars, both in India and abroad. Mini theories and interpretations have been produced with regard to the nature of peasant participation in the movement. The main objective of this study is to highlight the real significance of the movement which in my view has not been sufficiently emphasized in other studies.

It has been argued that the Champaran movement was the first important foundation stone that Gandhi laid for himself.[79] Jacques Pouchepadass finds that the rich peasants of Champaran "instigated" and "intimidated" the other peasants to "go along" and spread rumours to keep up the momentum of Satyagraha.[80] But he speaks very highly of the role of propaganda in the movement without going into the base for such rumours. Anand A. Yang considers that "indigo disputes were not clear-cut acts of peasant solidarity... but actions organised generally by local zamindars or substantial raiyats against the unpopular foreign planters".[81] In order to substantiate the prominent role played by the affluent raiyats he cites the example of a Brahmin cultivator, Raj Kumar Sukul, who had a money-lending business of rupees fifteen thousand. He quotes Pouchepadass and argues that the so-called "anti-factory oligarchy" was composed primarily of "high-caste peasants: Brahmins, Rajputs, Babhans(Bhumihar Brahmins), Kayasthas and Muslim Sheikhs". Girish Mishra opines that it was a high-caste, rich, peasant-money-lender's combination.[82] Although Papiya Ghosh admits at one place that "it would be wrong to overstress Gandhi's restraining role in Champaran", she however contradicts herself at another place by describing the "tenuous nature of Gandhi's control during 1917".83

It is essential for any study on Gandhi and the Champaran Satyagraha that his own writings should be first studied carefully followed by other writings.[84]

It may remain one of the big question marks of Gandhian studies whether Gandhi made Champaran or Champaran made Gandhi. In 1917 Gandhi was known only to the intelligentsia in India and he needed a Champaran to throw him into the Indian limelight. He did not know even the geographical location of Champaran. It was not the intelligentsia of Bihar but it was an "ignorant", "unsophisticated" and "resolute agriculturist", Raj Kumar Sukul's insistence that he committed himself to visit Champaran. Sukul had no friends in Patna and he was "perfectly innocent of everything".[85] Gandhi was not asked by the AICC to study the agrarian problems of the raiyats of Champaran. He did not even give his opinion on the resolution moved by Braj Kishore Babu in the Lucknow Session of the Congress in 1916, although he was pressed by Sukul to support it. The reading of Gandhi's *Autobiography* clearly indicates that he was reluctant to visit Champaran but was virtually hounded by Sukul, who followed him from Lucknow-Kanpur and then from Calcutta to Patna, Muzaffarpur and, ultimately, Champaran. He also wrote several letters to Gandhi requesting him to visit Champaran.

The reluctant Gandhi reached Patna on 10 April 1917 accompanied by Sukul. Sukul failed to guide him properly and it was Maulana Mazhrul Haq who showed him the way to reach Muzaffarpur first and then Motihari. At midnight on 17 April 1917 Gandhi was received by J.B. Kripalani with a "crowd" of students. On the next day a small group of *Vakils* including Ramnaumi Babu, met him. The lawyers of Bihar were afraid of the government even though they assured Gandhi of their help with some hesitation. Braj Kishore Babu, who had championed the cause of the indigo growing raiyats in the Council at the annual meetings of the Bihar Political Conference, reacted to Gandhi's call for help in an "exceptionally coolheaded" manner.[86] But later on he became one of the confidants of Gandhi. Gandhi was aware of the capacity of sacrifice of the middle class intelligentsia and therefore he sought "clerical assistance" in interpretating the language of the local people. He was fully cognisant of the limitations of the urban-based middle class intelligentsia, who had a narrow vision of the tenants and therefore could not have mass appeal.

Gandhi proceeded to Champaran in a spirit of enquiry. He made it very clear that his mission to Champaran was not to agitate the peasants there but to test the accuracy of the statements made to him about the *tinkathia* system of indigo plantation. He declared that his mission was that of "making peace with honour".[87] He even tried to convince the planters and local administration that he had no ill-will against them. He wanted to know even the planter's side of the case. But despite his open attitude he was branded by the planters as an "outsider" and was asked not to interfere between "their tenants" and the planters.[88] The Commissioner whom he wanted to see before conducting the enquiry even asked him forthwith to leave Tirhut. But showing the first signs of an indomitable will and devotion to duty, Gandhi persisted and decided to visit Bettia first where the raiyats belonging to indigo *Kothis* were the poorest of the district. On his way to Bettia he was stopped and served a notice by the government asking him to leave Champaran. In reply to the notice he wrote that he would not comply with it till his enquiry was finished. As a result he was summoned to the court the next day. The news of the notice and the summons spread like a wildfire. True to the tradition of protest movements in the land since the 1860s onwards thousands of peasants assembled in the court and around Gorakh Babu's house where Gandhi was residing. Assemblage of a "crowd" demonstrated the solidarity of the peasants. It cut across all barriers of caste/community/class and region. Gandhi was a Gujarati *bania* but the caste-conscious peasantry of Champaran had no hesitation in accepting him as their leader. It was for the first time that the peasantry was involved on a mass scale. This incidence emboldened the peasantry to come forward and forget the "fear of punishment". Thus the opinion that the movement was sustained by the rumours spread by Raj Kumar Sukul does not seem tenable. It was physically impossible for Sukul to collect thousands of peasantry at Motihari.[89] The Congress had no base in Motihari and communications were not developed. The spontaneous response from the "crowd" representing all segments of the agrarian society was evident for the first time. A whispering campaign from mouth to ear, and from village to village resulted in a mass assemblage in Motihari preventing Gandhi's arrest.

The presence of the crowd put the government on its trial. In such circumstances the Lieutenant Governor asked the local authority to withdraw the case against him . Gandhi's warnings given to the press and public not to indulge in violent activity were faithfully obeyed but the planters went on engineering poisonous agitation against him. They even burnt the school hut at Bhitiharva village run by Kasturba Gandhi and others. In the teeth of opposition Gandhi started taking down the statements of the raiyats. Prominent among those who assisted him included Braj Kishore Babu, Rajendra Babu, Shambhu Babu, Anugraha Babu, Dharnidhar Babu, Ramnaumi Babu, J.B.Kripalani and Maulana Mazharul Haq.

During the course of enquiry each peasant tendering evidence was cross-examined. An officer of the Intelligence Department was always present to watch the correctness of the statements. But the government was suspicious of the enquiry committee and therefore Gandhi was asked to serve on the Enquiry Committee constituted by it. He agreed to serve on the Committee provided he would be allowed the freedom to guide and advise the raiyats as to what line of action they should take.[90] Sir Frank Sly was made the Chairman of the Committee of Enquiry with L.C.Adani, Superintendent and Remembrance of Legal Affairs, Bihar and Orissa, Raja Harihar Prasad Narayan Singh, Member of Bihar and Orissa Legislative Council, D.J.Reid, member of Bihar and Orissa Legislative Council, G.Rainy, Deputy Secretary in the finance department of the government of India and M.K.Gandhi. E.L.Tanner, ICS, Settlement Officer, South Bihar, was appointed as the Secretary to the Committee.[91]

Of the fifteen recommendations made the most important was that the *tinkathia* system should be completely abolished. The *Satta* or agreement was made voluntary and its term was to expire in three years. The selection of fields in which indigo was grown was left to the raiyats; the rate of sale of indigo plants was to be settled by the raiyats; the realisation of *abwab* was declared illegal and labour was made voluntary.

It appears from the recommendations that *Nilaha Raj* came to an end in Champaran but it was not so. With some relief indigo continued to be grown there till the late 1920s.

Nevertheless the participation of the peasants in the movement radicalised Indian politics. The narrow base of Indian nationalism till then was confined to the Legislative Council and the press; it came into the street. Gandhi was, in fact, not face to face with *Ahimsa, God* and Truth. Rather he was face to face with the mass of the Indian people, ie the peasantry. The potentiality of the peasantry was tested and it was found that they were a force to be reckoned with as they could change the course of events. Champaran was no victory for the peasants in absolute terms but it was a testing ground where the peasantry, for the first time, flexed its muscles and showed its strength. The Champaran peasantry was in a very low stage of development but the social upheaval created by it horrified the colonial ruler. In terms of class characterisation, the peasants as a class were still in their birth throes. It was far from developed enough to assume leadership over and to transform the society on its own.

Thus a perusal of the primary sources enables us to say that the tenants of the indigo growing districts of Bihar were not only directly involved in the production of indigo but they were also the instruments of social and economic change in an agrarian society. The relentless resistance of the raiyats clearly proves that they were fighting in groups against the indigo planters, the landlords and the government not only for the sake of individual gains and self-aggrandisement but also for the peasant community as a whole. The number of petitions sent to the authorities against the planters clearly indicate that they possessed immense potentiality to bring about social and economic change. Their potentiality to fight against the *firangees* was realised by the Lieutenant Governor of Bengal and the Governor-General of Council who instructed the local officials to conciliate the tenantry to their side. The colonial authorities were so much afraid of the raiyats that the latter were not allowed to go out with umbrellas which had parts of bamboo in them for possible use against the planters.

The combination of the raiyats was not based on the identity of an individual group as caste or religious community as the sociologists and colonial historians have often found; they were united in a body to fight for a common cause affecting their livelihood. The allegation of the governmment that disturbance was inspired and engineered by a section of the affluent peasantry is untenable. Their representations/petitions to the government against the planters included the grievances of the ploughmen, the cart-drivers and the labourers. The assemblage of 20,000 raiyats in Motihari to register their grievances before the Commissioner of Patna in 1868, the angry protest march of 6,000 raiyats (in some records it is 4,000) as a consequence of Sital Rai's arrest in 1908 and a virtual demonstration of the raiyats before King George V at Narkatiaganj railway station in 1911 illustrate that even the lowest segments participated whole-heartedly in the movement and considered it their own cause.

The raiyats were, in fact, passing through a phase when any political party or disciplined outside leadership had not emerged but they were shrewd and prudent enough to claim a share in the planters' profits and an enhancement of the price of their indigo plant. Of course in the nineteenth century historical development it would be futile to expect indigenous movement against the planters to the complete exclusion of a relatively well off tenants. Clearly the ground had been prepared for the participation by the masses in political action in Bihar. Gandhi's Champaran movement in 1917, Vidyanand's movement in Darbhanga in the 1920s and the Non-cooperation movement in Muzaffarpur owe a lot to the socio-political tradition established by the nineteenth century tenantry in Bihar. It is wrong and superficial to suggest that Gandhiji was a subcontractor of the alien ruler or wielded a "magic stick"; Gandhi, in fact, was a man of the earth who could clearly see the strength and limitation of the traditional peasantry and had the character and strength to develop it into a powerful force against oppression and alien rule. The Mahatma, no doubt, discovered the revolutionary potentiality of the situation in Champaran and the people of Champaran first recognised his stature as the messiah of the oppressed and paved the way for his success as a national and world leader.

REFERENCES

1 A.N. Das, *Agrarian Unrest and Socio-Economic Change, 1900-1980* (New Delhi, 1983); A.R. Desai, ed, *Peasant Struggle in India* (Oxford University Press, New Delhi, 1979); D.N. Dhanagre, "Peasant Movement in India, 1920-1950", D. Phil. dissertation, University of Sussex, 1973 (unpublished); Ranjit Guha, *Subaltern Studies: Essays on South Asian History*, Vol.I (Delhi, 1983). Five more volumes have come out but none of them refers to this aspect. Dharma Kumar and Raychaudhury, ed, *The Cambridge Economic History of India* (Orient Longman, 1982); Sunil Sen, *Peasant Movement in India : Mid-Nineteenth and Twentieth Century* (New Delhi, 1982); F. Tomasson Jannuzi, *Agrarian Crisis in India : The Case Study of Bihar* (New Delhi,1974); K.K. Sharma, *Agrarian Movements and Congress Politics in Bihar* (New Delhi, 1989) (Chapter I, from page 17 to 46 is fully devoted to the "Agrarian Setting Before and After the Permanent Settlement", but it does not refer to the agrarian tensions in the indigo growing districts of Bihar in the nineteenth century). Important articles on the subjects which do not throw light on the agrarian tensions and peasants' protests in the indigo growing districts of Bihar include Girish Mishra, "Indigo Plantation and Agrarian Relations in Champaran during the Nineteenth Century" *Indian Economic and Social History Review hereafter IESHAR*, Vol.III, No.4, December 1966, pp.332-57; Girish Mishra, "Socio-Economic Background of Gandhi's Champaran Movement", *IESHR*, Vol.V, No.3, 1976; Stephen Henningham, "The Social Setting of the Champaran Satyagraha : The Challenge to an Alien Elite", *IESHR*, Vol.XIII, No.1, 1976; Stephen Henningham, "Agrarian Relations in North Bihar : Peasant Protest and the Darbhanga Raj, 1919-1920", *IESHR*, Vol.XVI, No.1, 1979; Jacques Pouchepadass, "Local Leaders and Intelligentsia in the Champaran Satyagraha (1917) : A Study in Peasant Mobilization", *Contributions to Indian Sociology* (NS), Number 8, 1974; B.B. Chaudhuri, "Growth of Commercial Agriculture in Bengal, Part I and II", *IESHR*, Vol.I, No.1, 1970; B.B. Chaudhuri, "Agrarian Unrest in Bengal and Bihar, 1900-1940" in B.R. Nanda, ed, *Socialism in India*, (New Delhi, 1972); B.B. Chaudhuri, "Process of

Depeasantisation in Bengal and Bihar, 1885-1947", *The Indian Historical Review*, Vol.II, No.1, July 1975, and many others.

2 A.N. Das, opcit., p.57.

3 B.B. Chaudhuri, "Agrarian Unrest in Bengal and Bihar, 1900-1940", op.cit.

4 Ram Narain Sinha, *Bihar Tenantry (1783-1833)* (New Delhi, 1968).

5 Ranjeet Guha, *Subaltern Studies : Essays on South Asian History*, Vol.I, op.cit.

6 *Bengal Judicial Criminal Proceedings*, No.167, 22 January 1830, from the Acting Magistrate of Tirhut to the Government of Bengal.

7 Ibid., No.174, from the Officiating Magistrate of Bihar (Patna) to the Government of Bengal, 30 January 1830. The peons of the factories also filed complaints against the raiyats where the indigo crops had been damaged or destroyed by the tresspass of the cattle. The raiyats were assaulted by the peons of the factories when the former tried to rescue their cattle on their being reported to the *thanas*.

8 Ibid., No.182, Acting Joint Magistrate of Munger to the Government of Bengal, 13 February 1830.

9 *Bengal Criminal Judicial Proceedings*, No.26, 27 December 1839. From the representatives of the indigo planters of Tirhut, Saran and Munger to the Secretary, Government of Bengal, 20 May 1839.

10 Ibid., Additional Notes by Shakespear, Member, Board of Revenue, 24 April 1830. Notes and enclosures were apprehended with the representation by the planter so as to convince the government about the desirability of a legislation to curb the "recalcitrant" raiyats, the ploughmen and the cart-drivers who did not enjoy the confidence and faith of their English masters.

11 *Bengal Judicial Proceedings*, No. 352,10 July 1856, Petition of Tekhand Mondal and others, inhabitants of Pargana Bhagalpur to the Junior Secretary, Government of Bengal, Fort William, 10 April 1856.

12 *Bengal Judicial Proceedings*, No.77, 2 October 1856. From the Commissioner of Bhagalpur Division to the Secretary, Government of Bengal, 30 August 1856.

13 *Bengal Judicial Proceedings*, No.386, July 1861. Circular letter from Messrs Gisborne and Co. to the managers of the seven concerns in Tirhut, 12 July 1861.

14 *Bengal Judicial Proceedings*, No.151, November 1864, from the Secretary to the Landholders and Commercial Association, Calcutta, to the Government of Bengal.

15 *Bengal Judicial Proceedings*, No.152, from A. Eden, Secretary to the Government of Bengal to the Secretary, Landholders and Commercial Association, No.575, 18 November 1864. The Lieutenant Governor desired that the raiyats should be allured towards the benefit of indigo. He felt that if the raiyats were attracted to "accumulation of wealth" which will make them ready enough to undertake the remunerative cultivation. But he did not want that the government agency should teach them the benefits of indigo as it would "give rise to very great abuse".

16 *Bengal Judicial Proceedings*, No.49, February 1867, from D.B. Barbour, Assistant Magistrate of Madhubani to the Officiating Magistrate of Tirhut, No.15, 1 January 1867.

17 Ibid.

18 Ibid., from A.T. Maclean, Officiating Magistrate of Tirhut to the Assistant Magistrate of Madhubani, No.11, 19 January 1867.

19 Ibid., from A.T. Maclean, Officiating Magistrate of Tirhut to the Commissioner, Patna Division, No.13, 21 January 1867, para I. It may be noted here that the slightest hint or an encouragement from any quarter was an important factor for the raiyats those days to stake their claim. But there was no leader to exploit the situation. This clearly illustrates that the raiyats were intelligent enough to understand what was good or beneficial to them.

21 Ibid., from the Commissioner of Patna Division to the Magistrate of Tirhut, 25 January 1867.

22 Ibid., No.51, Commissioner of the Patna Division to the Secretary, Government of Bengal, No.33, 29 January 1867.

23 Ibid., from A.T. Maclean, Officiating Magistrate of Tirhut to the Commissioner of Patna Division, No.17, 26 January 1867.

24 Ibid., No.52, from D.B. Barbour, Assistant Magistrate of Madhubani to the Officiating Magistrate of Tirhut, Letter No.49, 25 January 1867.

25 Ibid., No.33, from A.T. Maclean, Officiating Magistrate of Tirhut to the Commissioner, Patna Division, 19 February 1867.
26 Ibid., para 9.
27 Ibid. The enclosure along with the judgement delivered on 31 January 1867 against the raiyats contained a brief history of the case. In fact the raiyats were asked by one Govind Jha to cultivate his land. But the Manager proved that the land was not in the *jot* of Govind Jha but in the name of one Devi Prasad *thikadar* from whom he got the *thika*. Since Govind Jha did not pay the rent, the land was managed by the planter through Devi Prasad *thikadar* who paid the rent to the government.
28 Ibid. Enclosure.
29 Ibid., No.53, para 2.
30 Ibid., No.53, para 6. It was reported that the raiyats of Nawadah and Lahul factories had also refused to grow indigo.
31 Ibid., No.53, from A.T. Maclean, Collector of Patna to the Commissioner of Patna Division, 4 February 1867.
32 Ibid.
33 Ibid. The Collector of Patna accertained the reasons why the raiyats were opposed to indigo. He found out that too much of raiyats' land was taken by the planters. The ploughmen, cart-drivers and the labourers were also insufficiently paid. It was recorded by him that there had been one or two collisions in which exchange of blows occurred.
34 Ibid., No.129, from J.W. Dalrymple, Commissioner of Patna Division to the Secretary, Government of Bengal, Letter No.50, 7 February 1867.
35 Ibid., No.38. Demi-official letter from A.T. Maclean (no record as to whom the letter was sent), 22 February 1867.
36 *Bengal Judicial Proceedings*, No.25, May 1868.
37 Ibid. The Commissioner of Patna was on a tour to Motihari.
38 Ibid., Nos. 77 and 79, May (?). In fact there were three petitions sent by the raiyats of Champaran to the Lieutenant Governor of Bengal; the first was dated 27 March 1868 and the remaining two were dated 30 March 1868.
39 Ibid., No.131, May (?). Balpin was the planter who got some influential raiyats released from the jail.

40 Ibid.
41 *Bengal Judicial Proceedings*, No.34, July 1868. This petition was transfered to the Government of Bengal, *Home Department*, No.50, 6 June, 1868 for disposal.
42 Ibid., No.35, from C.T. Metcalfe, Officiating Collector of Champaran to R.P. Jenkins, Commissioner of Patna Division, 19 February 1868. According to the Collector Mahashaya Singh, Daulat Singh and others belonging to Bhawanipur village were the originators of the disturbances.
43 *Bengal Judicial Proceedings*, No. 209, October 1867 (?) from C.T. Metcalfe, Officiating Magistrate of Champaran to the Commissioner of Patna Division, 15 December 1867.
44 Ibid., No. 210, para 2 from H.L. Dampier, Officiating Secretary to the Government of Bengal to the Commissioner of Patna, No. 6787, 31 December 1867.
45 Ibid., para 5.
46 Ibid., No.211.
47 Ibid., para 19.
48 From C.T. Metcalfe, Officiating Magistrate and Collector of Champaran to R.P. Jenkins, Officiating Magistrate of Patna Division, para 5, 24 January 1868.
49 Ibid., para 8.
50 Ibid., para 48.
51 Ibid., para 51.
52 From C.T. Metcalfe, Officiating Magistrate of Champaran to the Commissioner of Patna, No. TC, 13 February 1868.
53 Ibid.
54 Ibid.
55 Ibid.
56 Ibid. Resolution by the Lieutenant Governor of Bengal, paras 1 & 3, 21 March 1868.
57 Ibid.
58 Ibid., No.228, from R.P. Jenkins, Officiating Commissioner of Patna Division to the Secretary, Government of Bengal, No. C, dated Camp (Muzaffarpur), 17 May 1868.
59 Ibid., para 15.
60 Ibid., para 24.
61 *Home Department* No.5581, from H.L. Dampier, Officiating Secretary to the Government of Bengal to the Secretary, Government of India, 17 October 1868.

62 Worsely, the Magistrate of Muzaffarpur. He recorded this incident in his diary on 19 October 1876, quoted in K.K. Datta, *Freedom Movement in Bihar*, Vol. I (Patna, 1957), p. 175.

63 *Proceedings of the Government of India in the Department of Agriculture, Revenue and Commerce*, January 1874 (Land Revenue and Settlement), No.80, Part B, No.2783, 5 August 1873 from the Secretary to the Government of Bengal to the Commissioner of Patna.

64 Ibid., from A. Forbes (Tajpur) to the Collector of Tirhut, 28 January 1873.

65 Ibid.

66 Ibid., D.O. letter from A. Forbes (Tajpur) to the Collector of Tirhut, 28 January 1873.

67 *Report on the Native Newspapers of Bengal*, September-December 1908.

68 Ibid., September-December 1908, *Amrit Bazar Patrika*. Sital Rai was released in 1908 by the High Court.

69 Ibid., *Howarh Hitaishi*, 7 November 1908.

70 Ibid., *The Dainik Chandrika*, 4 November 1908.

71 Ibid., *The Hitavadi*, 5 November 1908.

72 Ibid., *The Hindustan*, 7 November 1908.

73 *Bihar District Gazetteers*, Champaran, P. C Roy Chaudhury (Patna, 1960), p. 274.

74 *Bihar Land Revenue Proceedings*, Nos. 9-12 of March 1913.

75 Ibid., Nos. 22-23 of December 1915.

76 K. K. Datta, *History of Freedom Movement in Bihar*, Vol. I (Patna, 1957), pp. 185-86 quoted in B.B. Misra, ed, *Select Documents on Mahatma Gandhi's Movement in Champaran, 1917-18* (Patna, 1963), p. 19.

77 A. M. and S. G. Zaidi, ed, *The Encyclopaedia of Indian National Congress*, Volume Seven 1916-20 (Emergence of Gandhi), Resolution No. XI, Agrarian Trouble, p. 112.

78 G. P. Sharma, *Congress and the Peasant Movement in Bihar* (Bombay, 1987). Details of the agrarian programme of the Congress have been summarised in this book.

79 Judith Brown, *Gandhi's Rise to Power* (Cambridge, 1972), pp. 73, 78-79. His views have however been questioned by S. R. Singh in his article on "Historiography of Gandhian Movement" published in *The Indian Historical Review*, ICHR, July 1985-January 1986, Vol. XII, Nos. 1-2, pp. 226-27.

80 Jacques Pouchepadass, "Local Leaders and Intelligentsia in the Champaran Satyagraha (1917): A Study of Peasant Mobilization", *Contributions to Indian Sociology*, No. 8, 1974, pp. 79, 84-85.

81 Anand A. Yang, *The Limited Raj, Agrarian Relations in Colonial India*, Saran District, 1793-1920 (OUP, New Delhi, 1989), p. 237.

82 Girish Mishra, *Agrarian Problems of Permanent Settlement: A Case Study of Champaran* (New Delhi, 1978), Chapter seven.

83 Papiya Ghosh, "Peasants, Planters and Gandhi", a fifteen-page unpublished article. Although she quotes fifty-four references to substantiate her views, she does not refer to Gandhi's *Autobiography*.

84 B.B. Misra, ed, *Select Documents on Mahatma Gandhi's Movement in Champaran, 1917-18*, (Patna, 1963). It contains 243 documents besides notes, supplement and appendices which are easily not available in archives; Rajendra Prasad, *Satyagraha in Champaran* (Ahmedabad, 1961), M. K. Gandhi, *An Autobiography* (Ahmedabad, 1927), K.K. Datta, *Freedom Movement in Bihar*, Vol. I (Patna, 1957), Chapter VI, pp. 167-280; and B. G. Tendulkar, *Jab Gandhi Champaran Aaye* (in Hindi) (Patna, 1976) and many other books and articles.

85 M.K. Gandhi, op. cit., 305. More than three lakh copies of this book had come out till 1981 but it has not been cited by Anand A. Yang and Pouchepadass in their writings. In my estimation it should be dissected first.

86 Ibid., p. 308.

87 B. B. Misra, op. cit., Document Nos. 46 and 48, pp. 86-87, 89-91.

88 M. K. Gandhi, op. cit., p. 309.

89 Ibid., p. 311.

90 Ibid., p. 320.

91 For details see K. K. Datta, *Freedom Movement in Bihar*, Vol. I, op.cit., pp. 245-50.

CHAPTER VI

Conclusion

The study of indigo cultivation in Bihar from the beginning of the nineteenth century to the second decade of the twentieth century reveals that the colonial policy of the British empire in India was determined by the needs of the remittance as well as of the demand of the British cloth merchants. Indigo cultivation began to expand in Bihar with the rapidly increasing demand of the indigo products in the European markets. Although the indigo business was a private enterprise and the Company a trading corporation, indigo cultivation in the interior *dehat* was considered as a means of diffusing a large body of European planters not only for the production and manufacture of the raw material but also for sustaining the interest of the British empire from below.

An advance of a million pounds to the planters for capital investment through the Agency Houses, issuing licenses to British citizens to go to the interior *dehat* for indigo cultivation, leasing of land to the planters and making them landed proprietors, warehouse facilities extended to them and low rate on shipment for the export of indigo to the European markets were all designed to colonise the villages in Bihar. Bentinck favoured the presence of the Europeans in the *mufassil* as it would "civilize" the Indians by disseminating European arts and science among the natives. It was a clear indication of colonial designs and "white man's burden" to civilize the East. Pattle, a member of the Board of Revenue was more articulate and candid in his pronouncement of the colonial plan. Any hindrance towards British settlement in the countryside was considered by him to be detrimental to the revenue of the state; he also considered the British settlement as a political necessity. He observed: "Our permanency in this country must always be uncertain until attachment to the government is unquestionably the common interest of a principal and influential portion of the population.... it was only capitalists and their principal agents that will colonise India".[1]

He was fully aware of the "natural resources" of Bengal which were vast and "imperfectly developed". His view found expression in the philosophical and ideological school---the evangelical humanitarian wing in England which wanted to diffuse British civilization and Christianity in India. The Select Committee appointed by the British Parliament, though critical of the indigo planters for the fear that the American precedent would not be repeated, asked the Government of India to go ahead with settling British citizens.

The interests of the colonial government and the planters were identical – the latter argued that they were the producers of a staple commodity, the supply of which was of vast importance to the commercial prosperity of the mother country.[2] Halliday also believed that the economic future of Bengal depended upon the enterprise of the Europeans in the *mufassil*.

Although the indigo growing raiyats were treated as "working cattle", the government's attitude to the planters remained favourable to them. Even the wild rumour spread by the raiyats that the government was opposed to indigo cultivation began to be countered and strongly denied. Except J.P.Grant, no other administrators ever desired that the raiyats should enjoy freedom of enterprise in choosing the crops. The Governor-General in Council emphatically asserted that the value of indigo trade was higher than the pious wish of J.P.Grant as indigo fetched enormous profit from Russia, France, England and all "civilized countries" in the world. Mr C.Beadon, the Lieutenant-Governor of Bengal, did not want the withdrawal of indigo cultivation. Rather he wished an amicable settlement of disputes in every way. Lawrence merely warned the planters and asked them to conciliate the raiyats. The possibility of loss in case the disputes with the raiyats of Champaran were not settled frightened him. Sir Ashley Eden believed in the efficacy of the planters' reformatory measures. Even Richard Temple, the so-called "friend of the raiyats", turned down the suggestion of the Commissioner to appoint a Commission of Enquiry for reviewing the planters' dealings with the raiyats on the plea that it would "place capital in jeopardy". The Bihar Indigo Planters Association was formed with the blessings of the government with Sir Ashley Eden as its patron. Its main objective was to safeguard the interests of the planting committee.

The petitions submitted by the raiyats against the planters were either ignored or rejected under the pretext that the government had no jurisdiction in the matter. The transfer of power from the company to the Crown had no bearing on the nature of indigo cultivation and relations of production based on it. The system of cash advance had been suitably designed to ensure the planters' claim to the product as well as their control over millions of producers.

Over 400 indigo concerns in North Bihar during the period looked like a cobweb in which a large number of raiyats had been inextricably entangled. Though established over a period of time the planters held only fertile and alluvial land in the villages. Since this land was fit for double crops which were not used for growing food crops, shortage of foodgrains and famines occurred frequently in Bihar.

The planters were invariably the beneficiaries regardless of the fact that a particular piece of land was under the *assamiwar* system of cultivation or the *zeerat* system of cultivation. Statistical figures indicate that indigo covered only 1 per cent to 6.5 per cent of the net cropped area. But this figure is deceptive and misleading because over a period of 20 years the entire holding of a raiyat was involved in indigo cultivation which seriously affected the material condition of the raiyats. In the *zeerat* system of cultivation the raiyats lost their right to individual holdings and in the *assamiwar* they were never paid the balance due to them.

The indigo planters of Bihar got an opportunity to prove their loyalty to the *Raj* in 1857; they fought against the rebels, protected the government treasury from the rebellious masses and guarded Muzaffarpur from possible attacks. Such a help in the deepest crisis that the *Raj* had to face in Bihar gave the government full confidence in them. And in return they began to take every help from the government machinery for the cultivation of indigo.

Since popular participation of the common people in the Revolt in 1857 in Bihar threatened the foundation of the Raj, the colonial administration was in search of a permanent ally to buttress the British rule. Appeasement of landed aristocracy became the hallmark of the British policy in India after the Revolt of 1857. Lord Canning sought to buttress the British with the support of the upper class of the Indian society. The planters soon realised the importance of the zamindars in an agrarian society as the latter were the *de jure* owners of the land; they wielded influence on the agricultural population. In order to exercise control over the raiyats it was necessary to align and form a joint front with the zamindars. Since the planters had ready cash, they began to pay higher rent on time to the zamindars than the raiyats. The parasitic and greedy zamindars preferred the planters to the raiyats in leasing land . Thus a "triple" alliance of convenience between the government, the zamindars and the planters was formed in an agrarian society to control the actual producers. Once the land was leased to the planters by the zamindars for indigo cultivation, the planters began to excercise their authority over the raiyats through the influence of the zamindars.

Since a strong and powerful bulwork was formed to serve and sustain the interests of the *Raj* from below, the planters and zamindars were made honorary magistrates and also found positions on various committees and boards constituted by the government. Although occasional clashes occurred between the zamindars and the planters, these remained confined to the pre-1857 period. The planters of Bihar (Patna) were "honourable and upright men" to the zamindars. From Raja Rammohun Roy to the Raja of Bettia all appreciated the "good work" of the planters. Dwarkanath Tagore went to the extent of pronouncing his indebtedness to the non-official Europeans for their prosperity and progressive views. The Panchgachhia *Babus*, the Raja of Bettia, Kazi Ramzan Ali and even the Maharaja of Darbhanga took the side of the planters. When asked to intervene in the dispute between the raiyats and the planter, the Maharaja of Darbhanga maintained neutrality. The Raja of Bettia went further to support the planters. He issued a *hukumnama* and signed the *roobakari* in order to silence the raiyats who were agitating against the planters. The landlords' help to the planters was considered to be of immense importance by the Secretary to the Government of Bengal. He observed that the zamindars in Tirhut were on the planters' side, and their influence was so great that he did not apprehend the repudiation of the indigo contracts by the raiyats.[3] Needless to mention that while the planters were interested in enormous profit, the zamindars in enhanced rent and the colonial government in revenue and remittance -- all of them collaborated among themselves to the neglect of the starving raiyats.

The raiyats were the victims of this collaboration. They were neither converted into prosperous farmers nor were they allowed to remain free to cultivate the land with food crops. Indigo cultivation in Bihar entailed uncertainty, insecurity and oppression for the raiyats. Quite a few of them lost their holdings and became farm labourers.[4] Some of them also migrated to seek their fortunes in the Nepal *terai* where they hoped to avoid the planters' oppressive presence.

Leasing of land by the landed proprietors to the planters often resulted in giving full powers to the latter for their intense exploitation. Failure on the part of the poor raiyats to pay the rent on the stipulated date was considered disobedience and their cattle and utensils were seized to meet the revenue demand. Inability to pay the rent also resulted in imprisonment of the raiyats. Desperation sometimes drove the raiyats to commit suicide and sell their sons and daughters.

The raiyats however, did not prove to be meek and docile victims of oppression. They resisted it stubbornly, sent numerous petitions[5] to the higher authorities for remedying the situation and even showed symptoms of rebellion in 1867-68 and in the 1870s. Caste and religion failed to divide them and they fought unitedly for their cause against the *firangees*. The government realised the seriousness of the threat to the *Raj* and the Governor-General in Council asked the local authorities to take appropriate measures to prevent further deterioration in the situation. It not only enhanced the price of the indigo and fixed three *kathas* in a *bigha* for indigo cultivation but it also sought to mollify the aggrieved raiyats. This experience of fighting for justice against foreign nationals under a colonial set-up gave rise to a new consciousness and even nascent nationalism. The twentieth century therefore did not start on a clean slate. Gandhi, more than any one else, could read the situation most unerringly. He realised that the peasantry could be actively involved in political action and the middle class complexion of the Indian National Congress could be radically changed through the active participation of the peasantry and a mass of people. A man of action, he translated this vision into a reality and radically altered Indian politics. Gandhi's success in Bihar and the peasantry's role in that success was clearly gauged by the peasantry of Maharashtra, Madras and Andhra. They saw Gandhi as a Rama who had been born to kill the British Ravana. There was to be no going back to the dreadful past experience and the march to a future with hope became irreversible.

REFERENCES

1 *Board of Revenue,* No.57, J.P. Pattle's Minute, 20 November 1833.

2 *Bengal Judicial Criminal Proceedings,* No.26, from Messrs Taler Mackinnan H.Hill (representative of the planters of Tirhut, Saran and Munger) to F.J. Halliday, Secretary to the Government of Bengal, Fort William, 27 December 1839.

3 *Home Department* No.5581, 17 October 1868, Fort William, from the Officiating Secretary to the Government of Bengal to the Secretary, Government of India.

4 R.L. Shukla, "British colonialism at work in India and Egypt : A comparative view", Presidential address, Section IV, *Proceedings of the Indian History Congress,* Goa, 1987, pp. 604-5. Details of the working of British colonialism in regard to the production of commercial crops have been lucidly analysed with facts and figures.

5 One of the petitions sent by the raiyats of Champaran to the Lieutenant Governor of Bengal (May 1868) is given in Appendix IV.

APPENDIX I*

Satta for Indigo I

I, Kali Pande, son of Adit Pande, Brahmin by caste, am a resident of *mauza* Pandipur, tappa Madhaul, *pargana* Majhaulia, *thana* Motihari, sub-registry and district Champaran.

Taking of my free will and inclination, an advance of Rs 12 from Mr. . . . . Manager on behalf of . . . . proprietor of indigo concern, and its sub-tappa Mando, *pargana* Majhaua, *thana* and district Champaran, for cultivation of *Phaguni* indigo in an area of 7 1/2 *biswah* of land for a term of 20 years from 1304 to 1323 Fasli out of 2 *bighas* 1 *cuttah* of *kasht* land (measured with a *laggi* of eight *haths* prevalent in the factory) held as *thika* in *mauza* Pandipur mentioned above, I do hereby declare that in the said *thika kasht* the portion that will be "best suited to the cultivation" (emphasis mine) of indigo I shall cultivate, prepare and sow with as much seed of indigo as will be given by the Manager.

That I shall take every possible care and pain in preparing the fields and in sowing, weeding for the first, second and third time, and that I shall do in time all other necessary duties required for the cultivation of indigo in all its stages.

That if the *Phaguni* seeds do not germinate in this portion of indigo land I shall sow with *Baisakhi* and *Asarghi* indigo and shall all possible care thereof, and in any case they do not grow I declare not sow in it any other grain; if I do, "I shall be liable to forfeiture of all sums falling due from the Manager in my account of indigo for which no objection on my part or that of heirs shall be considered valid" (emphasis mine).

That when the indigo plants are ready to be cut, I shall cut and have them loaded on all carts whenever sent from the *kothi* during the time fixed for *mohai*.

---

* Reproduced from the *Final Report on the Survey and Settlement Operation in the district of Champaran*, 1892-1899, C.J. Stevenson-Moore (Calcutta, 1900), pp. 155-56. The *Satta* was excuted between the two unequal partners -- the virtual ruler and the ruled and therefore it was favourable to the planters. Emphasis has been placed on the portion of the *Satta* which had adversely affected the raiyats.

That regarding remuneration it is agreed upon that in case of good outturn Rs 16 per *bigha* and in failure Rs 6 per *bigha* according to factory measurment be accepted by me every year during the time of lease.

That if owing to my neglect and inattention any portion of indigo field be prepared and sowed at the cost of the factory, that Manager will be at liberty to deduct their cost from my dues of indigo, and "if that be insufficient to cover the demand he will be entitled to realise the amount from my person and properties" (emphasis mine).

That the landlord's rent for the land set apart for cultivation of indigo by the Manager shall be paid by me and not by the factory.

That it is optional with me the Manager or his *Amla* to select and measure any other patch of field in the said *thika kasht* for cultivation of indigo, but this should be specified in the month of *Baisakh*, and "I shall cultivate and prepare that without objection being raised on my part or that of my heirs" (emphasis mine).

That if I fail to do so any year and cultivate and sow indigo in fields other than those selected and set apart by the Manager or his *Amla*, I for the breach of contract shall be liable to pay to the factory damage, after the expiry of sowing season, of "Rs 48 per *bigha* every year till the end of the term of the lease" (emphasis mine).

That in default of the payment of the damage mentioned above the factory is entitled to bring a civil suit against me and recover the amount from my movable and immovable properties for which "no objection will be raised on my part or that of my heirs" (emphasis mine).

That at the expiry of the term of lease, I am entitled to get from the Manager of the factory "whatever amount may fall due to me in my account of indigo deducting therefrom the amount of the advance mentioned above" (how vague is the clause, emphasis mine).

I therefore write this agreement for 20 years for cultivation of indigo that it may be of use in time of need.

APPENDIX II*

Contract

"It, Jube Ruot, part proprietor of *Mauza* Gedha, *pergunna* (pargana) Girdsara, of my own free will and consent agree to cultivate for Mr. George Nicholls, Manager of Powelputtie factory, 24 *bighas* of indigo every year from the commencement of 1231 *Fasly* to the end of 1235 *Fasly* a period of 5 years. The whole amount of cultivation being 120 *bighas* and have received in advance on account thereof the sum of *sica* Rupees 48. I therefore engage that these lands to the amount of 24 *beegahs* which the Manager of the factory or his servants may approve of, shall be properly prepared before the full moon of *Kartick* every year till the expiration of the term of this contract. At the season for sowing, weeding and horrowing I will sow, weed and horrow "as often as I shall be ordered to do so" (emphasis mine). The seed to be given from the factory and when the plant may be ripe for manufacturing I will on the order of the Manager of the factory or his servants cause it to be cut in proper time and loaded on articles that may be sent from the factory and "whatever stubble may be left for a second cutting shall be ploughed as often as may be ordered" (emphasis mine).

I shall receive yearly for every *beegah* full of plants as measured by the servants of the factory; 6 Rupees per *beegah* and such fields in the crop may fail shall remain empty till the 15th of June when they shall be given up and I will receive 2 rupees 8 annas per *beegah*. I will go to the factory every year and receive my advance in the proportions and at the periods below mentioned. In all this I will not in any manner fail. If by neglect or unwillingness in the performance of any of the conditions on my part any loss or hindrance should occur to the factory, "I subject myself to a penalty of 12 rupees 8 annas for each *beegah*...".

Sd. E. S. Campbell
Officiating Magistrate

Juba Ruot
Witness

---

* *Bengal Judicial Criminal Proceedings*, No. 167, 1 June 1830, from Acting Magistrate of Tirhut to the Government of Bengal, 22 January 1830. The Tirhut Magistrate informed the Bengal Government about the nature of the indigo disputes and system of advances. *Contract* was in practice in Tirhut (Muzaffarpur and Darbhanga) and Saran districts.

APPENDIX III*

Planters and *zamindars* fight their battles in civil courts. A row of this kind was a great windfall to the police. The *darogah* (now called head inspector) arriving on the spot, both sides make arrangements that the best of food and every comfort should be available for this great man (for the time being); and the side he honoured with his company was looked upon as the winning one. His head clerk, or *mohurrir*, had also to be suitably provided for, and after him the *burkandazes*, now called constables, made *koosh* (pleased). Then came the game of "What will ye tak, or what will he gie?" both sides being powerful and wealthy. The *darogah sahib* wrote out his report, and having been well tipped by both sides, contented himself with announcing, that both were equally guilty, and sending up for trial before the Magistrate two or three of the smaller fry of each side. In due course they appeared before the *Huzoor*** who, following up the cue set by the police, punished men of both sides by a short imprisonment. We, after consultation, made up our minds to let possession slip through our hands, and try the civil court. A very amusing incident occurred some years ago in connection with the police. The *Burra Sahib* of the police was to come to Sonepore, his camp having preceded him; the district police were consequently fussing about getting everything ready, so that he and his officials might have every comfort. The great man arrived with a number of guests, and all retired to rest after the fatigues of the day. At about 4 o'clock in the morning there was an alarm of thieves. A good deal of shouting, and noise followed; and, after a time, it became known to the people in the camp, that the big man's camp had been robbed -- he and his guests having been relieved of a quantity of jewellery. The *darogah* was at once summoned. Hearing what had happened, his distress was great, and he forthwith went to arrange for the capture of the thieves. By

---

* Reproduced from Minden Wilson, *History of Behar Indigo Factories*, op. cit., pp. 142-43. It speaks about the corrupt system of administration in the British *Raj*.

** *Huzoor* = Presence, a term of respect used to officials.

seeing this *darogah*, a clever, energetic, and intelligent policeman, ordered his promotion, and that a sword of honour should be given to him. The "outer world" will tell you how it was all done; the *darogah* paid some *domes* (men of the lowest caste), to go and commit the burglary - they would get a few months' *jail*, but they did not mind that, being accustomed to it. The stolen property was to be kept handy, and made over to the *darogah*. This was all carried out: the *domes* getting their reward in cash, went to *jail*, and the *darogah* got promotion, and a sword of honour.

APPENDIX IV*

Ryots

The humble petition of Meer Enaet Kurreem, Dowlee Shah Kulwar, Goolee Burree, inhabitants of Mouzah Siswah Ajgurreah, Tuppehs Mudowal and Seronah; Huree Rawot Koormee of Tuppeh Ninora, Hur Ghurn Lal Patwaree of Ninora, Shaik Burras Kalee of Tupeeh Seronah, and several others, whose names are given in the annexed list:_

TO THE HON'BLE W. GREY, Lieutenant Governor of Bengal. Most respectfully showed,

That the Indigo Planters of the Factory Seharho, Pergunnah Mugoorah in Moteeharee, the subdivision of Chumparun, in the Zemindaree of the Maharajah of Bettiah, are exercising such cruelties upon your petitioners that it is impossible to describe them fully in this petition; your petitioners therefore most humbly beg to submit the following brief narrative of their grievances for your Honor's humane consideration and justice:

That your petitioners being the ryots of Tuppeh Madhole and Nanore Seronah, Pergunnah Majooah in Motiharee subdivision of Chumparun, zillah Sarun, Zemindaree of Maharajah of Bettiah Serahar, have their habitations and cultivation there, and the said *Mouzahs* were in the Ticca of Lala Tej Pertub Narain of Bhowanypore, Pergunnah Majooah (Majhaua).

That the said Ticcadar in the year 1272 Fuslee gave the said Mouzahs in Kutkina to Messrs. Balpia and Hulwunt, and on the occasion of the execution of his *Kutkina*, your petitioners for fear of the said planters entreated the Ticcadar to protect them. The Ticcadar gave your petitioners hopes and stated that there was no fear. Shortly after the said planters called up your petitioners and ordered them to cultivate indigo on their lands your petitioners were at first unwilling to do so but from fear of the said planters they began, from the commencement of the year 1272 Fuslee, to

**Bengal Judicial Proceedings* No. 75, (?) May 18, 1868. It was one of the petitions of some raiyats of the subdivision of Champaran in the Bettia estate sent to the Lieutenant-Governor of Bengal (undated).

sow indigo on 4 cottahs from a beegah, at a rental of 20 Rupees and 8 *annas* annually, while the cost of your petitioners was Rupees 17-8 or 18 annually.

That for this return the said planters gave your petitioners in some year 2 Rupees and in others 3 Rupees per beegah, and promised to pay the balance afterwards. Unier such a sacrifice your petitioners in hope of receiving the balance hereafter continued to cultivate indigo on their lands. In the present year 1275 Fuslee, all the ryots went to the factories to ask for the promised balance due to them respectively, when they were told to cultivate corn, & c., on their lands, or whatever your petitioners may like, and the said planters promised ti pay the balance according to any arrangement Mr. Thomas, the Manager of the Rajah of Bettiah, may make your petitioners then commenced to cultivate *cheena* (a species of gram) *jye* (barley) *jow* (dats) sugarcane and cotton, in the meantime the people of the factories came and pulled off the plants. Each Factory has about 200 men ready to destroy and plunder your petitioners' cultivation.

Owing to this breach of promise, some of the ryots, viz., Eneet Kurreem, Dowlee Sahoo and others filed a petition of complaint before the Magistrate, containing the above facts, but owing to your Petitioners' misfortune that officer paid no attention to their complaints; an attested copy of the said petition with the order thereon, as also a Pettah granted by Tej Pertab Narain, the said Ticcadar to Dowlse Sahoo and others are herewith annexed for your Honor's information. The planters now insist upon the whole of your Petitioners' lands being cultivated with indigo and are attempting to plunder the whole of the fruits of your Petitioner's labours. Parties who made objections were illegally made defendants, both in the Civil and Criminal Courts, by the said planters, but fortunately for your petitioners *Baboo* Jadoonath Ghose, the Deputy Magistrate, and the *Moonsiff* dismissed the cases thus fraudulently instituted. Failing in this, the Planters with the assistance of the Factory peons, brought away your Petitioners to the Factory, where some were punished and others fined in sums varying from 100, 50 and 40 Rupees each. Many of the ryots have in consequence of this oppression left their abodes and settled themselves in *Mouzahs* bordering in Nepal. While your petitioners were confined in the

Factory, your Petitioners' relatives came forward with whatever amount they could procure and paid the fines which had been imposed upon your Petitioners, and which was accepted on condition that your Petitioners should cultivate indigo on their lands and receive the balance due to your Petitioners according to the arrangement made by the Manager of the Rajah of Bettiah, and it was on these conditions your Petitioners were rescued from confinement. But the said Manager made no advantageous or better arrangement on behalf of your Petitioners, nor was the balance even paid to your Petitioners. The said Manager, however, allowed your Petitioners the option of taking 8 Rupees per *beegah* for the past years and 12 Rupees per *beegah* for the future, or to cut down the cultivation or desert the lands and go to Nepal.

The reason of the said Manager not making better arrangements in favour of your Petitioners is, that he is himself proprietor of five factories and holds a 4 *annas* share in the factory of Lal Serayea. Your Petitioners are in possession of sealed receipts and *Farkhatties* of the said *Kutkinadars*, who as well as other Indigo Planters fraudulently instituted suits against your Petitioners for arrears of rent. The Maharajah of Bettiah having conferred full power upon his estates, resides at Peryag (Prayag, Allahabad) and Benares, consequently the Local Authorities deny all justice to your Petitioners.

On the visit of the Commissioner of the Division at Moteeharee, 20,000 men went forward before that authority with complaints of their grievances and for redress, but unfortunately they returned to their house, hopeless and disappointed. Now the Planters being thus encouraged have commenced to plunder our dwelling houses, corn, & c., confine your Petitioners and punish them in various ways. Madar Bux of Jowkutya, belonging to the Factory of Lal Serayea, Pergunnah Majooah, in which the Manager of Bettiah holds a 4 *annas* share, has acquainted your Honor with the above facts, on which your Honor was pleased to pass an order on the Commissioner for inquiry and report, and for this reason no attention is paid by the Magistrate to the complaints of your Petitioners, on the contary, they are attempting to turn your Petitioners out of the Court yard. The Planters have dismissed from service Lala Hur Churn Lall Putwaree and others, for siding with your Petitioners out of sheer humanity. For the want of means your Petitioners are unable to institute suits for the balance due to them, as they cannot pay for stamps required by the Pleaders and *Mooktears*. Again, *gharries* or conveyances are forcibly taken from the ryots for the use of Government and paid for at 2 *annas*, when the rate fixed by the Magistrate is 8 *annas*. The hire of labour is paid at 9 *pie* where the rate is 2 *annas*, and plough bullocks at 5 *pie* where 3 *annas* is the rate. Under such a state of affairs it is difficult for your Petitioners, without incurring risks on their life, to reside in such a place and suffer such cruelties and punishments, consequently your Petitioners, such of them as have been able to pay train hire, have arrived here with the hope of obtaining redress from your Honor, having left their families destitute and unsupported. Your petitioners would not be surprised that the ryots left behind have been already murdered, as the time of cutting down their cultivations have arrived.

Your Petitioners have been informed that hundreds of the people have settled down in Nepal and their houses and villages have been deserted.

Your Petitioners humbly pray under the above circumstances, that your Honor will be pleased to appoint a Commission for enquiry without delay, as your petitioners apprehend bloodshed and destruction to property to a great extent, and the present state of the District to be exceedingly distrubed, as by the violent oppression of the Planters your Petitioners as well as all the ryots are in perfectly dissatisfied, state of mind and body, and the remedy which is urgently required is in the hands of your Honor.

Your Petitioners beg to solicit the return of the original papers with Your Honours** order in their case.

And your Petitioners as in duty bound shall pray.

**Please address Lala Kesho Pershad, No. 2. Bhowanypore, Kassariparah.

Bibliography

Archival Sources (unpublished),

Bengal Judicial Department, 1830-1869, A & B Proceedings, 1859-1912

Bengal Judicial Progress 1830-1869

Bengal Land Revenue Department, A & B Proceedings, 1859-1912

Bengal General Miscellaneous Department, A & B Proceedings, 1859-1912

Bengal Political Department, A & B, 1859-1912

Bengal Political Special Department (Confidential), A & B Proceedings, 1907-1912

Proceedings of the Board of Trade (Commerce), Govt. of Bengal

Proceedings of the Board of Revenue (Land Revenue), Govt. of Bengal

Proceedings of the Govt. of Bengal (Police)

Proceedings of the Govt. of Bengal (Legislative Deptt.), 1858-1880

Government of India House (Political) Department, A & B Proceedings

Government of India House (Judicial) Department, A & B Proceedings

Government of India

Revenue and Agriculture Department, A & B Proceedings

Government of India House Department (Revenue) General Branches, 1859-1880.

Government of India, Department of Agriculture

Revenue and Commerce (1871-1880)

Branch of Land Revenue and Settlement. (Paper relating to indigo cultivation in Champaran and Tirhut). It contains a detailed report on the state of public feelings in regard to indigo cultivation in Tirhut

Bihar and Orissa Political Special Department (Confidential), A & B Proceedings

Bihar and Orissa Land Revenue Department, A & B Proceedings

Bihar and Orissa Political Department, A & B Proceedings

Confidential Proceedings of Champaran Agrarian Committee 1917

Published

Agriculture Statistics of Bihar (published annually)
Bengal Administration Reports (Annual)
Bihar and Orissa Legislative Council Debates, 1912-18
District Fortnightly Narratives of the Drought of 1873-74
(Tirhut North, monthly report for November - December 1873)
Fifth Report (Parliamentary Papers) of the select committee of the House of Commons, 1812 (ed, W.K. Firminger)
Papers relating to Indigo cultivation in Bengal (Preliminary to the appointment of Commission): Selection from the correspondence connected with the indigo cultivation, April 1854 - May 1860
Proceedings of Hansard's Parliamentary Debates, House of Commons 1860-1880
Proceedings of the Bengal Legislative Council, 1862-1880
Proceedings of the Legislative Council of India, 1858-1880
Report of the Indigo Commission with Minutes of Evidence, 1860
Report of the Proceedings of the East India Company in regard to the culture and manufacture of Indigo, Calcutta, 1836. (It contains the decision of the Court of Directors of the EIC as to why, and with whom the contract should be made to start indigo cultivation)
Report of the Select Committee of the House of Commons on Colonization and Settlement of India, 1857-58
Report of the Select Committee of the House of Commons, Revenue, Judicial and General Appendix, 1832
Report on the Native Newspapers (Weekly), Bengal Presidency
Report on the Indian Newspapers and Periodicals published in the provinces of Bihar and Orissa
Selection from the Records of the Government of Bengal: Indigo Cultivation in Bengal, XXIII (Calcutta, 1860)
Selection of Papers at the East India House, 4 volumes(London, 1820-26)

Books, Dissertations and Articles

Ahmad, Z.A., *Agrarian Problems in India* (1936).
Andrews, C.F., *Mahatma Gandhi's Ideas including Selections from his Writings* (Allen and Unwin, London, 1929).

Anon, *Sketch of the Career of Honourable Ashley Eden* (Calcutta, 1877).

Anon, *Zamindari Settlement of Bengal*, 2 vols (Reprint, B. R. Publishing Corporation, Delhi, 1985).

Baden-Powell, B.H., *Land Systems of British India*, 3 vols (Oxford, 1892).

Bagchi, A.K., "Deindustrialization in Gangetic Bihar, 1809-1901" in Barun De, ed, *Essays in Honour of Professor S. C. Sarkar* (People's Publishing House, New Delhi, 1976).

Bagchi, A.K., (The) *Evolution of State Bank of India: The Roots, 1806-1860; Part II: Diversity and Regrouping, 1860-1876* (Oxford University Press, Bombay, 1987).

Bagchi, A.K., *Political Economy of Underdevelopment* (Orient Longman, Hyderabad, 1983).

Bagchi, A.K., *Private Investment in India, 1900-1939* (Orient Longman, New Delhi, 1980).

Bagchi, A.K., "Reflections on the Nature of the Indian Bourgeoisie", in *Social Scientist*, No. 214-15 (New Delhi, 1991).

Basu, B.D.Z., *Colonization of India by Europeans* (Calcutta).

Beames, John, *Memoirs of a Bengal Civilian* (Reprint, Manohar, New Delhi, 1984).

Besant, Annie, (The) *Future of Indian Politics* (Theosophical Society, Adyar).

Bhattacharya, Sabyasachi ed, *Essays in Modern Economic History*, Indian History Congress, Golden Jubilee Year Publication Series, Volume Four (Munshiram Manoharlal, Delhi, 1987).

Bhattacharya, Sabyasachi, *Financial Foundations of the British Raj* (IIAS, Shimla, 1971).

Bhattacharya, Sukumar, (The) *East India Company and the Economy of Bengal from 1704-1740* (Firma K. L. Mukhopadhyay, Calcutta, 1969).

Blyn, G., *Agricultural Trends in India, 1891-1947: Output Availability and Productivity* (Philadelphia, 1966).

Bose, S.R., *Economy of Bihar* (Firma K. L. Mukhopadhyay, Calcutta, 1971).

British Indian Associations, Report (Annual) 1860-1875: Public Correspondence and Petitions (Calcutta, 1856).

Buchanan, D.H., (The) *Development of Capitalist Enterprise in India* (New York, 1934).

Buchanan, F.H., (An) *Account of the District of Bhagalpur, 1809-11* (Patna, 1939).

Buchanan, F.H., (An) *Account of the District of Purnea, 1809-11* (Patna, 1928).

Buckland, C.E., *Bengal under the Lieutenant Governors, being a narration of the principal events and public measures during their periods of office 1854-1894* (Reprint, B. K. Publishers & Distributors, New Delhi, 1976).

Chakravarty, Suhash, *Anatomy of the Raj* (People's Publishing House, New Delhi, 1982).

Chakravarty, Suhash, (The) *Raj syndrome: A Study of Imperial Perceptions* (Chanakya Publications, Delhi, 1989).

Chandra, Bipan, *Nationalism and Colonialism in Modern India* (Orient Longman, New Delhi, 1984).

Chandra, Bipan, (The) *Rise and Growth of Economic Nationalism in India: Economic Politics of Indian National Leadership, 1880-1905* (People's Publishing House, New Delhi, 1969).

Charleswarth, Neil, *Peasants and Imperial Rule* (Cambridge, 1985).

Chaudhuri, B.B., "Agrarian Movements in Bengal and Bihar, 1919-1939", in B. R. Nanda, ed, *Socialism in India* (Delhi, 1972); also in A.R. Desai, ed, *Peasant struggles in India* (Oxford University Press, New Delhi, 1981).

Chaudhuri, B.B., *Growth of Commercial Agriculture in Bengal 1757-1900*, 2 vols (Indian Studies, Past and Present, Calcutta, 1964).

Chaudhuri, B.B., "Land Market in Eastern India, 1793- 1940", in *Indian Economic and Social History Review*, Vol. 13, Nos 1 & 2, 1975.

Chaudhuri, B.B., "(The) Process of Depeasantisation in Bengal and Bihar, 1885-1947" in *The Indian Historical Review*, Vol. 2, No. 1, New Delhi, 1977.

Chaudhuri, B.B., "(The) Transformations of Rural Protests in Eastern India, 1757-1930", Presidential Address, *Proceedings of the Indian History Congress*, Section III, Waltair session, 1979.

Chaudhuri, M.K., ed, *Trends in socio-economic Change in India* (IIAS, Shimla, 1969).

Chaudhary, R.B., (The) *British Agrarian Policy in Eastern India, Bengal and Bihar, 1859-90* (Janki Prakashan, Patna, 1980).

Chaudhary, R.B., "Lawrence and Indigo cultivation in Bihar", in the *Proceedings of the Indian History Congress*, Muzaffarpur session, 1972 (33), pp. 545-52.

Chaudhary, V.C.P., ed, *Unclassified Class Oppression under the Crown: An Archival Probe* (Patna, 1991).

Chermyak, Y., *Advocates of Colonialism*, translated from the Russian by Taras Kapustim and edited by Roger Silverman (Moscow, 1968).

Chirols, Valentine, *Indian Unrest* (Light and Life Publication, New Delhi, 1979).

Crane, R.I., (The) *Indian National Congress and the Indian Agrarian Problem, 1919-38: A Historical Study* (Yale University, Yale, 1951) (Microfilm, NMML, New Delhi).

Das, Arbind N., *Agrarian Unrest and Socio-economic Change in Bihar, 1900-1980* (Manohar, Delhi, 1983).

Datta, K.K., *History of Freedom Movement in Bihar*, 3 vols (Government of Bihar, Patna, 1958).

Datta, K.K., ed, *Writings and Speeches of Mahatma Gandhi relating to Bihar, 1917-1947* (Patna, 1960).

De, Amalendu, ed, "Indigo Plantation in Bengal, its Social, Economic and Political Effects", in the *Proceedings of the Indian History Congress*, Ahmedabad session, 1954 (17), summary, p. 382.

Desai, A.R., ed, *Labour Movement in India, Documents, 1918-1920* (Indian Council of Historical Research, New Delhi, 1988).

Dhanagre, D.N., *Agrarian Movement and Gandhian Politics* (Institute of Social Sciences, Agra University, 1975).

Dhanagre, D.N., *Peasant Movement in India, 1920-1950* (Oxford University Press, New Delhi, 1986).

Diwakar, R.R., ed, *Bihar Through the Ages* (Orient Longman, Calcutta, 1959).

Dutt, R.C., (The) *Economic History of India under Early British Rule* (Routledge & Kegan Paul, London, 1950).

Dutt, R.C., (The) *Economic History of India in Victorian Age* (Routledge & Kegan Paul, London, 1950).

Dutt, R.P., *India Today* (Manisha Granthalaya, Calcutta, 1979).

Fisher, C. M., "Indigo plantation and agrarian society in North Bihar in the nineteenth and early twentieth centuries" (unpublished dissertation of Cambridge University) (NMML, New Delhi).

Gandhi, M.K., *An Autobiography* (Navjivan, Ahmedabad, 1969).

Gandhi, M.K., *Collected Works*, Vol 13A (Navjivan, Ahmedabad, 1969).

Garner Staig, Mary Sue, "(The) Historical evolution of rights in land in Bihar, India" (unpublished Ph.D thesis, University of Texas, 1975) (Microfilm, ICHR Library, New Delhi).

Ghosal, H.R., *Economic Transition in Bengal Presidency, 1793-1833* (Firma K.L. Mukhopadhyaya, Calcutta, 1966).

Ghosal, H.R., "Indigo in North Bihar and Mahatma Gandhi", in the *Proceedings of the Indian History Congress*, Gwalior session (15), 1952.

Ghosh, K. K., *Agricultural Labourers in India: A Study in the History of their Growth and Economic Conditions* (Indian Publica- tions, Calcutta, 1969).

Ghosh, Papiya, "Peasants, Planters and Gandhi" (unpublished article, 1991, ICHR Library, New Delhi).

Ghosh, Papiya, "(The) Rural base of the Bihar Congress, 1920-36" in *Social Science Probings* (New Delhi, March, 1986).

Gopal, S., *British Policy in India, 1858-1905* (Orient Longman, Delhi, 1975).

Griffith, Percival, (The) *British Impact on India* (Frank Cass & Company, London, 1965).

Guha, Amalendu, *Planter Raj to Swaraj: Freedom Struggle and Electoral Politics in Assam, 1826- 1947* (ICHR, New Delhi, 1977).

Guha, Ranjit, "Nil Darpan, the Image of Peasant Revolt in a Liberal Slum", in the *Journal of Peasant Studies*, Vol. 2(1), 1975.

Guha, Ranjit, *Rule of Property for Bengal: An Essay on the Idea of Permanent Settlement* (Orient Longman, New Delhi, 1982).

Guha, Ranjit, *Subaltern Studies: Essays on the South Asian History*, 6 Vols (Oxford University Press, New Delhi, 1982).

Gupta, Sulekh Chandra, *Agrarian Relations in Early British Rule in India: A Case Study of Ceded and Conquered Provinces (Uttar Pradesh, 1801-1833)* (Asia Publishing House, Bombay, 1963).

Gupta, Vindhyachal Prasad, *Neel Ke Dhabbe* (in Hindi) (Bettia, Bihar, 1986).

Hauser, Walter, "The Indian National Congress and the Land Policy in Twentieth Century", in *Indian Economic and Social History Review*, Vol. 1(1), July-September, 1963.

Henningham, Stephen, (A) *Great Estate and its Landlords in Colonial India, Darbhanga 1860-1942* (Oxford University Press, New Delhi, 1990).

Henningham, Stephen, *Peasant Movements in Colonial India: North Bihar 1917-1942* (Cambridge, 1982).

Henningham, Stephen, "The Social Setting of Champaran Satyagraha: The Challenge to an Alien Elite", in *Indian Economic and Social History Review*, Vol. 3, 1976.

Hobsbawm, E.J., "Peasants and Politics", in *Journal of Peasant Studies*, No. 1, October 1973.

Hunter, W.W., *Annals of Rural Bengal* (Reprint, Cosmo Publishers, Delhi, 1975).

Hunter, W.W., (A) *Statistical Account of Bengal*, Vols 21 and 24 (Reprint, D. K. Publishing House, Delhi, 1976).

Imperial Gazetteers of India: The Indian Empire, Vols 1-4.

Irfan Habib, *Agrarian System of Mughal India* (Asia Publishing House, Bombay, 1963).

Irfan Habib, "Process of Accumulation in Pre-colonial and Colonial India", in *The Indian Historical Review*, Nos 1-2, New Delhi, July 1984 and January 1985.

Irfan Habib, "The Social Distribution of Landed property in Pre-British India: A Historical Survey", in R.S. Sharma and V. Jha, ed, *Indian Society: Historical Probings in Memory of D. D. Kosambi* (People's Publishing House, New Delhi, 1974).

Irfan Habib, Sayera, "Colonial Exploitation and Capital Formation in England in the Early Stages of the Industrial Revolution", in the *Proceedings of the Indian History Congress*, Aligarh session (36), 1975.

Jannuzi, F. Tomasson, *Agrarian Crisis in India: The Case Study of Bihar* (Sangam Books, New Delhi, 1975).

Judith Brown, M., *Gandhi's Rise to Power: Indian Politics 1915-22* (Cambridge University Press, 1972).

Kling, B.B., (The) *Blue Mutiny: The Indigo Disturbances in Bengal, 1859-1862* (Philadelphia, 1966).

Kumar, Deepak, ed, *Science and Empire: Essays in Indian Context* (Anamika Prakashan, New Delhi, 1991).

Kumar, Dharma and Desai, Meghnad, ed, *The Cambridge Economic History: Vol. 2: 1757-1970* (Orient Longman, Delhi, 1984).

Kumar, Kapil, "Peasants, Congress and the Struggle for Freedom, 1817-1939", in Kapil Kumar, ed, *Congress and Classes: Nationalist Workers and Peasants* (Manohar, New Delhi, 1988).

Lehman, Frederick Lousi, "(The) Eighteenth Century Transition, in Response of some Bihar Intellectuals" (unpublished thesis, 1967, University of Wisconsion, USA) (ICHR Library, New Delhi).

McAlpin, M. B., "(The) Effects of expansion of market on rural income distribution in the nineteenth century India", *Exploration in Economic History*, No. 12, 1975.

Mehta, Makrand, "The leader and his Milieu: Gandhi and Ahmedabad, 1915-1920", in *The Indian Historical Review*, Vol. XII, Nos 1-2, July 1985 and January 1986.

Misra, B. B., ed, *Select Documents on Mahatma Gandhi's Movement in Champaran, 1917-18* (Government of Bihar, Patna, 1963).

Mishra, Bharat Prasad, "Land utilisation in Champaran Plain" (Ph.D thesis, University of Bihar, Muzaffarpur, now published by Anamika Publications, New Delhi, 1991).

Mishra, Girish, *Agrarian Problems of Permanent Settlement: A Case Study of Champaran* (People's Publishing House, New Delhi, 1978).

Mishra, Girish, "Indigo Plantations and Agrarian Relations during the Nineteenth Century", in *Indian Economic and Social History Review*, Vol. 3(4), 1966.

Mishra, Girish, "Socio-economic Background of Gandhi's Champaran Movement", in *Indian Economic and Social History Review*, Vol. 5(3), 1968.

Mishra, Shipra, "Plantation Economy during the Colonial Period: A Study of its Impact on the Rural Society of North Bihar" (unpublished M.Phil dissertation, Delhi University, 1987).

Mitra, Nilbandhu, *Nil Darpana* (The indigo planting mirror) (Calcutta, 1861).

Mittal, S.K., "History of Indigo Industry in North Bihar 1817-1917: A Political and Economic Study with Special Reference to Champaran" (unpublished manuscript, ICSSR Documentation Centre, New Delhi).

Mittal, S.K., *Peasant Uprisings and Mahatma Gandhi in North Bihar: A Politico-economic Study of Indigo Industry 1817-1917 with Special Reference to Champaran* (Anu Prakashan, Meerut, 1978).

Moore, James Daniel, (Jr) "Plantation Development and the Labour Response in Nineteenth Century Mysore" (UMI, unpublished dissertation, 1983) (ICHR Library, New Delhi).

Natarajan, L., *Peasant Uprisings in India, 1850-1900* (Bombay, 1953).

Pandey, S.N., "Agrarian Unrest and Political Consciousness, Indigo Plantation in Bihar and Peasant Resistance, 1860-1877", in the *Proceedings of the Indian History Congress*, Kurukshetra session (43), 1982.

Pouchepaders, Jacques, "Local Leaders and the Intelligentsia in the Champaran Satyagraha (1917): A Study of Peasant Mobilization", in *Contributions to Indian Sociology*, No. 8, 1974.

Qeyamuddin Ahmad, "Some Historical Records Service in the Bettia Raj Archives" in the *Proceed- ings of the Indian Historical Records Commission*, Vol. 37, Pt 2 (National Archives of India, New Delhi, 1962).

Rajendra Prasad, *Champaran Mein Mahatma Gandhi* (in Hindi)

Ranga, N. G., *Revolutionary Peasants* (Delhi, 1949).

Ray, Rajat, "(The) Crisis of Bengal Agriculture, 1876-1927: The Dynamics of Immobility", in the *Indian Economic and Social History Review*, No. 10, 1973.

Ray, Ratan Lekha, *Change in Bengal Agrarian Society, 1760-1850* (Manohar, New Delhi, 1979).

Reid, W. N., (The) *Culture and Manufacture of Indigo* (Calcutta).

Royal Commission of Agriculture in India Report (Bombay, 1928).

Roy Chaudhury, P.C., *Gandhi's First Struggle in India* (Navjivan, Ahmedabad, 1962).

Roy Chaudhury, P.C., *Gaya Old Records* (Patna, 1958).

Roy Chaudhury, P.C., *Muzafarpur Old Records* (Patna, 1959).

Saha, Radhamadhav, "Early Indigo contracts in a Bengal District: Their Importance for the Future of Indigo Plantation", in the *Proceedings of the Indian History Congress*, Varanasi session (31), 1969.

Sangwan, Satpal, *Science, Technology and Colonialisa- tion: An Indian Experience 1757-1857* (New Delhi, 1991).

Sarkar, Sumit, *Popular Movements and Middle Class Leadership in Late Colonial India: Perspectives and Problems of a History from Below* (K. P. Bagchi and Company, Calcutta, 1983).

Schendel, William Van, *Three Deltas: Accumulation and Poverty in Rural: Burma, Bengal and South India* (New Delhi, 1991).

Sen, Nandini, "Indigo Rebellion", in N.R. Roy, ed, *Challenge: A Saga of India's Struggle for Freedom* (People's Publishing House, New Delhi, 1987).

Sen, Sunil, *Agrarian Relations in India, 1793-1947* (People's Publishing House, New Delhi, 1979).

Sewak, Ram, *History of Bihar between the two World Wars, 1910-39* (New Delhi, 1985).

Shahid Amin, "Gandhi as Mahatma in Gorakhpur District", in Ranjit Guha, ed, *Subaltern Studies*, Vol. 3 (Oxford University Press, New Delhi, 1984).

Shahid Amin, *Sugarcane and Sugar in Gorakhpur: An Enquiry into the Peasant Production for Capitalist Enterprise in Colonial India* (Oxford University Press, New Delhi, 1984).

Shanin, Teodar, ed, *Peasants and Peasant Societies* (Penguin, 1972).

Sharma, G. P., *Congress and the Peasant Movement in Bihar* (Somaiya, Bombay, 1987).

Sharma, K. K., *Agrarian Movements and Congress Politics in Bihar, 1927-47* (Anamika Prakashan, New Delhi, 1989).

Sharma, R. S., ed, *Survey of Research in Economic and Social History of India* (ICSSR, New Delhi, 1986).

Shukla, P. K., "Indigo Plantation and the Rural Crisis in North Bihar in the second half of the Nineteenth Century", in the *Proceedings of the Indian History Congress*, Dharwad session (49), 1988.

Shukla, R. L., "British Colonialism at work in India and Egypt: A Comparative View", Presi- dential Address at the Indian History Congress, Section 4, Goa Session, 1987.

Singh, N. P., "The Indigo Industry of Bihar and the Oppression of Ryots 1833-1858", in the *Proceedings of the Indian History Congress*, Bodh Gaya session (42), 1981.

Singh, Shyam Narayan, *History of Tirhut: From the Earliest Time to the end of the Nineteenth Century* (Calcutta, 1922).

Singh, S. R., "The Historiography of Gandhian Movement: A Critique", in *The Indian Historical Review*, Vol. XII, Nos 1-2, New Delhi, July 1985 and January 1986.

Sinha, Anugraha Narain, *Mere Sansmaran* (in Hindi) (Patna, 1942).

Sinha, N. K., *Economic History of Bengal*, Vols 1-3 (Reprint, Firma K. L. Mukhopadhyaya, Calcutta, 1985).

Sinha, Ram Narain, *Bihar Tenantry, 1783-1833* (People's Publishing House, Bombay, 1983).

Stokes, Eric, (The) *Peasant and the Raj: Studies in Agrarian Society and Peasant Rebellion in Colonial India* (Vikas Publishing House, Delhi, 1978).

Tripathi, Amales, *Trade and Finance in the Bengal Presidency, 1793-1833* (Oxford University Press, Calcutta, 1979).

Voelcker, John Augustus, *Report on the Improvement of Indian Agriculture* (Reliance Publishing House, New Delhi, 1986).

Wadhwa, D. C., "*Transferability of Raiyati Holdings in Bihar: A Long Journey 1793-1950*", in D. N. Panigrahi, ed, *Economy, Society and Politics in Modern India* (NMML, New Delhi, 1985).

Watt, George, (A) *Dictionary of the Economic Products of India*, Vol. 4 (Reprint, Cosmo Publica- tions, New Delhi, 1983).

Watt, George, *Pamphlets on Indigo* (Shillong, 1890).

Weston, Christine, *Indigo* (The Reprint Society, London, 1946).

Wilson, Minden, *History of Bihar Factories: Reminscences of Bihar, Tirhut and its Inhabitants of the Past, History of Bihar Light Horse Volunteers* (General Printing Company, Calcutta, 1980).

Wolf, Eric, *Peasant Wars of Twentieth Century* (London, 1971).

Yang, Anand A., (The) *Limited Raj: Agrarian Relations in Colonial India: Saran District, 1793-1920* (Oxford University Press, New Delhi, 1989).

Zaidi, A.M. and G.S., ed, *The Encyclopaedia of the Indian National Congress, Vol. 7 (1916-20): Emergence of Gandhi* (Indian Institute of Applied Political Research, New Delhi, 1979).

Journals

Asiatic Society, Calcutta Journal, Caicutta, India.

Bengal Past and Present, Calcutta, India.

Calcutta Review (monthly), Calcutta, India.

Comparative Studies in Society and History, Cambridge, U.K.

Contribution to Indian Sociology, New Delhi, India.

Economic History Review, Cambridge, U.K.

Exploration in Economic History, USA.

Indian History Congress, Proceedings, New Delhi, India.

(The) Indian Economic and Social History Review, New Delhi, India.

Indian Historical Quarterly, India.

Indian Historical Records Commission, Proceedings, New Delhi, India.

The Indian Historical Review, New Delhi, India.

Journal of Asian Studies, USA.

Journal of Bihar and Orissa Research Society, Patna, India (now *Journal of Bihar Research Society)*.
Journal of Economic and Social History of The Orient, Netherlands.
Journal of Economic History, Wilmington, Delaware, USA.
Journal of Indian History, Trivandrum, India.
Journal of Peasant Studies, London, U.K.
Modern Asian Studies, Cambridge, U.K.
Nineteenth Century Studies: (Trade and Commerce), No. 8, October, 1974, Calcutta, India.
Quarterly Review of Historical Studies, Calcutta, India.
Social Science Probings, New Delhi, India.
Social Scientist, New Delhi, India.
Studies in History, New Delhi, India.

Newspapers

Akhbar-ul-Akhiar (Urdu bi-monthly), Muzaffarpur, India.
Al Punch (Urdu), Patna, India.
Amrita Bazar Patrika (weekly), Calcutta, India.
Bangabandhu, Calcutta, India.
Bangabasi, Calcutta, India.
Basumati, Calcutta, India.
Behar Bandhu (Hindi weekly), Patna, India.
(The) Behar Herald, Patna, India.
Bharat Mitra, Calcutta, India.
Bir Bharat, Calcutta, India.
(The) Calcutta Review, Calcutta, India.
Dainik Chandrika, Calcutta, India.
Durbin (Urdu weekly), Calcutta, India.
Education Gazette (weekly), Hooghly, India.
Ekata, Howrah, India.
Hindi Bangabasi, Calcutta, India.
Hindoo Patriot, Calcutta, India.
Hindu Hitoishni (weekly) Dacca, Bangladesh.
Hitavadi, Calcutta, India.
Hitvarta, Calcutta, India.
Howrah Hitaishi, Calcutta, India.
Hunkar (Hindi), Patna, India.
Indian Mirror, Calcutta, India.
Jame-i-Jehan (Persian weekly), Calcutta, India.
Janata (Hindi), Patna, India.

Medini Bandhav, Midnapore, India.
Navayuga, Calcutta, India.
Nayak, Calcutta, India.
Planters Gazette, Calcutta, India.
Pratap Press Leaflet, Kanpur, India.
Sadharani (weekly) Chinsurah, India.
Sahachar (weekly), Calcutta, India
Sambad Prabhakar (daily) Calcutta, India.
Sandhya, Calcutta, India.
Sanjivini, Calcutta, India.
Saptahik Sambad (weekly), Calcutta, India.
Som Prakash (weekly), Calcutta, India.
Sonar Bharat, Howrah, India.
The Statesman, Calcutta, India.
Sumay, Calcutta, India.
Tirhut Samachar, Muzaffarpur, India.
Urdu Guide (weekly), Darbhanga and Calcutta, India.

Glossary

The meanings of the terms given in this glossary reflect the sense in which they are used in this book.

Abwab: illegal cess; it was a kind of a cess assessed on land over and above the original rent.

Adalat: a civil or criminal court of justice.

Amla/Amlah: a subordinate official employed by the planter/zamindar for collection of rent.

Amahi: a cess imposed on the tenant by the planter acting as landlord in Champaran at the rate of one rupee per year for growing mango.

Amin/Ameen: a specialist in measuring the village land.

Anaj: all kinds of grains.

Anna: one-sixteenth of a rupee.

Assami/Assamee: a tenant under the zamindar/landlord on whom a claim was made.

Assamiwar: it denotes a system under which tenants had to enter into an agreement with the planters to grow indigo at a fixed rate per *bigha*.

Asharhi: it pertains to a month of June/July in which *Asharhi* indigo was sown.

Aya/Ayah: maidservant.

Babu: it was a term of respect used for the people of the upper caste/strata of the society.

Badlain: exchange of land.

Badmash/Badmasha: notorious or bad character.

Bakast: it was a piece of land enclosed by the landlords after evicting the tenants who failed to pay arrears of rent.

Baishakhi: it pertains to the month of April in which the crops of *Baishakh* were reaped and grains prepared.

Bhadai: it pertains to the month of *Bhado* (September) in which the crops of the season were reaped and prepared.

Bania: grocer.

Bataidar: share-cropper. Generally the tenant was entitled to a share of fifty percent of the crops produced by him on a piece of land belonging to the landlord.

Bapahi-Putahi: it was a kind of cess/death tax imposed on the tenant after his death and was realised from his son/heir.

Babhun: Bhumihar Brahmin.

Bara-Saheb: planters were generally addressed as *Bara-Saheb* by the tenants.

Batchhapi: it was a kind of a cess realised from the sellers of oil and milk in Champaran district.

Begari: one who renders unpaid service to the landlords.

Bethmahi: those indigo seeds which could not grow.

Bheeth/Bhit: it was a kind of upland near the homestead which was more fertile, better manured, more carefully cultivated and adapted for growing superior kinds of crops.

Bhitha/Bheeth: it was term used in Champaran and Tirhut for upland. It was also called *Goinra* land in Muzaffarpur district.

Bichai: a cess realised from the dealers of grain in Champaran distict.

Bijmar/Beejmar: the land on which indigo seed could not germinate. The tenant was however entitled to receive the minimum price for *Bijmar* land if the indigo seed could not grow for no fault of his own.

Biswah/Biswa: more than a *katha* of land or one-twentieth of a *bigha*.

Chamar: a tanner. It is one of the lowest castes in Bihar.

Chaitnaumi: celebration of the birth anniversary of a mythological God, Lord Rama. It is celebrated in the month of *Chaitra* (March).

Cheena: a food crop grown in the summer season.

Chittka of ghee: one *chittka* is less than a gram.

Chulhakar: a person employed to generate heat for boiling indigo leaves.

Chulahi-Awan: a cess realised from the persons who worked for boiling and preparing turmeric.

Dal: pulse.

Daroga: Inspector of police; head of a police office.

Dashhari/Dashhara: a Hindu festival of ten days in the second half of the month of *Asin* (October) dedicated to Goddess Durga. Cess was realised from the tenant for celebrating this festival.

Dastur: custom; customary practice; customary dues; a commission or percentage on the collection of rent/cess.

Dawatpuja: a Hindu festival observed exclusively among the *Kayasthas* in honour of their mythological God Chitragupta. Cess was realised from the tenant for celebrating this festival.

Dehat: village adjoining the sphere of influence of an indigo factory.

Dhur: one-twentieth of a *katha*.

Dhanuk: (intermediary) caste engaged in agriculture.

Diwan: Superintendent of land who collected land revenue from the tenant.

Doom/Dom: a lowest caste of Bihar.

Fasly/Fasli: the harvest era introduced by Akbar. To convert it into the Christian era an addition of 593 years is made, that is, 1380 *Fasly* is equivalent to AD 1380+593=1973.

Fauzdari: criminal case.

Fauzdar: office superintendent of criminal court.

Firangee/Firangina: alien ruler.

Gharries/Garis: bullock cart.

Guddhur: a kind of a grain of Tirhut.

Ghawahi: cess realised from the tenant of Champaran by the planter for the expenses incurred on the sore of the *Saheb* (planter).

Goala: milkman; (intermediary) caste engaged in agriculture.

Goom: lost.

Gorkha: a member of a regiment in the British or Indian army made up of the soldiers from Nepal.

Gumasta: an agent.

Gairmazrua: uncultivated land; the common pasture land in the village.

Hajat: police lock-up.

Hath: a hand; a cubic measured from the elbow to the tip of the middle finger; a foot and a half.

Harja/Harza: demurrage.

Hathiahi: a cess realised from the tenant of Champaran for the purchase of an elephant.

Hazoor: an expression of respectful address like "Sir" in English.

Hunda: fixed quality of grain/indigo was settled with the tenant who was given unprofitable land for cultivation.

Hukumnama/Hookumnama: letter of order.

Ilakadar: a person responsible for the protection of indigo land.

Istifa: surrender; settlement after surrender.

Islas/Izlas: court or office.

Jail: a place where the convicts are kept.

Jamadar: a subordinate officer of police; a leader of peons; a subaltern.

Jama: acount of assessment.

Jamabandi: the rent-roll; settlement of revenue accounts.

Jot: a piece of land or land under the landlord's cultivation.

Jiladar: a person responsible for maintaining the indigo farming land under the *zeerat* system of cultivation.

Katha: unit of land measurement (1/20 of a *bigha*).

Kayastha: a Hindu caste with clerical profession.

Kabuliat: an agreement to pay rent; deed of acceptance.

Kandhahi: cess realised from the tenant for growing sweet potato.

Karpardar/Karpardas: a village accountant.

Karinda: an expert in preparing indigo.

Khoodkast/Khudkas: a tenant who cultivates the land himself; land was given for cultivation to such a tenant.

Khatian: record-of-rights.

Khuski: a system under which indigo was cultivated without condition.

Kodo: a kind of summer crop.

Koeri: a Hindu sub-caste (intermediary caste) specialised in growing vegetables.

Kothi: an indio concern; a commercial building from where the management of indigo cultivation was looked after.

Kothial/Lathial: persons kept on voluntary contact by the planters for unlawful activities.

Kurmi: a Hindu sub-caste (intermediary caste) generally employed by the high-caste landlord for domestic service; an agricultural labourer.

Kutchhari/Kachahari: a court house.

Kusraili: a system of land tenure. It is also called *Shikmi*. Under this system the planter took land from the tenant and grew indigo with his own labour.

Laggi: a bamboo rod of little over eight feet length used for measuring land in Muzaffarpur district.

Lagan: rent.

Lathi: a bamboo rod used by the planter for unlawful activities.
Mahya/Mahai: the beating of indigo.
Mahal: area of an estate.
Malik: proprietor; owner.
Mahapatri: priest engaged by the planter of Champaran for worshipping.
Makai: maize.
Maharani: the pricipal wife of a Hindu Raja/Zamindar.
Mahajan: money-lender.
Mauza: village.
Marwach: cess realised from the tenant at the time of girl's marriage.
Mehanatana: wage.
Mokchas: to get rid of planters.
Mufassil: the countryside.
Mokhtar/Mukhtar: a person authorised to act or plead for someone in the court.
Mori-mate: a person in charge of the water.
Mokkaarie/Mukarrari: a fixed tenure of land.
Motarahi: a cess imposed on the tenant for the purchase of a car for the planter.
Mujeeb: a provincial battalion who supplied men as guards for the treasury during the 1857 Revolts in Bihar.
Munshi: a village accountant.
Nazrana: usually a gift given to the superior boss, but in the case of the Champaran tenant the Lieutenent-Governor asked the local government to offer some relief to the agitating tenants in the form of *Nazrana*.
Nawahi: cess imposed on tenant for the purchase of a boat.
Nilaha: planter.
Nil/Neel: indigo.
Nil maha: a person employed for mixing the leaves of the indigo plant in the pot.
Paikast: a non-resident cultivator or one who came from another village of the *pargana* to cultivate land.
Panchkathia: it was a system of indigo cultivation in Purnia district under which five *kathas* in one *bigha* were fixed for growing indigo.
Panikharcha: cess realised from the tenant for using water; irrigation fee.

Powah/Puuah: less than one-fourth of a kilogram.
Panch/Punch: a village head.
Pargana: an administrative division equal to a subdivision of a district.
Patwari: a village accountant.
Parwana: an order from a senior officer to his subordinate.
Patta: a deed of cess; a document given to the revenue payer indicating his obligation.
Parti: fallow land; uncultivated land.
Pechawa: an employee of the indigo factory.
Phaguni: the crop sown in the month of *Phagun* (February/March) is called *Phaguni*.
Pie: a coin of the smallest denomination was called *pie*.
Phirangian: Europeans. The tenants usually addressed the planter as *phirangee*. This is the plural form of this word.
Rabbi/Rabi: wheat.
Rahar: *Arhar dal*/pulse.
Raiyat: cultivator, tenant.
Ryot/Raiyati land: land under the cultivation of a *raiyat*/cultivator.
Rasad/Russad: provision; store of grain.
Robokari/Rubkaree: proceedings of a case.
Raj-ank: a cess realised by the planters in their assumed capacity of a king.
Raj: stands for the British Empire.
Saheb/Sahib: a lord; a term of respect equivalent to Sir. The planter was usually called *Saheb* by the tenant.
Sagaura/Saghai: remarried woman; a cess realised by the planter at the time of the marriage of a widow in Champaran.
Salami/Salaami: presents; it was a kind of cess which was imposed on the tenant who had to pay *Salami* to the planter on meeting him.
Sarkar: Government; a district.
Satta/Sutta: an agreement to supply indigo or something else for which some advance money was paid.
Shama/Sama: a kind of *kharif* crop.
Sharabbeshi: an increase upon the existing rent.
Sulahnama: a compromise paper.
Tehsildar: collector of revenue of rent of the landlord.
Talbana: daily-wage.
Tawan: fine; demurrage.

Taluk: a particular area.
Teel: oil seed.
Thika/Theeka: a kind of contract; *hunda*.
Terai: sub-mountainous region.
Thana: police station.
Thikadar/Ticcadar: contractor.
Thikadari: a system under which a village farm was taken for farming.
Tokedar: village functionary.
Tola: part of a village.
Tinkathia: a system of land tenure in the indigo growing districts of Bihar in which the tenant is forced to set apart three *kathas* per *bigha* of his holdings for indigo cultivation.
Vakeel/Vakil: lawyer.
Zamindar/Zemindar: a big landlord, landholder, landed proprietor, landowner.
Zabardast: powerful.
Zilladar: a person responsible for maintaining the indigo farming land under the *Zeerat* system of cultivation.
Zeerat/Zairat: land under the *khas* cultivation of a zamindar or a planter.
Zar-i-peshgi/Zerpeshgi: advance; impressed money.

Index

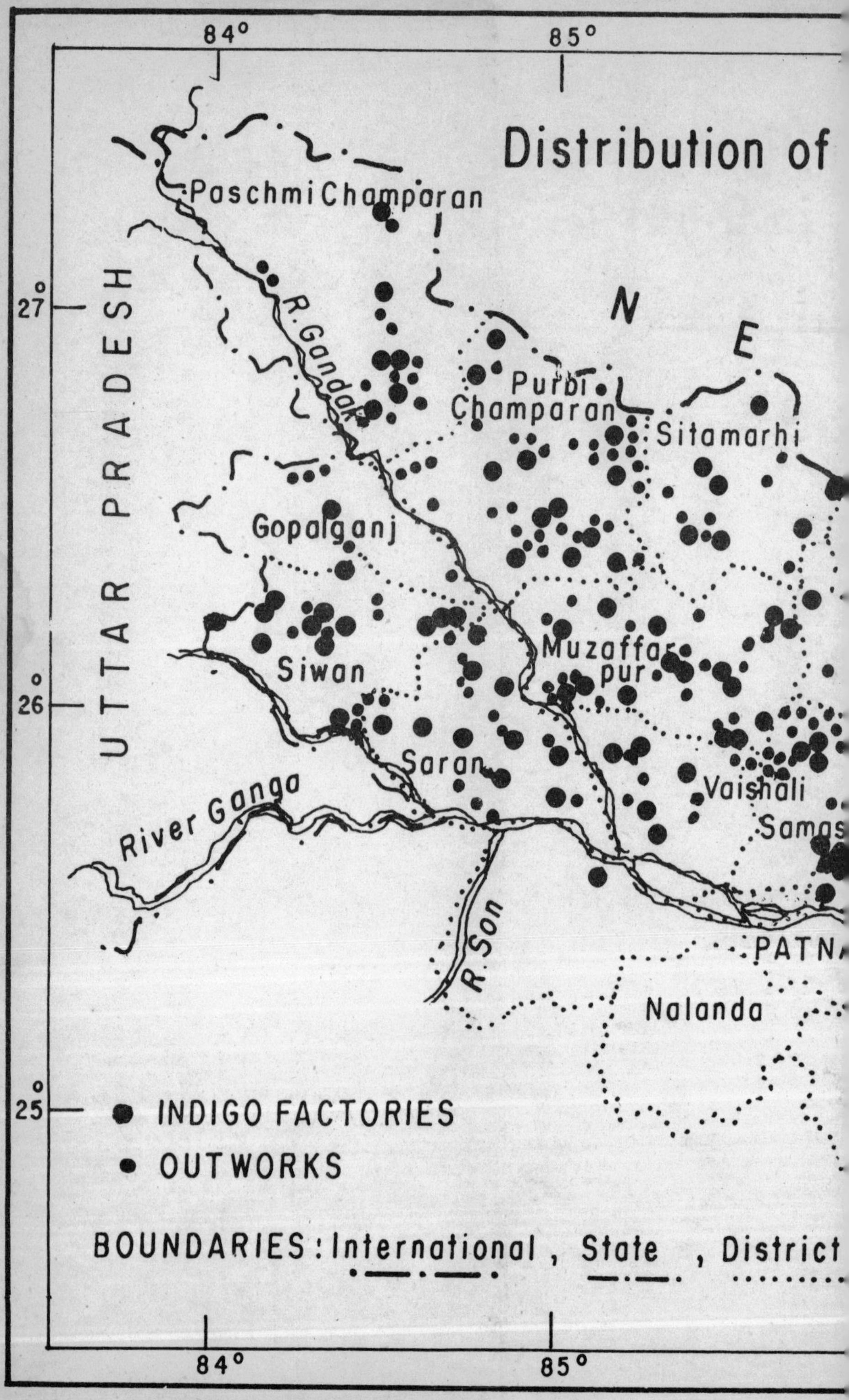

Distribution of
84°
85°
27°
26°
25°
UTTAR PRADESH
N
E
Paschmi Champaran
Purbi Champaran
Sitamarhi
R. Gandak
Gopalganj
Siwan
Muzaffarpur
Saran
Vaishali
Samas
River Ganga
R. Son
PATN
Nalanda
INDIGO FACTORIES
OUTWORKS
BOUNDARIES: International, State, District